Changing Alliances

Changing Alliances

DAVIS DYER, MALCOLM S. SALTER, AND ALAN M. WEBBER

The Harvard Business School Project on the
Auto Industry and the American Economy

MALCOLM S. SALTER AND MARK B. FULLER, *Directors*

Harvard Business School Press
Boston, Massachusetts

HARVARD BUSINESS SCHOOL PRESS

© 1987 by the President and Fellows of Harvard College
All rights reserved.
Printed in the United States of America.

90 89 88 87   5 4 3 2 1

LIBRARY OF CONGRESS CATALOGING-IN-PUBLICATION DATA

Dyer, Davis.
  Changing alliances.

  Bibliographic references
  Includes index.
  1. Automobile industry and trade—United States.
I. Salter, Malcolm S.   II. Webber, Alan M.,
1948–   .   III. Harvard Business School Project
on the Auto Industry and the American Economy.
IV. Title.
HD9710.U52D94   1987   338.4'76292'0973   86-33619
ISBN 0-87584-175-9

Contents

79311

Preface

Many important books have been written in recent years about our nation's industrial performance. Some have been targeted at presidential candidates and their supporters searching for a more competitive industrial policy that the public sector could initiate. Others have been targeted at managers to increase their companies' performance in the global marketplace. Finally, some have been aimed at labor leaders and their constituencies who have profound interests in domestic employment levels and employment practices. Rarely have studies of industrial performance addressed the overlapping concerns of all three groups. This book attempts to do so.

As the title *Changing Alliances* suggests, this book focuses on relationships—relationships among the institutions of management, labor, and government and how they have affected industrial development and continue to affect corporate performance in the world auto industry. These relationships comprise, both in the United States and its competitor nations, systems of "industrial governance" that can be procompetitive or anticompetitive. What differentiates our study from its predecessors is our argument that these relationships affect corporate performance; that with respect to industries like autos, the new technologies, new labor contracts, and new public policies cannot by themselves lead to sustained improvements in the performance; that future increases in competitiveness and corporate performance will depend upon American management, labor, and government adopting new attitudes and developing new institutions that together add up to a more procompetitive industrial governance system.

In the chapters that follow, we spare the reader technical language often associated with theory building and research monographs. Indeed, the phrase *industrial governance* rarely appears in our story of the U.S. auto industry in crisis. We are more likely to speak of enterprise systems when referring to the conduct of relationships among management, labor, and government as each attempts to influence the development of business policies that affect its separate and shared interests.

The concept of industrial governance and the enterprise system it produces permeates our treatment of the recent auto crisis and the future of the U.S. auto industry. The concept guided our analysis of the nature of the competitive challenge facing the American automobile industry and helped shape our ideas about what would improve the industry's competitive performance.

In the course of a four-year project, the Harvard Business School Project on the Auto Industry and the American Economy, we conducted hundreds of interviews in executive suites, factories, union halls, and government offices around the world. Beginning in the United States, we spoke with the leaders of the Big Three: corporate strategists, economists, financial officers, product planners, human resource managers, government relations specialists, environmental analysts, and division managers. We interviewed up and down the organizations, as well; we met men and women who work as factory managers and shop-floor foremen, people who work in the middle of the bureaucracy and people who work in the middle of a components plant, people who turn out memos and people who turn out cars.

We did the same extensive interviewing within the United Auto Workers. Top labor officials met with us, as did retired leaders and rank-and-file union members. Finally, we spoke with scores of government officials, including White House policy makers, members of the cabinet, members of Congress, governors, and state-level leaders. To gain added perspective we interviewed former government officials who had helped establish public policy toward the auto industry during their time in office.

We then repeated this process in a selected group of competitor nations. We examined the auto industries in the United Kingdom and in Germany as representative of the least and most competitive industries in Europe, respectively. And we focused intensively on the Japanese auto industry, which has established new standards for competitiveness against which the American automakers must now be measured. In each of these nations we conducted lengthy and detailed interviews with top corporate executives, labor leaders, and government officials, returning several times to each country over the four-year life of the project.

Our observations, analyses, conclusions, and recommendations are presented here and should speak for themselves. We believe that the challenge to the U.S. auto industry is systemic—that it is rooted in each nation's enterprise system, the relationships between management and labor and between management and government that govern corporate decision making in each country. In our view, the enterprise systems of other nations, notably Japan, are the source of their competitive advantage; a fundamental change in the environment from national to global competition has changed the terms of competition from company rivalry to system rivalry. But even though the context has changed dramatically, the American enterprise system has been slow to adapt. Managers, union leaders, and government officials continue to adhere to ways of thinking and acting that fit the old environment but not the new one. As a result, American automakers are now competing at a severe disadvantage. Finally, we believe that this challenge requires basic and far-reaching changes in the philosophy and practice of the American enterprise system, led by private sector managers, if the U.S. auto industry is to regain its competitive footing or, indeed, survive over the long term. These findings, in abbreviated form, represent the general conclusions of our work.

Just as important as the results of this project, we believe, are its origins. Our study of the auto industry grew from a strong conviction about the position of the industry in the American economy. First, we regarded the auto industry as an American original, an enterprise of enormous power and scale where the issues of economy and politics are cast on a giant screen. After all, the names of American heroes are deeply entwined with the history of this industry: Henry Ford, Alfred Sloan, Walter Chrysler, Walter Reuther. Names we take for granted today as products—Chevrolet, Olds, Buick, Champion, Firestone, and more—bear testimony to the genius of the entrepreneurs who invented an industry. Moreover, their industry became an American way of life, imprinted on the landscape in the form of sprawling freeways and elaborate cloverleafs and in our life style in the form of the single family home and the two-car garage.

The industry became the economic center of a web of production that touched steel and iron, rubber and glass, machine tools and plastics, textiles and electronics, and a host of other industrial products. It even provided the template for the design of America's enterprise system: Ford created the model of industrial production and company after company copied from the master; Sloan identified the principles of corporate structure and strategy and General Motors became the standard of modern management; Reuther established the United Auto Workers as the elite of unions and its bargaining positions and economic rewards became the measure of organized labor's performance.

As we began to visit the sites of the auto industry, our inchoate feelings for this industry were given form. It is impossible to walk through an engine plant in the gigantic River Rouge facility, or to witness the technological research in the GM Technical Center, or to examine the workings of Chrysler's highly automated Windsor, Ontario, assembly plant without being reminded over and over of the complexity, expense, and scale of this one industry. It does little good simply to cite numbers: billions of dollars, millions of units, hundreds of thousands of workers. The physical reality of immense factories covering acres of ground, filled with endless lines of fast-moving, noisy machines, and occupied by armies of workers performing the repetitious and arduous tasks of building cars is the source of the power and magic of the auto industry.

Enlarged to the level of a worldwide enterprise, this physical reality of the auto industry casts an overwhelming shadow. It is, quite simply, the world's largest manufacturing industry. Around the world, it is a leading source of jobs and a commanding source of investment. Every developed nation that has an auto industry has, at one time or another, sought to protect it from foreign competition. For that reason, as well, countries that currently have no auto industry but are searching for paths to national economic development are now trying to develop their own producers, as a source of employment, investment, and growth.

Around the world, nations also regard the auto industry as an important source of technological leadership. In just a few years, the automobile industry has undergone a dramatic transformation, from a stodgy mature smokestack industry to a cutting-edge high-tech industry where technological innovation is creating not only the car of the future but also the factory of the future.

The auto industry also contributes substantially to the trade balance—or imbalance—among nations: In 1984, almost half of the U.S. $34 billion bilateral trade deficit with Japan came from auto trade. For all these reasons—employment, investment, economic growth, technological leadership, balance of trade—the auto industry has assumed a central role in both global economics and global politics.

In part, then, we selected this industry because of its economic and political salience. The issues confronting it are complex; the stakes immense. In this one industry there are fundamental issues that may define the social, economic, and political agenda of the 1990s: the philosophy of the corporation, its purposes and practices; the fate of organized labor; the role of the government in a global economy and the national competitive position of the United States.

From this discussion, it might seem that the auto industry is unique. It is not. In fact, our second consideration in selecting it for study was its value as a metaphor, a powerful symbol for a substantial part of the larger American economic landscape. We are not the first to recognize this role of the auto industry. In his 1946 study of General Motors, *The Concept of the Corporation*, Peter F. Drucker commented on it explicitly.

> The automobile industry stands for modern industry all over the globe. It is to the twentieth century what the Lancashire cotton mills were to the early nineteenth century: the industry of industries. The performance of all industry is likely to be judged by it. Any solution it might find to give the worker citizenship in industrial society would become the general solution. No solution found elsewhere would have much meaning unless it could successfully be applied in the automobile industry.[1]

The more we examined the auto industry, the more we became convinced that its situation was exemplary rather than unique. When we began our work, it was popular to frame the competitive challenge facing America as nothing more than a painful transition, an economic passage in which the old mature smokestack industries like iron, steel, and autos were inevitably giving way to the glistening new high-tech industries of the future. If the auto industry was in trouble, it was to some extent to be expected, an outgrowth of natural economic causes, evidence of the product life-cycle theory at work. Some observers saw the plight of the auto industry as an example of Joseph Schumpeter's theory of "creative destruction." The distress from the shrinkage of the auto industry would, in time, be more than compensated for by the growth of healthy new industries.

We thought then that theory was being applied to evidence and inappropriately so. We saw a different set of circumstances: globalization sweeping across American industry at a steady, if uneven, pace, transforming the context of competition as it moved. What happened to the American auto industry in 1979 would, we thought, happen in turn to virtually any manufacturing industry in which the organization of people or the intervention of government could make a difference—any industry, in other words, in which the enterprise system played a role. Subsequent events involving the semiconductor industry, the computer industry, the communications equipment industry, and the airframe industry, to name but a few, have confirmed our view.

The critical shift under way today is not simply from a smokestack economy to a high-tech economy, or even from a manufacturing to a service economy. Rather it is a change from a national to a global economy and, thus, from a competition between American companies operating within one enterprise system to a competition between enterprise systems.

Seen in this light, the challenge to the American auto industry is a challenge to the American economy. The capacity of the auto industry to respond to foreign competition and transform itself in accord with the new environment will tell a much larger story about the future shape of the American economy. The efforts of management, labor, and government to forge a strategic alliance are crucial indicators of the kinds of companies we will have in this country in the future, the kinds of jobs we will have, the standard of living we will enjoy, and, perhaps, the role we will play in the world. In writing this book we hope to contribute not only to the debate over these crucial issues but also to outcomes that we will all want to live with.

The book is divided into four parts. Part I provides an overview of the competitive challenge facing the U.S. auto industry. Part II is historical in content. It analyzes how the relationships among management, labor, and government have affected the development and performance of the American, European, and Japanese auto industries. Part III looks at the U.S. auto industry today, accenting the dilemmas facing each of the key industrial actors—the Big Three, the UAW, and what we have come to call the government—as they, separately and in concert, attempt to respond to the new competitive challenges brought by industry globalization. Finally, Part IV presents both our views of the prospects of the U.S. auto industry and our vision of what outcomes and procompetitive policy processes are within our reach.

Boston, Massachusetts   Davis Dyer
September 1986   Malcolm S. Salter
                                                   Alan M. Webber

Acknowledgments

Many people in business, labor, government, and academia helped us with this project and to them we are deeply indebted. They are, quite literally, far too numerous to mention, but several deserve special thanks, since they provided access to important sources of information or shared their ideas and time beyond the call: Richard John of the U.S. Department of Transportation, Richard F. Davis and William Chew of General Motors, David M. McCammon and Jeffrey Hitchcock of Ford, Wendell Larsen and Thomas Miner of Chrysler, and Douglas Fraser and Don Ephlin of the UAW. In addition, Candace Howes and Sheldon Friedman of the UAW Research Department gave chapter 7 a thorough and critical reading. We continue to disagree with them on some matters of interpretation, but the chapter is much the better for their efforts. John O'Donnell of the U.S. Department of Transportation served as a continual source of industry data and spent long months preparing and revising Appendix A. More than providing statistical backup, he became an informal member of and knowledgeable contributor to our research team.

Within our own institution, Dean John H. McArthur and E. Raymond Corey, research director, played key facilitating roles. Both helped us assemble the team and Corey in particular provided steady support and personal encouragement throughout the years of field research. We were fortunate to receive counsel and criticism from other colleagues: Christopher S. Allen, Keith Bradley, Leslie Hannah, Janice McCormick, George C. Lodge, D. Quinn Mills, Thomas K. McCraw, Michael Reich, Bert Spector, and Bruce A. Scott. John T. Dunlop also served us well as a source of friendly criticism and encouragement based on his long experience with dispute resolution in industry. Kenneth R. Andrews of the *Harvard Business Review* gave generous research leaves to Associate Editors Dyer and Webber, as did Dean Jack Neuhauser and James Bowditch of Boston College, who provided research time to Davis Dyer when he served on the faculty of that sister institution. To them, as well as to the others who helped us in our work, our most sincere thanks.

PART **I**

Overview

CHAPTER 1

The Competitive Challenge

For most of the past decade, the Big Three American automakers have been locked in a battle with their Japanese rivals. In 1986, while the struggle continues and our methods of financial reporting obscure the results, the outcome is evident: The Big Three are losing.

At the low end of the market, where conflict was first felt and was most intense, the battle is now over. No American producer makes a competitive small car; none has concrete plans to replace its existing models with American-designed or American-made versions when the current generation expires. Chrysler and GM already import substantial numbers of finished vehicles and Ford will shortly follow. GM's Saturn model, which the company heralded in 1983 as a model that would "leapfrog" Asian competitors and gain back lost market share, is now presented as a sporty, upscale car aimed at buyers in a different segment.

In the midsize and sports car markets, the Japanese are gaining ground every day. Although the voluntary restraint agreement (VRA) negotiated by the Reagan administration and in effect from 1981 to 1985 caused Japanese imports to level off and influenced Asian companies to build assembly plants in the United States, it also led these companies to enrich the mix of vehicles sold here. Unit sales of Japanese cars in the United States have crept up slowly since the VRA, but the dollar value of Japanese cars sold in the United States continues to soar. Toyota, Nissan, Honda, Mitsubishi, and Fuji (Subaru) have launched successful models in midsize and sporty segments.

The Japanese are even beginning to penetrate the high end, luxury markets, where the Americans already face stiff competition from European specialty producers.

Indeed, the American automobile industry of the late 1980s scarcely resembles that of only a decade ago. Each of the Big Three produces in coalition with Japanese partners, and the Japanese partners increasingly call the shots in the design and supply of the most important parts and components of shared vehicles. GM is endeavoring to strengthen its ties to Toyota, Isuzu, and Suzuki; Ford to Mazda; and Chrysler to Mitsubishi; and all three have found partners in other Asian countries as well.

By 1990, according to one estimate, GM will source 11 percent of its models from overseas or joint ventures, Ford will import 26 percent, and Chrysler 27 percent.[1] The cars will be imported from all over the world, from Japan, Korea, and Taiwan, from Brazil and Mexico, and from Germany. And even among the cars built in the United States, the foreign content will steadily increase, especially in important power train components.

And no longer is the American auto industry synonymous with the Big Three. In 1986, VW, Honda, Nissan, Toyota (through a joint venture), and Hyundai already operate assembly plants in the United States and Canada. By 1990, foreign-owned companies assembling cars in North America will include Mitsubishi (via joint venture with Chrysler), and Fuji and Isuzu (via joint venture), with additional plants or capacity planned for Toyota, Nissan, and Honda.

The picture of the North American automobile market emerging from these trends is alarming. By 1990, according to our estimates (see Appendix A), these "local assemblies" will account for more than 2.0 million units. Together with about 3.5 million units imported (including "captive" imports by the Big Three), foreign-based and foreign-owned production will total about 60 percent of cars sold in the United States. And this may be a *conservative* estimate, for each passing month brings announcements of new capacity, investments, and coalitions targeted at the U.S. market.[2]

The cost of the Big Three's retreat is extremely high, so high that many nations would consider it unbearable. Besides the hundreds of thousands of jobs and billions of dollars in investment the U.S. automakers are continuing to lose, the effects of change will ripple outward to suppliers and dealers, to communities and public institutions. Nor will the foreign-based investment in the United States begin to offset this damage. In addition to the direct impact of the lost auto wars, the indirect effects—lost skills, lost investment, lost opportunities—will prove adverse for years to come.

Management, government, and labor have found it difficult to frame a concerted response to the forces subsuming the industry. A principal problem has been the misinterpretation of the reports from the front lines. Since 1978, the United States has been on an unprecedented economic and political roller-coaster ride. From high-flying prosperity, the economy plunged into a deep collapse of basic industries, exposing what seemed to be near-fatal flaws in the fundamentals of American business. In July 1980 the *Harvard Business Review* published an article entitled "Managing our way to economic decline," which offered the definitive analysis of the country's business crisis. The article began, "During the past several years American business has experienced a marked deterioration of competitive vigor and a growing unease about its economic well-being." In fact, the sense of unease seemed depressingly well founded. By the end of 1982 one industry after another was mired in depression-level performance; nationally unemployment had soared to over 10 percent. In the auto industry, unemployment reached almost 22 percent.

But just when national confidence seemed to have sunk to a new low and experts were heralding Japan as the new number one, a booming recovery pushed American industry past even the record peaks of 1978. Gone was the self-doubt and self-criticism of 1980, replaced by a buoyant feeling of confidence. After all, wasn't American business committed *en masse* to a national search for excellence? America had met the crisis and was back on top. Or so it seemed to many.

But beneath the surface of a boom-bust-boom cycle, there were more significant and more fundamental changes, largely overlooked or misunderstood by observers and participants in national economic affairs. Why had so much of American industry suddenly performed so poorly? What were the real causes of the competitive collapse that took place in 1979? What measures were behind the spectacular recovery that had produced record profits a few years later? How permanent was the new-found prosperity? Would it last, or did the roller coaster have another plunge ahead?

The best way to answer these questions is to focus on the most prominent story in the larger national drama—the story of the U.S.

auto industry in global competition. For some, the competitive challenge is explained simply by pointing to the Japanese automakers' twin advantages: lower costs and higher quality. But a closer reading of recent events indicates that high cost and poor quality are only surface symptoms of a deeper structural crisis. The challenge posed by the auto industry is how to explain—how to think about—three conflicting pictures.

The first, from early 1979, is a picture of a robust and thriving enterprise basking in record profits of $4.9 billion, record sales of 12.9 million cars and trucks, and record employment of over one million autoworkers. In this photo, the smiling Detroit automakers and the United Auto Workers have just negotiated a healthy new contract calling for a 34 percent raise and the addition of fourteen paid personal holidays over the agreement's three-year life. Clogging the docks, in the background, sit 500,000 imports, an unwanted backlog of Japanese cars.

Next is a montage of the years between 1979 and 1984, a sequence tinged with crisis. These shots show industry analysts calculating the $1,500 to $2,000 per car Japanese cost advantage and consumers discovering the Japanese quality advantage. There is a picture of a grim Lee Iacocca pleading with the Congress for a government loan to save Chrysler workers' jobs—and then having to lay off 50,000 of the 110,000 workers to save the company. There are glimpses of more than 300,000 unemployed autoworkers and twenty-five mothballed auto plants across the country. Finally, there is a picture of American government officials gathered at the Hotel Okura in Tokyo with their Japanese counterparts working out the last minute details of a voluntary restraint agreement that will limit the number of cars allowed into the United States.

Then there are the most recent photos, once again showing dramatic change. Instead of vacant plants, the snapshot shows $50 billion worth of modernized, robotized factories and equipment. Once again there is a shot of a contract signing—but instead of mushrooming wages and benefits, this one features a historic redefinition of management rights and union responsibilities. Like the 1978 photo, this shot is brightened by huge profits—more than $9.8 billion. And the pictures of top management now show the faces of American corporate heroes: Chrysler's Lee Iacocca on the cover of *Time* magazine and GM's Roger Smith in the *New York Times* magazine, hailed as innovators and men of vision.

Simply focusing on the Japanese cost and quality advantages will not explain these starkly contrasting images. Nor will conventional thinking regarding labor wage rates, the use of technology in the production process, or any one of a dozen other intellectual pigeon holes. Instead there are two underlying developments that give order and a sense of meaning to the apparent contradictions and discrepancies in the auto industry's story—and that also suggest what kind of images may appear in the next snapshots.

First is the change from a national competition to global competition—globalization. This change has signaled a deep and permanent shift in the terms and conditions in the auto industry: For example, there is no longer a discrete set of domestic competitors that constitutes the U.S. auto industry; there is only a world auto industry. Nor can the United Auto Workers any longer claim a monopoly on the supply of labor for cars and trucks made and sold in the American market. Nor, for that matter, can the federal government take actions that ignore the global market and the pressure of tough foreign competitors. As a crosscurrent, globalization has signaled the need not only for reinvestment but even more for rethinking the bases of competition.

Second is the change from rivalry among American companies within the U.S. enterprise system to rivalry between differing national enterprise systems. Before globalization, the relationships between management and labor and between management and government in the United States made little difference in the performance of the auto companies. After all, each of the Detroit automakers dealt with the same union, under the same contract, and with the same government, under the same laws and regulations. But after globalization, the American companies confronted competition from foreign automakers operating within enterprise systems governed by different philosophies and different practices. From the enterprise system has come the capacity to compete: For the Japanese, the relationships between management, labor, and government ensure low cost and high quality.

The record of the past forty years illuminates the evolution of the Japanese enterprise system, one of the most successful in the world today. In the wake of World War II, the Japanese rebuilt more than their factories; they rebuilt their enterprise system. At the heart of the new system were two tenets of business philosophy with far-reaching economic and political implications. First, trade with the

world would determine the economic well-being of the nation; therefore, national companies would have to be competitive on a global
scale. Second, only the integrated, negotiated efforts of management,
labor, and government could produce globally competitive companies. None of the three sides could succeed by itself; none could
succeed unless all succeeded.

Over a period of decades Japan evolved distinctly non-American
definitions of institutional purposes, goals, and performance, an enterprise system with six key characteristics.

Shared authority and responsibility

Management explicitly accepts as legitimate the authority wielded by
labor and government in helping govern the performance of the company. Labor and government recognize that with authority comes
responsibility.

Shared interests

The primary interests of the three sides are different: profits, jobs, a
rising national standard of living. But they are not necessarily incompatible; indeed, they are interdependent. Each side, by recognizing the
legitimacy of the interests of the other, makes it possible to achieve its
own.

Efficient, effective, economic decision making

The mechanisms within the enterprise system for dealing with information, communication, and negotiation stress these three qualities.
They are efficient: decisions are made in a timely fashion and at the
lowest appropriate level. They are effective: decisions address real
problems, are calculated to produce results, and once made, stay made.
They are economic: all sides give careful consideration to the impact on
real costs of any decision.

Flexibility and adaptability

All sides assume that change, not stability, is the operating norm in
the economic environment. Accordingly, the relationships not only
allow for but consciously design mechanisms and agreements that
permit quick adaptation to new circumstances.

Strategic thinking

Not only management but labor and government as well focus on the
long-term accomplishment of goals and systematic approaches to achieving a sustainable advantage over competitors.

Focus on the company in the global market

The relationships are formed at the level of the individual company,
rather than the entire industry, and stress the competitive status of the
company in the world, rather than only in the nation.

These six characteristics, as well as the philosophy and practices implicit in the Japanese system, represent a dramatic contrast to the American system, which was largely in place before World War II and grew to full expression in the 1950s and 1960s. This is not a criticism of the American approach. Its attributes fit the environment; overall the system delivered what was asked of it: high profits, high wages, and a high standard of living. It had its own internal logic. Management was presumed to be the sole authority in the operation of the enterprise, and with sole authority went sole responsibility for company performance. Workers were a variable cost of production; management's key to dealing with the union was to minimize labor problems by buying out their interests with high wages and generous benefits and to channel communication and conflict into adversarial and periodic bargaining. The government was largely considered external, a factor that inflicted added costs and was best kept at arm's length. Developed over a lengthy period of stability and limited to economic competition within the United States, the system stressed quantity over quality and control of assets over control of costs.

For almost fifty years it was a system that worked and worked well. But with the onset of globalization, the American system no longer fit the environment; in the new global competition, the system simply could not deliver what it was not designed to deliver. When the environment temporarily returned to the preglobal conditions—for example, through the negotiation of a voluntary restraint agreement with the Japanese—the system once again appeared to perform smoothly. But in an open and free world market, the American system is a fundamental disadvantage for American companies.

Seen in this light, globalization poses a direct challenge to the American auto industry and the American economy. Since 1979, the plight of the auto industry has most visibly and dramatically demonstrated the powerful impact of global competition, but the same story can and will unfold across the economy as globalization touches one industry after another, high-tech and service. The question facing American managers, workers, and government officials, therefore, is how to respond to this challenge.

There are three options. First, it is possible to attempt to ignore or resist the change. In the case of the auto industry, both have been attempted. The initial response to the challenge was to ignore it or, alternately, blame the crisis on another: management's shortsightedness, labor's greed, government's ineptitude. The second response, led by the UAW and supported by several of the auto companies, was

to block globalization by changing the rules of trade: either a voluntary restraint agreement or local content legislation would return the
competition to a predominantly American one, within the old system.
It is not hard to understand the appeal of this option. But its attractiveness does not make it any more viable as a solution to a serious,
long-term political and economic problem. Denial and avoidance,
over time, only increase the cost of finally addressing the problem
and may, ultimately, diminish the chance of finding an effective
remedy.

The second option is to insist that the foreign competitors change
their system. There has been some of this, directed toward Japan, a
mixture of inaccurate and wrongheaded insistences—"Japan bash-
ing"—and legitimate objections to their brand of economic nationalism. Within narrow limits, this approach can help reduce the
competitive crisis, forcing the Japanese to open their market, invest
in the United States, and make the overall operation of their system
more transparent and sensitive to outside interests. But this approach
cannot resolve the underlying problem, which remains an American
rather than a Japanese problem. Nor can American political and
economic pressure, applied within reasonable limits, ever succeed in
remaking the Japanese system according to American dictates.

The last option, although the most difficult, is the only one of the
three that holds any promise of responding to the challenge: the
American system adapts to meet foreign competition; management
and labor learn to share interests; management and government
negotiate a role for the government as a catalyst for competitiveness.
This is neither a far-fetched nor hopelessly idealistic prescription. At
least in the relationship between management and labor some
progress has been made since the crisis of 1979. Both the 1982 and
1984 contracts between General Motors and Ford and the UAW made
significant improvements in the areas of shared responsibility and
authority and shared interests.

The contracts established a series of joint committee structures
covering an extensive range of previously reserved managerial tasks,
everything from shop-floor, day-to-day matters to joint administration of a multimillion-dollar venture capital fund for new start-ups.
In the area of shared interests, the 1984 contract centered around a
historic quid pro quo: the UAW agreed to a moderate wage settlement—particularly in light of record profits—and even surrendered
some expensive benefits; management agreed to create a $1 billion

employment security fund. In effect, the contract represented a first step toward adapting the American enterprise system in new and important ways. More sweeping change is reflected in the systemic change being attempted by GM and the UAW in the Saturn project and the joint venture with Toyota.

For a number of reasons, no similar change has taken place in the relationship between American management and government. Moreover, despite the adaptations of management and labor, difficult questions persist. Can the American system, as a whole, make the needed changes? Can it change enough and in time? Or will we witness the steady erosion of the American auto industry, in this case by the transfer of jobs and investments overseas and the loss of technological leadership?

The responsibility for answering these questions, as well as the responsibility for leading change, if it is to come, rests with American management. There are three reasons why the task of leadership necessarily falls to management. First, in practical terms, we are an economy of companies. It is ultimately through the company that competition is conducted, just as it is the company that ultimately deploys the resources that carry out the competition. Labor and government, through their relationships with management, always influence and often govern the decision-making process. But the company is the instrument of competition and its managers play the lead role.

Second, in the United States there is a historical reason for management's predominant role—tradition. The appearance of professional managers commanding complex, large-scale enterprises substantially predates the development of a corresponding labor organization or the federal government. As business historian Alfred Chandler notes,

> With the coming of large-scale business enterprise, first on the railroads and then in industry, a new class of businessmen appeared—full-time salaried managers who made a lifetime career of working up the managerial ladder. Comparable administrative hierarchies came later in local and federal government . . . . At the federal level, the number of public administrators remained small until the coming of the Great Depression pushed the government into taking an active role in restoring the nation's economic health. Then with World War II and the continuing cold war, the number of government workers and administrators rose at an unprecedented rate.[3]

The clear historical dominance of management over government is captured by the relative size of the two institutions over time: In 1929, for example, the total government work force in Washington, D.C., was substantially smaller than that of General Motors. As Chandler points out, this pattern of managerial dominance is unique to the United States: "In no other country, however, were large managerial business hierarchies created before the formation of an extensive government civil service."[4]

Finally, in philosophical terms, the arena for change is, first and foremost, management's. The philosophical issue here is whether American management is prepared to acknowledge the joint authority and responsibility that in fact today govern the corporation. Common sense and practical day-to-day experience confirm that labor and government in the United States do already share the authority for decision making—and escape the responsibility for competitive performance. Only management can remedy this disequilibrium by negotiating with labor and government. As the futile debate over industrial policy has shown, neither force of logic nor offers of assistance can persuade an unwilling management to accept labor and government. Until American management recognizes its own self-interest, there will be no fundamental change of the national enterprise system and American industry will be disadvantaged in global competition.

PART II

The Development
of the World
Auto Industry

CHAPTER 2

The Context
of Competitiveness

Competitive advantage in manufacturing flows from two sources. First, a company makes or delivers a product at a lower cost than its rivals. Alternatively, a company need not worry about competing on cost if it can earn a premium price by differentiating its product or service from those of its rivals. Cost and differentiation advantages, in turn, reflect the processes and systems whereby products are made—how production is organized, the interest of managers and workers in doing their jobs well, and whether public intervention supports or impedes the company's efforts to go about its business. In a domestic industry, these factors tend to be similar or constant for all competitors. In global industries, however, national enterprise systems have a major impact on relative cost and quality. Furthermore, these systems can themselves be a source of competitive advantage.

The relationships between management and labor, on the one hand, and between business and government, on the other, are the key dimensions of these enterprise systems. The first relationship determines a company's ability to organize and motivate employees to make cost-efficient and quality products, and the second structures the incentives that prompt companies to invest and grow. Together, these relationships determine the setting or context in which companies compete in global industries.

The competitive impact of national enterprise systems appears most vividly in the modern auto industry. For example, in the factories where workers assemble cars, production is organized not only

13

according to the dictates of efficient industrial engineering and the capacities of machinery and equipment but also according to the language of collective bargaining contracts. By the same token, in the executive offices and board rooms where managers formulate plans for building new models and locating new plants, investment decisions and strategies are shaped not only by economic and financial logic but also by national macroeconomic policies, industry-specific government programs, and regulations.

In this chapter and the three that follow, we look closely at the effects of enterprise systems on automakers' competitiveness—their ability to make low-cost, high-quality cars—in four countries.

INSIDE THE PLANT

Strolling through an assembly plant in Germany, England, Japan, or the United States, an observer would notice many more similarities than differences. Companies that build automobiles for the mass market perform essentially the same functions the world over. Although manufacturers may differ in the number of parts they make or buy and the number of people they employ, and no two plants are exactly the same in scale, layout, and operations, the process everywhere is similar. At one end of the plant, raw materials, parts, and components arrive, and at the other, finished vehicles emerge for final inspection.

Inside the plants, where this remarkable transformation takes place, the organization of people and machinery is critical to success. The manufacturing process is enormously complicated and sophisticated. A finished automobile contains roughly 5,000 parts and components. Depending on how many of these parts are made and subassembled in the plant, the building may require 2.5 million square feet and sit on 200 acres of land.[1] As many as 3,500 managers and workers may be in a plant during a single shift. These people work with and around machinery and equipment worth hundreds of millions of dollars: gigantic, noisy presses to stamp body parts; robots and welding equipment to fit these parts together; automated transfer lines to move the body and chassis along as the car takes form; machines that coat and paint the body; the computer systems that control the flow of the entire process and monitor progress at each stage. Between and among the machines and lines are the baskets and bins containing small parts for assemblies and subassemblies.

Many plants include separate lines for assembling instrument panels, seats, and other interior parts. Some plants even have separate lines devoted to the final assembly of the engine, itself an extremely sophisticated product. Here manual and numerically controlled machine tools grind and bore metal parts to precise specifications before workers gather and inspect them, fit them together, test the final product, and mate it to the chassis.

A final assembly plant in operation hums with activity and movement. The main assembly line, moving at a pace that completes a car every sixty to ninety seconds, flows like a river into which countless tributaries pour. In modern plants, suppliers move in and out of the loading docks, making deliveries as often as every two hours. Inside the plant, workers driving forklifts are busy delivering parts to work stations and removing empty bins. Managers roam the aisles and corridors in electric golf carts, and it is not unusual to see supervisors and maintenance workers moving about the plant on bicycles.

In the most efficient factories, this activity is orchestrated smoothly, hour after hour, shift after shift, day after day. It is an enormously difficult process to manage. And it is expensive. The direct capital costs run in the hundreds of millions of dollars, and operating costs can reach $1 million per day. A single assembly plant consumes enough electricity, coal, or fuel oil for its machinery, heating, and air conditioning systems to power 40,000 households—a city the size of Davenport, Iowa, for example. Labor costs are also significant. Consider this: In a plant employing 3,000 workers on each of two shifts, a one-cent-per-hour wage increase adds up over a single year to $115,200.[2] Multiply that by the number of plants in a company, making allowances for plants of different size. Throw in overtime, cost-of-living adjustments, allowance for productivity increases, the cost of benefits, and higher wages for skilled workers and management employees' salaries, and it becomes obvious why wage settlements are so hotly contested in collective bargaining, and why negotiating skills are critical to competitive success. At General Motors, each penny-per-hour increase in wages represents an annual payroll increase of nearly $8 million.[3]

Recent comparative studies of the economics of automaking suggest that other management and personnel costs are more important sources of competitive advantage than differences in direct wage costs. In particular, manpower levels, job classifications, training, inventory management, and overhead vary significantly between the more productive and less productive plants.[4] Most of these factors

EXHIBIT 1 *The Scope of Collective Bargaining*
Negotiated Issues in the 1984 GM-UAW Contract

For the plant:	job classification
	work rules
	overtime
	hiring and firing
	training
	transfers
	discipline
	safety
	subcontracting
	introduction of new technology
	quality of work life (QWL)
For the company:	grievance procedure
	plant closings
	outsourcing
	training and retraining
	transfers between locations
	employment security
	new product development (Saturn)
	new venture development
	medical, dental, and legal benefits
	employee discounts
	QWL
For the industry:	pattern wages
	hours of work and overtime
	compensation
	seniority rights
	pensions
	unemployment benefits

are negotiated directly in collective bargaining. (See Exhibit 1 for the range of significant competitive issues covered in a modern labor contract.) The general relationship—the nature and frequency of interactions—between managers and workers in the plants affects competitive performance as well. And these are only the effects of labor on cost; labor's impact on quality is another matter. Here again, evidence is accumulating to show a positive link between good relations between managers and workers, "quality of work life" in the plants, and product quality.[5]

In sum, key determinants of competitive success in the modern auto industry are the management of logistics, the ability to coordinate and control the flows of thousands of parts and components, and shop-floor management, the ability to keep workers and machines working together steadily, rhythmically, safely, and carefully. In turn, the relationship between management and labor in general and collective bargaining agreements in particular have a marked influence on the management of people and processes in modern assembly plants.

OUTSIDE THE PLANT

The final assembly process is the most visible and critical part of automaking, the place where, literally, it all comes together. Yet much that happens outside the plants also affects competitive performance. Planning, finance, design engineering, purchasing, marketing, advertising, and public affairs management play important roles. It may cost as much as $4 billion to develop a new car—the bill for the first Saturn cars will be even higher—and involve four to six years of planning, engineering, negotiations with suppliers about quantity, price, quality, and delivery times, and discussions with national, regional, and local governments on matters ranging from the condition of local roads and rail lines to arcane matters of regulatory compliance. Thus, how these matters are handled is enormously significant. In all of these issues, the relationship between the government and the industry is critically important. In every auto-producing nation, governments do many things that affect their companies' competitiveness. Macroeconomic policies—the mix of monetary, fiscal, and trade policies—have immediate and obvious effects on the automotive market. Because a car normally represents a consumer's second-largest lifetime purchase (after a house), interest rates have a disproportionate impact on demand. But interest rates also affect supply, since in lean times the automakers borrow money to invest in new plant and equipment. If the cost of this money is too high, investments may be canceled or postponed. Tax policies—such things as depreciation schedules, investment credits, and "loss-carry-forwards"—also directly influence strategic decisions and competitive performance. Trade policies also affect the competitive environment by controlling (or not) the price and level of imports and exports.

Macroeconomic policies, by definition, are not supposed to discriminate among industries, although in practice large, politically prominent industries such as autos are hurt or helped more than others. In addition to macroeconomic policies, national, regional, and local governments can affect the competitiveness of companies under their jurisdiction. For example, policies toward industry structure (antitrust), corporate governance, contracts (with labor, suppliers, and dealers), education and training, health care and pensions, unemployment insurance, collective bargaining, and workers' rights and safety affect a company's cost of doing business. Such policies, added to management of the macroeconomy, represent the obvious effects of government action.

But governments around the world also intervene in the auto industry specifically, at a microlevel. Every auto-producing nation has an auto sector policy, explicit or implicit, concerning such matters as road building, highway safety, air quality, energy cost and availability, auto-specific taxes, licensing and registration, and inspections. Since the mid-1970s, most nations have had auto-specific trade policies as well. Some European governments even own auto companies partially or wholly.

Each government policy, whether targeted at the auto industry or not, has an impact on the competitive performance of the auto companies. In the United States, government involvement with the auto industry has mixed effects and is poorly coordinated (see Exhibit 2).

Since there is government involvement in the auto industry wherever autos are made, it follows that the nature of the relationship between business and government—the substance of policies and the processes by which these policies are made and implemented—affects competitive performance. Together with the relationship between management and labor, then, the relationship between business and government defines the context in which companies compete.

HOW IT MATTERS

In every auto-producing nation similar institutions carry out similar economic functions. The instrument of competition everywhere is the company, be it General Motors, Volkswagen, or Toyota. Unions represent workers in every major auto-producing nation. Government oversight of the industry, implicit or explicit, exists in each nation.

If the functions are similar everywhere, so are the goals. Managers in each country want to control costs and increase profits. Union

EXHIBIT 2 Government Policies and Competitive Effects
in the U.S. Auto Industry

Policies

		Direct	Indirect
	P o s	federal purchases tariffs import quotas	highway programs cheap energy
E F F E C T S	M i x e d	fuel-economy standards	macroeconomic policies employment laws
	N e g	antitrust regulation of safety, emissions	general social, environmental, & work-place regulation

officials around the world strive to raise real wages, provide job guarantees and income protection, and ensure fair treatment of workers. National governments are all alike in that each worries about employment levels, investment policies, capital flows, and trade balances.

Despite this commonality of functions and goals, companies in some nations are clearly more effective competitors than rivals elsewhere. Many of the differences in competitive performance stem from differences in the structure and operation of national enterprise systems. These enterprise systems, in turn, reflect choices and turning points in the historic development of each competitor nation.

The United States, the United Kingdom, West Germany, and Japan provide a range of contrasts in development, structure, and performance. In the past generation, Japan has risen from the ranks of minor producers to become the world's leading auto-producing nation, setting global standards in cost and quality. The story of the British auto industry illustrates the opposite extreme. As recently as the 1950s, the United Kingdom boasted the second-largest industry in the world (after the United States). Today, the British industry ranks below Spain's in production, and is arguably the weakest in Europe. West Germany and the United States are cases in the middle. Until the late 1970s, the business world regarded each as a principal contender for global dominance. Since then, of course, the Japanese producers have clearly taken the lead.

In comparing these four national experiences, we should review the six characteristics of Japan's economic success identified in chapter 1:

shared authority and responsibility;

shared interests;

efficient, effective, economic decision making;

flexibility and adaptability;

strategic thinking; and

focus on the company in the global market.

It cannot be emphasized too strongly that these characteristics reflect choices that Japanese managers, workers, and government officials made explicitly in rebuilding the nation's economy after World War II. For all the attention recently focused on Japan's economic success, few commentators seem aware of how much this success depends on deals that the key economic actors struck, and on institutional procedures and arrangements worked out during the 1950s.

The key relationships between managers and workers and between business and government in Japan are structured to promote competitiveness. Inside the factories, managers and workers pull together to reduce costs and improve product quality. A worker who stays on after hours to participate in a quality circle sees a tangible relationship between his effort, his employer's success, and his own reward in the form of a bonus and "lifetime employment." Japanese managers are willing to concede some so-called management rights that their counterparts in the United States or Europe guard jealously, because the Japanese see the connection between authority and responsibility shared with workers and competitive performance.

On the business-government side, the Japanese automakers acknowledge that the government played an important, legitimate role in rebuilding the economy after the war and that continued government involvement in the industry is appropriate within certain bounds. For its part, the Japanese government is well aware both of the auto industry's economic salience as a mass employer and major exporter and of its own role in influencing competitive conditions. The government strives for good relations with the automakers, and much as the companies and their enterprise unions do, government officials and business leaders in Japan frequently consult about major decisions, events, and trends before policies are formed.

In short, the Japanese enterprise system is designed to enhance corporate competitive performance. As such, the Japanese system contrasts sharply with those of the United States and Europe, where the principal economic actors have approached their agendas in ways that emphasize differences and produce conflict.

In the national industry studies that follow, certain features of enterprise systems bear close scrutiny. Patterns of competitive behavior and the key relationships between the parties were defined in particular historical circumstances. Although these circumstances have changed everywhere, some enterprise systems have adapted to change more easily than others. The ways in which corporate strategies and organizations developed within home markets continue to shape competitive practices in global rivalry. Why, when, and how unions came into being in each country, and the development of labor's roles and responsibilities similarly affect how the auto companies are faring in world competition. Finally, the nature of government decision making in each nation—its origins, content, structure, and process—bears directly on the automakers' current competitive performance. Differences in these features of national enterprise systems go a long way toward explaining particular companies' ability to make low-cost, high-quality automobiles and to compete effectively in the global marketplace.

CHAPTER 3

"The Only Market That Matters":

The American Automakers and Domestic Rivalry

The American auto industry has endured cyclical ups and downs for decades, but the recent boom-bust-boom cycle described in chapter 1 signifies something out of the ordinary. The wild fluctuations in profits and losses, from record peak to record valley and back again in the space of five years, highlight a fundamental change overtaking the industry: the globalization of competition. U.S. automakers are no longer competing among themselves on familiar terms. Rather, they are locked in a fierce worldwide struggle for market share with rivals in Europe and Japan. And despite the record profits of recent years, the American Big Three are competing in this global struggle at a serious disadvantage.

This disadvantage, in brief, stems from the attempt to compete in a new environment with habits and institutions formed in the past. The dynamics of competition in the industry developed when the American market, the largest and most lucrative in the world, was essentially the private preserve of the Big Three. In these extremely favorable circumstances, the automakers settled into competitive practices appropriate to a stable oligopoly. Moreover, in the decade following World War II, the UAW succeeded in taking wages out of competition through pattern bargaining. As a result, a labor monopoly matched the automakers' oligopoly. Finally, the government did little to promote greater rivalry among the players. By permitting the dominance of the Big Three, the decline of the independent auto companies, and pattern bargaining, the government tacitly accepted a standard of competition that would prove inadequate once the Japanese automakers invaded the American market.

Before the late 1970s, the companies, the union, and the public had few incentives to change their ways. For most of this century, the auto companies occupied center stage in the economy: the nation's biggest employers; consistent creators of high profits; dominant forces in the world's richest market; the elite of American manufacturing industries. Investors in auto companies annually reaped returns well above those that other corporations could generate; autoworkers enjoyed wages well above those of employees in comparable jobs outside the industry; a public on the move enjoyed inexpensive, always improved cars; and taxes on corporate profits, high salaries and wages, and autos themselves helped fill government coffers at the local, state, and federal levels.

With competitive practices so well entrenched, institutions so well established, and economic benefits so evenly apportioned, it is little wonder that the auto companies, the UAW, and federal policy makers are now encountering great difficulties in adapting to change. This chapter describes how the American auto industry formed and developed its distinctive ways of organization and competition—its enterprise system—and looks at how this system is performing in the face of global competition.

THE RISE OF THE BIG THREE

The American auto industry of the mid-1980s was largely in place by the mid-1930s. By then the Big Three—General Motors, Ford, and Chrysler—already dominated the domestic market. Following GM's lead, the automakers had settled on enduring methods of making and selling cars as the market matured and the public's preferences in transportation fell into a predictable pattern. From the 1930s on, the industry developed consistent patterns of pricing, profitability, organization, and management. The companies and their products changed little during the next four decades.

Two Revolutions

The origins of the American auto industry date to the 1890s, when several companies began producing "horseless carriages" on a commercial scale. The industry quickly attracted hundreds of entrants, but it also became concentrated economically and geographically at an early date. By 1909, the year after the first Ford Model T and the founding of General Motors, three companies—Ford, GM, and the ancestor of Studebaker—already controlled about 50 percent of the market. The largest automakers were located in southeastern Michigan, where existing railway carriage and metalworking industries and natural resource and transportation advantages supported the mushrooming growth of auto manufacturing.[1]

Two revolutions led to the industry's concentration. The first was a revolution in production, Ford's discovery of how to build autos on a massive scale. The second was a revolution in marketing, the General Motors strategy to cover the market nationwide with products appealing to different segments of the buying public.[2]

Ford's ability to mass-produce cars—a much larger and more sophisticated product than any that had been built on an assembly line before—was a tremendous competitive advantage. Producing more cars meant selling more. It also meant reducing costs per unit, lowering prices, and stimulating additional demand. In 1909, the first full year of Model T production, Ford built 12,292 cars; in 1914, the first full year of the moving assembly line, Ford built 260,720 Model T's. Ford's share of the market ballooned to more than 50 percent by the end of the decade.[3] To dispose of the cars pouring off the assembly lines, Ford's partner, James Couzens, set up a nationwide network of dealers who capitalized on the Model T's low price and reputation for durability. As early as 1913, more than seven thousand Ford dealers blanketed the United States. The company's slogan— "Watch the Fords go by!"—well expressed the transportation revolution sweeping the country.[4]

Combination and merger, the strategy pioneered by William C. "Billy" Durant at General Motors, provided the second general route to success. Using stock swaps and other speculative financial methods, Durant pieced together an automotive empire. In 1908, Durant merged a mass of automobile and supplier companies, including the Olds Motor Works, Cadillac, and Oakland, into the General Motors

Corporation. In the following decade, Durant added still more companies: Hyatt Roller Bearing, Chevrolet, Fisher Body, Delco and Remy, Frigidaire, and many more.[5] Durant was fortunate that at least a few of these were substantial operations, including several automakers with national dealer networks. Four of the new subsidiaries—Cadillac, Oakland (later Pontiac), Oldsmobile, and Buick—served different, overlapping market segments. Whereas Ford competed with a single product tailored to buyers with little cash to spare, GM potentially offered a line of cars for consumers of various incomes.

In Durant's time, the strategy of covering and dividing the market was more accidental than intentional. When Durant's precarious deals caught up with him during the recession that followed World War I, GM's rescuers, the Du Pont family (represented by Pierre du Pont) and the young Alfred Sloan, made the new strategy explicit. The central elements of GM's plans were the careful segmentation of the market in terms of cost and quality and annual model changes based on new styling. As Sloan recalled, there was no way that GM could compete with Ford on the basis of cost; instead, the only hope seemed to lie in luring new customers with other features. Instead of competing with a single model as did Ford, GM chose to produce "a car for every purse and purpose."

GM segmented the market according to its price pyramid. At the bottom, the company priced the Chevrolet slightly higher than the Model T, but offered more features and a variety of colors. Above Chevrolet, Du Pont and Sloan positioned the other auto divisions from Durant's holdings—Pontiac, Oldsmobile, Buick, and Cadillac—into an ascending hierarchy of cost and quality. "This amounted," observed Sloan, "to quality competition against cars below a given price tag, and price competition against cars above that price tag."[6]

The implementation of the new strategy was as important as its formulation. To this end, Du Pont and Sloan rationalized the chaotic organization that Durant had left behind. The new leaders segregated GM's various businesses into groups—cars and trucks, parts and accessories, and nonautomotive businesses—and the groups into divisions headed by general managers. Each of the five automotive divisions became responsible for the complete assembly operations for its nameplate and its various models. Thus the GM organization designers separated and differentiated the company according to the strategy of serving different markets. But they also created interdivisional committees (later called policy groups) to coordinate functions such as purchasing, engineering, and research common to the entire group. This new corporate structure allowed GM to reap the benefits of two different sorts of organization: decentralization and wide market coverage (the groups and divisions) and centralized planning, financial services, and other administrative functions coordinated at various levels of management, including the top.[7]

To support this new structure, managers at GM also created or adapted a host of managerial policies and processes: statistical quality control and demand forecasting, periodic (ten-day) reports on factory and dealer inventories, and sophisticated cost accounting. Top managers were therefore regularly supplied with information critical in running a complex logistical business. Du Pont and Sloan also designed ways to professionalize the company's management. Durant had founded the General Motors Institute (GMI), an engineering vocational school in Flint, in 1908. His successors poured resources into GMI and used it to train managers as well as engineers. To motivate these new managers, Sloan offered a bonus: each year, based on divisional performance, managers were rewarded with varying amounts of stock.

In the later 1920s, Walter Chrysler, a former GM executive, set out to build his own company, successfully copying the strategies—but not the managerial innovations—of Du Pont and Sloan. Chrysler bought up and consolidated the remains of several failed automakers, including Maxwell Motors, whose middle-priced cars had an "indifferent mechanical reputation." Several years later, Chrysler introduced a premium line under his own name and in 1928 acquired the properties of the deceased Dodge brothers, thereby adding a low-cost competitor to Ford and Chevrolet.[8]

The Transformation of the Market

Ford's production methods and GM's marketing strategy complemented the changing needs of the auto-buying public. Looking back on the 1920s from the end of his career, Sloan asserted that "the watershed which divides the present from the past" was built upon four elements: "installment selling, the used-car trade-in, the closed body, and the annual model."[9] All of these factors worked to the advantage of the largest firms and against their smaller rivals. Under Sloan's guidance, for example, GM created the General Motors Acceptance Corporation, a credit agency, to enable dealers to carry inventories and customers to afford more expensive cars. The used-car trade-in signaled a new order of competition. Although not exactly saturated, the automotive market of the 1920s became crowded with companies that, for the first time, competed beyond regional borders for the same customers across the nation. The early casualties were smaller automakers with local markets and narrower margins. Between 1920 and 1930, the number of automakers in the United States plummeted from 160 to 23—a drop of 86 percent.[10]

The automakers' ability to make closed-roof cars, a necessity for selling in the harsher climates of the North, proved critical to success as well. Once more, however, smaller companies could not compete; the capital investment in machinery, tools, and dies was greater than many of them could afford. Finally, the annual model change proved beyond the means of most smaller companies. In the industry's earliest decades, new models had been introduced irregularly as new features or technological innovations became available. In the mid-1920s, however, Sloan and GM designer Harley Earl stumbled onto a new characteristic of the market: changes in automotive fashions, like the latest styles of clothes, could sway potential buyers. Consumers became increasingly willing to exchange recently acquired cars for the latest models. Stuck with unchanging models increasingly perceived as stodgy and out of date, many small automakers found it impossible to attract investment capital and left the business.

GM's success in selling on the basis of style—as opposed to cost or technological innovation—signaled a fundamental change in the market. GM understood that as better roads were built around the nation and per capita income climbed, the principal advantages of the Model T—its durability and low price—became less important. Consumers were beginning to favor cars with cosmetic features and creature comforts, road cruisers rather than runabouts.[11] In such a world, the biggest companies, which could afford to support nationwide dealer networks and advertising, enjoyed a substantial competitive advantage over their smaller rivals.

In sum, scale economies in production and marketing transformed the nature of competition in the industry. By the end of the 1920s, GM, Ford, and Chrysler dominated the market. And the industry had become big business. In 1929, only AT&T and U.S. Steel surpassed GM's $609.9 million total investment in plant, property, and equipment, and only AT&T employed more people than the 233,286 who worked for GM.[12]

Standard Practices and Predictable Patterns

As the market settled down and the rivalry of the Big Three took shape, the automakers developed standard practices and systems for managing the business. Auto company executives were responsible for enormous investments while also having to manage large-scale production systems involving thousands of people. High-volume manufacture of a product as complex as the automobile, with thousands of interdependent parts, required careful attention to plant location, layout, and job design. Indeed, logistics, the coordinated scheduling and delivery of parts to the assembly line, became one of the fundamental managerial responsibilities in the business.

The principal ways in which the Big Three ensured control over logistics included standardizing the layout of plants and streamlining production networks. Techniques pioneered at Ford's Highland Park plant, home of the Model T, became industry standards. According to researchers for the Federal Trade Commission, "a noteworthy feature" of the Highland Park plant was that

> it was designed and laid out on what has come to be known as the "line production system." In the plant previously used, as in other ordinary factories, machines, such as drill presses, milling machines, lathes, boring mills, planers, etc., were located in groups according to the type or class of operation; and the material in the process of manufacture was conveyed from group to group according to the sequence of operations. This resulted in a large amount of crisscrossing of the lines of progress and a large amount of shop transportation. The Highland Park plant was designed to avoid this by having the machines and the employees operating them placed in such sequence that the material would move in a predetermined line of production without interruption or loss of time in transporting material from the place of one operation to the place of the next. This means a production line for each part that is to be processed within the factory.

The new system not only enabled a greater volume of output but also "reduced inventories, eliminated storage rooms and eliminated the transportation of materials from one department to another—materially lowering the cost of production."[13]

Ford is also credited with the idea of centralizing and coordinating different stages of auto production in a single location. Although Ford's Highland Park plant and the River Rouge complex built in the 1920s were massive, integrated factories, Ford's operations were, in fact, decentralized at an early date. As the market for cars boomed, Ford discovered that it could reduce transportation costs sharply by locating final assembly plants near major markets. The company continued to operate specialized machining and parts manufacturing plants in the Detroit area while stampings, engines, and other parts were shipped to final assembly plants around the country. Before 1920, Ford had opened branch assembly operations in Kansas City, Long Island, Chicago, San Francisco, Memphis, Los Angeles, Denver, Portland, Seattle, Cambridge (Mass.), St. Louis, Columbus, Dallas, Houston, Minneapolis, Indianapolis, Pittsburgh, Atlanta, Cincinnati, Cleveland, Louisville, Buffalo, Milwaukee, Washington, Oklahoma City, and Omaha. Many independent suppliers were encouraged to locate plants near these branch operations in the interests of efficiency.[14] GM and Chrysler followed Ford's lead, although declining freight costs after World War II reduced the advantages of decentralized operations, and in the face of current foreign competition, the automakers have lately been attempting to retreat to the Midwest.

The Big Three also gained control over logistics through backward integration—the management of subsidiaries specializing in raw materials and parts. This process began at an early date. By the end of World War I, for example, all of the large automakers built their own engines and axles.[15] Over the years, GM went farthest in manufacturing parts. Durant had acquired a number of supplier firms during his buying sprees, and by the time GM rationalized these scattered operations in the 1920s and 1930s, it purchased less than 50 percent of the materials and supplies that ended up in its cars. Henry Ford, stubbornly determined to do things his own way, spurned GM's approach in favor of purchasing interests in raw materials and manufacturing his own steel, glass, and lumber. He even considered building his own rubber plants. The Ford Motor Company, however, purchased about 60 percent of its supplies from independent companies. Chrysler was the least vertically integrated of the major automakers, manufacturing a significant percentage of its parts only in the years after World War II.[16]

If the methods of making cars were becoming standardized in the 1920s, so was the product itself. The basic technological characteristics of the modern automobile emerged at an early date. The internal combustion engine was invented in the nineteenth century. Standardized parts and design, shock absorbers, electric headlamps, asbestos drum brakes, and steering wheels all appeared before 1910. In the next two decades came the electric self-starter, the closed chassis, low-pressure pneumatic tires, and synchromesh transmission; disc brakes and power steering made driving simpler, safer, and more comfortable, although there is ample evidence to support Sloan's 1962 observation that "great as have been the engineering advances since 1920, we have today basically the same kind of machine that was created in the first twenty years of the industry." Over time, as well, the auto companies' ongoing quest for volume and efficiency eclipsed the creative engineering achievements behind the revolution in mass production. Given such managerial emphases, the possibilities of radical technological change in autos, or in the methods of making them, diminished.[17]

The Big Three's pricing behavior also followed a predictable pattern once the oligopoly formed. In brief, General Motors set prices, and the other companies followed suit. Sloan's associate, Donaldson Brown, explained GM's pricing in the 1920s: The company set prices "to gain, over a protracted period of time, a margin of profit which represents the highest attainable return, commensurate with capital turnover and the enjoyment of wholesale expansion with adequate regard to the economic consequences of fluctuations in volume." This worked out to be an annual rate of return (net profits after taxes divided by net worth) that averaged about 20 percent over the years. The other automakers' payoff was considerably less, but they had little flexibility in pricing—they had to follow GM's lead. On the rare occasions that Ford or Chrysler announced its prices first, the company ended up cutting them if GM announced a lower figure. As Ford executive Theodore Yntema later testified before a Senate subcommittee, "We have to look at our competitive situation. Ordinarily, what we find is this: We have very little leeway. If we would reduce the price very substantially to meet competition, we would not make a very respectable profit."[18]

A Domestic Mindset

Like so much else in the industry's history, the automakers' approach to international competition took shape in the 1920s and 1930s. The Big Three became multinationals at an early date—by 1929 Ford and GM had assembly plants on six continents, and Chrysler had factories in several European countries and Canada—but high transportation costs, host country government policies, and distinctively different national tastes inhibited global integration of these operations. These factors, in addition to the tremendous size and profitability of the domestic market, explain why the Big Three concentrated their energies in North America.

Ford was the first major automaker to move outside the United States, licensing manufacturing operations in Canada in 1904. Ford linked its Canadian factories closely with those in the United States, but the company also used its Canadian operations to export throughout the British Commonwealth. GM and Chrysler copied Ford in both respects. Because it was cheaper to export "knocked-down kits" of parts than fully assembled cars to many countries, the American multinationals set up branch assembly plants around the world.[19]

Protectionism overseas curtailed this strategy, however. European governments adopted high tariffs on imported autos during World War I. Such policies led Ford to build fully integrated plants in England and Germany. GM entered the same markets for similar reasons, but did so by acquiring foreign subsidiaries, Vauxhall and Opel, in 1925 and 1929, respectively. Elsewhere in Europe, French and Italian government policies restricted American direct investment, and the primitive development of the market in other countries discouraged the Big Three from setting up operations. Many European nations also adopted energy, tax, or road-building policies that led consumers to prefer different sorts of cars from those favored in the United States. As a result, in the late 1920s Ford and GM began to run their European subsidiaries as decentralized companies with minimal links to operations in North America.[20]

Governments around the world raised tariffs again in the aftermath of the Depression to protect native industries and discourage imports. In Japan, the government took more extreme measures, forcing the Americans to abandon their branch assembly operations in the 1930s. Tariffs, other forms of protectionism, and the divergence of national preferences in autos led the American automakers to disengage domestic and international operations and to view the industry worldwide as a series of discrete national markets rather than as a single, global market.

The American market, moreover, had attractions of its own. To begin with, it was enormous. Auto sales in the United States outranked sales in the rest of the world combined until the 1960s. As late as 1955, nearly 80 percent of all car registrations in the world occurred in North America. Per capita income was the highest in the world; the system of roads was unmatched anywhere; and the infatuation of the public with cars had no parallel. Not only was the market large and growing, it was also lucrative. Between 1947 and 1967, the Big Three averaged a return of 16.7 percent on net worth, nearly twice the rate earned by other manufacturing companies. With an average return of 20.7 percent in this period, GM was one of the most consistently profitable corporations in the world.[21]

Best of all, the American market belonged essentially to three companies. For nearly four decades after the formation of the oligopoly in the late 1920s, the Big Three controlled nearly 90 percent of auto sales in the United States. The smaller independent producers—Kaiser and Willys, Studebaker and Packard, Nash-Kelvinator and Hudson—merged or left the business. By the mid-1960s, only the last pair, merged into American Motors, remained to build cars for the mass market. Imports from Europe, led by Volkswagen and Renault, generally remained below 10 percent of sales before the coming of the Japanese in the late 1960s raised the total import share dramatically.

In such favorable circumstances, with such limited and well-understood competitive rivalry, the American automakers deviated little from the strategies and methods they had settled on during the 1920s. The Big Three's market position remained remarkably stable over the decades. GM controlled more than 40 percent of the American market, and Ford and Chrysler never achieved more than 28 percent.[22] The auto companies grew alike in their business policies and practices. To stay close to GM, Ford and Chrysler slowly adopted GM's market segmentation and model change strategies.[23] The companies competed across the market but most vigorously in particular niches. GM's Chevrolet division and Ford competed evenly at the low end of the market, and GM dominated in the upscale segments. Ford enjoyed success with sporty cars such as the Thunderbird and Mustang, while Chrysler sold most of its cars at the low end of the market or in specialty niches such as those for small trucks and vans. Yet in the important respects, the automakers were far more alike than different. In terms of strategy, organization, operations, behavior, and, above all, their focus on the domestic market, the Big Three settled into predictable and profitable routines at an early date.

MANAGERS AND WORKERS

An irony of the American enterprise system is that management strategies and policies that emphasized efficiency and output emerged alongside employment policies that grew more rigid and counterproductive over time. The Ford method of production transformed the nature of jobs in the factories and reduced the amount of training and skill required to make cars. The work became less interesting and the pace more frantic, and the automakers' shift to annual models worsened the employment effects of an already seasonal and insecure business. Along with deskilled and insecure jobs came other problems: a prevailing, one-sided ideology of employer's rights; employment policies that gave short shrift to workers' needs and interests on the shop floor; patterns of immigration that reinforced social divisions between the two groups. As a result, auto managers tended to ignore or disregard constructive contributions and suggestions from the work force, and workers had few incentives to care about improving the cost and quality of the cars they made.

The coming of collective bargaining and the rise of the UAW did little to change this situation. Employers had been willing to pay good wages from the earliest days of the business. Collective bargaining institutionalized the practice, took wages out of competition among the domestic automakers, and greatly improved workers' security and benefits. In effect, the companies bought off labor's concerns about a work system that stressed "getting cars out the door," and further discouraged employees from contributing to production improvements.

Except for providing seniority rights and a formal grievance system, then, collective bargaining did not address fundamental problems in the relationship between managers and workers raised by technology of mass production and an ideology of efficiency. Moreover, formal contracts recognized and froze into place job classifications and work rules that inhibited flexibility and change. Finally, bargaining and grievance handling—inherently adversarial processes—actually increased divisions between employers and employees. Indeed, between the Ford revolution and the auto crisis of the 1970s, managers and workers pursued their own interests and agenda with little regard for the competitive implications of their actions.

Factory Life

The history of factory work in the auto industry after the coming of mass production makes gloomy reading. In earlier days, most employees had been autonomous craftsmen, responsible for their own tools and equipment, hours, and pace and quality of work. These workers had normally decided the best means of tackling a particular job and usually had seen their work on a product through from beginning to end. For example, work teams or gangs, each responsible for assembling an entire vehicle, had built the first autos.[24]

All this changed with high-volume production and the need to fill the insatiable demand for cars in the early twentieth century. The amount of skilled work in the factories dwindled while managerial and supervisory roles grew more important. Between 1908 and 1913, employment at Ford grew from 450 workers to more than 14,000. This influx of labor required more elaborate control systems. Industrial engineers carefully designed and segmented jobs at Ford's Model T factories. Most assembly-line jobs became interchangeable and involved little training. In 1922, Henry Ford estimated that 85 percent of his factory workers required less than two weeks of training, and 43 percent required less than one day. To keep the assembly process running at full speed and to avoid costly stoppages and breakdowns, foremen assumed more arbitrary and directive powers. They were typically charged "to see to it that the men under [them] turn out so many pieces per day and personally work to correct whatever may prevent it."[25]

These contrary tendencies—workers losing status and control and foremen acquiring both—had important effects on the evolution of employment practices and labor relations. Managers began to perceive workers as interchangeable machine parts. Carefully designed assembly processes, wrote Henry Ford, reduced "the necessity for thought on the part of the worker," and also reduced his discretion and "his movements to a minimum. As nearly as possible, he does only one thing with one movement."[26] The changing ethnic and social characteristics of the work force reinforced management's view of the worker and the barriers between the two sides. Statistics compiled at Ford in November 1914 show that only 29 percent of company employees were American born. There is no record of the percentage of American-born employees who were managers, but contemporary visitors to the factory frequently commented on the difficulties experienced by English-speaking foremen and non-English-speaking workers. In later years, when blacks entered the plants in increasing numbers, racial tensions compounded the divisions between managers and workers.[27]

As workers lost standing in the shops, they also fell prey to arbitrary management practices and the seasonableness of the business. One assembly-line worker, Clayton Fountain, recalled that

> the annual layoff during the model change was always a menace to the security of the workers. Along about June or July it started. The bosses would pick the men off a few at a time, telling them to stay home until they were notified to come back. There was no rhyme or reason in the selection of the fortunate ones chosen to continue working. The foreman had the say. If he happened to like you, or if you sucked around him and did him favors—or if you were one of the bastards who worked like hell and turned out more than production—you might be picked to work a few weeks longer than the next guy. . . . In October and November we began to trickle back into the plants. Again, the bosses had the say as to who was rehired first. Years of service with the company meant nothing . . . generally speaking, the laid-off worker had no assurance of any kind that he would be called back at any specific time.[28]

Although visitors to Ford's Highland Park plant noted high spirits among employees during the early days of Model T production, the work itself was unpopular. In 1913, the first year of the assembly line, absenteeism at Ford averaged about 10 percent and employee turnover reached an extraordinary level—370 percent.[29] Subsequent visitors reported the same observations time after time: work in the assembly line was boring, repetitious, dangerous, and exhausting. In 1914, Progressive journalist John A. Fitch recorded worker complaints that "each man . . . has just one small thing to do—and do over and over again. It's push and bustle and go." In 1923, the president of the leftist Automobile Workers Union quoted a worker's lament: "If I keep putting on Nut No. 86 for about 86 more days, I will be Nut No. 86 in the Pontiac bughouse." A Yale undergraduate who spent a summer working for Ford echoed the refrain: "You've got to work like hell in Ford's. From the time you become a number in the morning until the bell rings for quitting time you . . . can't let up. You've got to get out the production . . . and if you can't get it out, you get out."[30]

Such problems, early efforts to organize unions, and the social consequences of immigration and urbanization disturbed some employers, who attempted to counter them with "enlightened" personnel policies. At Ford, the company created separate skilled wage classifications, an employee savings plan, and high wages for qualifying workers—the famous "five-dollar day." In 1914, Ford followed these reforms by founding a Sociological Department to instill middle-class values, virtuous behavior, and the work ethic among employees. Other automakers also paid high wages to attract and retain workers. At GM, for instance, employees earned 40 percent more than the average American factory worker and were eligible for a savings program and a life insurance program in the 1920s.[31]

Most of these paternalistic efforts in "welfare capitalism" came to a halt in the early 1930s as the Depression hit the auto industry with devastating force.[32] Between 1929 and 1932 vehicle production fell 75 percent, from over 5.0 million units to 1.3 million. At the same time, the number of jobs in the industry dropped from 447,448 to 243,614—a fall of 45 percent. Those employees fortunate enough to keep their jobs worked fewer hours for less pay. The average weekly earnings of autoworkers fell 32 percent, from $35.14 to $20.00, between 1928 and 1932. In these years, according to historian Sidney Fine, Detroit experienced "the worst relief crisis of any major American metropolis and the highest jobless rate in the United States."[33]

Enter the UAW

The modern American system of industrial relations took shape amid the terrible conditions of the Great Depression. In earlier years, a combination of circumstances—management paternalism or intimidation, factional divisions in the labor movement, and worker indifference—had defeated efforts to organize unions in most manufacturing industries, including autos. In the 1930s, however, the automakers could not withstand public pressure to do something to shield workers from the effects of the Depression. Although the Big Three eventually recognized the United Auto Workers (UAW), the companies succeeded in circumscribing labor's advances and in limiting the scope of collective bargaining. Born in conflict, the relationship between the automakers and the UAW continued to feature the marks of struggle for decades: management's reluctance to recognize the union's legitimacy; ongoing fights over the scope of collective bargaining; and the institutionalization of adversarial relations.

Auto company executives portrayed the struggle in the starkest ideological terms. During the sit-down strike at GM's works in Flint, Michigan, Alfred Sloan's message to the workers posed the issues.

Will a labor organization run the plants of General Motors Corporation or will the management continue to do so? On this issue depends the question as to whether you have to have a union card to hold a job, or whether your job will depend in the future, as it has in the past, upon your own individual merit.

In other words, will you pay tribute to a private group of labor dictators for the privilege of working, or will you have to have the right to work as you may desire? Wages, working conditions, honest collective bargaining, have little, if anything, to do with the underlying situation. They are simply a smoke screen to cover the real objective.[34]

The Big Three tried many ways to evade being organized by an independent autoworkers' union, including threatening union organizers and setting up company-specific employee representation plans. Although the National Industrial Recovery Act (NIRA) of 1933 formally guaranteed employees "the right to organize and bargain collectively through representatives of their own choosing," free from "interference, coercion, or restraint" by their employers, the statute neglected to include enforcement procedures. Ford simply ignored it. GM and Chrysler interpreted the act to support management-designed employee representation plans, which opened communication with workers and provided a means to handle grievances, but included no provision for wage bargaining.[35]

The automakers also resorted to intimidation and violence to keep the unions out. Ford used its plant security force, the Service Department, to bully organizers and workers. GM and Chrysler employed Pinkertons and other private detectives to investigate suspected union sympathizers and infiltrate union meetings. The companies summarily dismissed employees for union activities. During the frequent strikes of the early 1930s fights between picketers and scabs were common. Occasionally worse happened. In 1932, Dearborn police and Ford Servicemen killed four strikers and wounded twenty others at the River Rouge complex. Five years later, when Ford security guards beat up a handful of union leaders (including Walter Reuther) at the famous Battle of the Overpass, national attention focused on the UAW's cause.

GM and Chrysler formally recognized the UAW in 1937; Ford held out until 1941. Recognition of the union, however, did not end the conflict; instead, the struggle continued within institutional boundaries. The automakers continued to oppose union representation elections across the country on a plant-by-plant basis. In the late 1930s, GM upgraded its Personnel Department and gave "preventive" employee relations a high priority to contain the union's growth.[36] Not until 1979 did the company finally agree to recognize the UAW in all of its facilities. The Big Three also worked to limit the scope of collective bargaining. The Wagner Act, successor to the NIRA in 1935, acknowledged employer's rights and confined bargaining to "wages, hours, and other terms and conditions of employment." Thereafter, the companies construed this clause narrowly while the union sought to expand its purview. The clause has been a continuing focus of debate between management and labor over the years.

GM's adamant position during a 113-day strike in 1945–1946 illustrates how strongly the company felt about its managerial prerogatives. Walter Reuther, the UAW vice-president in charge of negotiations with GM, had announced unprecedented goals: a reduction in the work week from 48 to 40 hours and an immediate thirty-cent-per-hour wage increase with no price hike passed on to consumers. The UAW would be willing to accept less, Reuther said, if GM would open its books to show how much of a wage increase could be afforded without raising prices. To show his seriousness, Reuther took the GM workers out on strike.

GM executives recognized "a crucial issue of principle" behind this proposal, a direct threat to its own responsibility and control of the business. The company responded to Reuther's demands with demands of its own:

1. That wages, hours of employment and other conditions of employment are the only matters which are subject to collective bargaining.
2. That the products to be manufactured, the location of plants, the schedules of production, the methods, processes, and means of manufacturing, the right to hire, promote, transfer, discharge, or discipline for cause, and to maintain discipline and efficiency of employees, are the sole responsibility of the Corporation.[37]

In the end, GM simply outwaited the union. In March 1946, the UAW, out of money and without support elsewhere in the labor movement, accepted a wage increase patterned after settlements in the steel and electrical industries. The UAW gained no say in the company's pricing decisions.

The UAW owed defeat in 1946 to its own internal problems as well as to GM's obstinacy. One Reuther associate recalled much later that the union leaders were too absorbed in their own internal affairs to pursue the strike: "We had enough to do in managing our own house without getting more involved in company affairs." Certainly, national

UAW leaders were struggling to centralize control of collective bargaining.[38] Like the Congress of Industrial Organizations (CIO), the new UAW was a federated organization. The national union had a centralized staff and responsibilities but ultimately depended on grass-roots organizing and financial support from member unions. Local unions retained wide powers and varied considerably in ideology, policies, and behavior. Local unions also differed in their agreements with management.

The Wagner Act and the coming of industrywide bargaining did little to change traditional patterns of wage classification, job evaluation, seniority rights, and other issues that remained subject to local custom. These matters continued to be settled at the shop or plant level, and their resolution depended on local conditions and leaders' attitudes and experience on both sides. These circumstances made it extremely difficult for the national UAW leadership to establish centralized standards and control, or to push for broad changes in the relationship between the companies and the union.

Civilizing the Relationship

Walter Reuther's rise to power in the UAW signaled a general willingness to accept management's terms for control of the work place. The struggle would be fought within the confines of collective bargaining. In the meantime, the workers would be well paid. Reuther presided over the UAW from 1947 until his death in a plane crash in 1970. During that time, his leadership was never seriously contested. His success stemmed from his advocacy of programs benefiting the economic interests of the union membership and his ability to deliver at the bargaining table.

Reuther repeatedly urged the fair distribution of America's tremendous wealth among the people who helped create it. "We will meet the problem of industrial tension only if we learn to distribute abundance," he wrote. "Our problem is to create the largest possible economic pie and to divide up an ever-increasing abundance based on human needs." Although such views could be interpreted as socialistic, Reuther was no revolutionary. Indeed, he embraced the American system of managerial capitalism wholeheartedly. He acknowledged management's rights to make decisions concerning new technologies and plant location and layout, but he insisted on protection of workers' rights as well. He pushed consistently for a shorter working week as a means of creating more employment opportunities. He sought standardized wages, "equal pay for equal work," throughout the industry: "Unless we succeed in thus taking labor out of competition . . . management will be able to depress our wage standards by locating production wherever labor is cheapest." He wanted protection of unemployed workers, health and safety benefits, and security at retirement through company-funded pensions.[39]

Most of these points were achieved in a series of national contracts Reuther negotiated with the Big Three in the decade following the failed strike at GM in 1946. These postwar agreements, which provided for an orderly rise in real wages, a cost-of-living adjustment (COLA), multiyear contracts, and substantial pension, health care, and unemployment benefits, routinized collective bargaining and stabilized the relationship between labor and management.

An enduring pattern of auto bargaining took shape in 1948. Rather than face annual confrontations over wage issues, GM president Charles L. Wilson proposed to augment autoworkers' wages yearly by an "annual improvement factor" (AIF) reflecting productivity increases in the American economy generally. Wilson also suggested a formula for adjusting wages with the cost of living as measured by the consumer price index. These two wage principles appeared in every national contract from 1948 to 1982. They guaranteed rising real wages for autoworkers and ensured that they would rank among the highest paid of all American workers. And through the AIF and COLA, Reuther took a long step toward his principle of "full distribution" of the industry's economic abundance. Between 1948 and 1981, wages rose by more than 300 percent, and benefits accumulated at an even faster rate.[40]

Subsequent national contracts marked other bargaining milestones: multiyear agreements after 1950, premiums for night shifts and overtime, longer vacations, and increasingly exotic economic benefits. In the 1949 Chrysler contract, the UAW negotiated company-funded pensions of $100 per month for retired workers; in 1950, new benefits included partial funding of hospitalization and medical care; in 1955, Ford agreed to "the guaranteed annual wage," or supplemental unemployment benefits (SUB) to aid laid-off workers. Subsequent bargaining innovations were periodic but less spectacular. In 1958 came severance pay. In 1961, the UAW negotiated a profit-sharing plan with American Motors and longer relief time at the major automakers; extended vacations in 1964; expanded pensions and health insurance in 1967 and 1970; personal paid holidays in 1973 and 1976.

In 1955, the UAW finally succeeded in taking wages out of competition through "pattern bargaining." After that year, national contracts with the Big Three expired on the same day every three years. In a contract year, the UAW selected one of the major automakers as its primary target. Once agreement was reached with that company, the union negotiated similar terms with the others, including, eventually, the independent automakers and suppliers. Pattern bargaining thus answered Reuther's call for "equal pay for equal work." It also had two other effects. First, it made the UAW into a monopoly union. Labor's negotiating power greatly increased, since a strike would penalize the union's targeted company disproportionately. Second, pattern bargaining served to increase the economic disparity between the Big Three and the independent manufacturers, since the large companies could more easily spread their labor costs across greater sales volume.[41]

Local bargaining also followed a relatively consistent pattern, though confined to narrow economic issues after the early postwar years. Nonetheless, within these bounds, the UAW locals made a slow series of advances that severely constrained plant and shop-level managerial authority to control the volume, efficiency, and quality of work. In particular, the union gained control over training and apprenticeship of skilled workers, work scheduling, hiring, transfer and promotion policy, work assignments and jurisdiction, job descriptions and wage classifications, and, occasionally, the type and amount of work that could be subcontracted.[42]

As conflict became channeled and factory life more structured and orderly, collective bargaining institutionalized adversarial relations between management and labor. Union officials continued to view employers with hostility. The personal histories of the UAW leadership partly encouraged this attitude. Reuther and most of his supporters had been young men in the 1930s, and they dominated union politics for four decades. Memories of the union's struggle for recognition seldom lay buried for long. Both Reuther and his brother Victor, moreover, had been wounded in the late 1940s by unidentified snipers. Although the gunmen were never found, both Reuthers suspected that hoodlums known to be associated with antiunion employers were responsible.[43] Over the years, the UAW also refused to let the stories of the sit-down strikes, the Battle of the Overpass, and other managerial excesses of the early years die. The union's magazine, *Solidarity*, continued for decades to run articles on the early struggles on anniversaries and in collective bargaining years. The union's orientation and educational literature also stressed a view of management lifted straight from the Depression.

Adversarial attitudes also reflected the nature of collective bargaining itself. The process of negotiation entailed periodic "battles" that had to be "won" at the expense of the other side. Belligerent posturing and rhetoric preceded contract agreements. And there was some truth to the union's belief that bargaining victories came only after struggle—concessions had to be wrested from an unwilling management. In the early contracts especially, the union negotiated from weakness. It had little knowledge of business and financial techniques and analysis and, at best, limited access to company records. Finally, the collective bargaining arena was the only place where leaders of both sides met to discuss each other's concerns. As Reuther put it, "Too often collective bargaining is a kind of brief encounter every two or three years under circumstances that do not contribute to objectivity."[44] Separated by barriers of politics and social class, and in the absence of occasions to communicate, representatives of labor and management had few opportunities or incentives to improve their relationship.

Over time, the era of violent opposition and ideological divisions gave way to what Leonard Woodcock, Reuther's successor, called "a civilized relationship."[45] Strikes and other extreme measures of worker discontent diminished, replaced by legal forms and the orderly procedures of modern industrial relations.

Change under Pressure: QWL and EI

Although unionization helped put an end to arbitrary and vindictive personnel management, the UAW was slow to address other shop-floor problems. The pace and segmented nature of assembly-line work continued to plague the work force. A famous study of a GM assembly plant in the late 1940s revealed workers still resentful of the discipline of the line. "The work isn't hard," said one, "it's the never-ending pace. . . . The guys yell 'hurrah' whenever the line breaks down . . . you can hear it all over the plant." Every few years, journalists, sociologists, and doctoral students observed the same malaise in the plants, giving it such names as "alienation," "the Lordstown syndrome" (after a much-publicized and largely misrepresented strike by workers at a GM plant in Lordstown, Ohio, in 1972), or "the blue-collar blues."[46] Interestingly, although the UAW helped publicize this form of worker discontent, it consistently overlooked the problem for decades. As a result, workers remained at war with their jobs, and management failed to tap a rich resource on the shop floor: employees' experience, ideas, and enthusiasm.

In the late 1960s, increasing import penetration, labor discontent, and growing problems with quality led the companies and the union to reexamine shop-floor attitudes. GM, which faced high levels of turnover, absenteeism, and grievances, began experimenting with organization development and job enrichment programs to increase worker participation and improve morale. These efforts were later collected under the rubric of "quality of work life" (QWL) at GM and "employee involvement" (EI) at Ford and given formal sanction in collective bargaining agreements.

Although managers and union officials have pushed for programs throughout GM and Ford, QWL and EI activities take different forms in different locations. In some cases, labor and management participate together in quality circles or task forces to tackle shop-floor problems such as absenteeism, supervisor training, product quality, and efficiency. In others, the two sides work together on problems of plant layout and job design. In still others, labor-management committees work outside the plant on community and social action programs.[47]

In most locations, the results of QWL and EI programs have been good. Absenteeism and grievance loads have dropped, and product quality and productivity have improved. Leaders on both sides believe that QWL and EI programs are a good idea and acknowledge that workers' job satisfaction and the competitive performance of the companies are intimately related. The programs have not succeeded everywhere, however. Several plants scrapped the efforts when local officers moved on or left office. Some managers dislike relinquishing authority and control in the work place; some union leaders attack the programs as a cover for assembly-line speedups, as a way to avoid involving workers in meaningful business decisions, and as a managerial ruse to circumvent the authority of shop committees.

Where they have taken root, QWL and EI programs and other joint labor-management programs are gradually modifying a long tradition of adversarialism. Managers and workers have begun to work together to attack competitive problems of cost and quality. This change has been slow and has come in fits and starts, however. The formal system of collective bargaining, designed and used for decades to divide wealth, has proved difficult to adapt to the task of increasing wealth by promoting competitiveness. Leaders on both sides continue to hold assumptions and subscribe to myths about decision making and responsibility that reflect the balance of power before unionization.

WASHINGTON AND DETROIT

"There are two cities in the country that are known by their industries," says Wendell Larsen, a former group vice-president at Chrysler, "Washington and Detroit." This shorthand for the federal government and the auto industry highlights the power and influence of two mammoth institutions. As an enormous employer, a large-scale consumer of steel, glass, rubber, and other basic products, and an important reservoir of engineering, research, and managerial talent, the auto industry occupies the center of America's industrial economy. And, of course, the growth of the federal government and its reach into the management of the economy are two major themes of twentieth-century American history.

The links between Washington and Detroit are many and varied. Over time, however, a general pattern is clear: the federal government has become increasingly involved in the affairs of the auto industry. This involvement ranges from targeted actions such as procurement and trade policies and auto-specific regulations to indirect measures such as macroeconomic policies, highway programs, and energy policy. The government's attention to the industry has been intermittent and inconstant over the years; periods of mild support and benign neglect have alternated with periods of fierce scrutiny and sharp intervention. The government, moreover, has made few efforts to coordinate the mixed effects of its actions, and has taken little note of its cumulative impact on the automakers' competitive performance.

For their part, the auto companies have regarded federal interventions in different ways in different periods. At times, particularly in the early days, the automakers were grateful for federal support. Later on, the industry even became a conspicuous supplier of executive talent to Washington.[48] In the 1960s, however, when the government began to intervene in industry affairs more actively through regulation of safety, emissions, and fuel economy, the automakers reacted defensively and made little effort to understand the government's new role. Executives complained bitterly about regulations and antitrust actions, and tended to regard federal intervention of any sort as an unwelcome intrusion. As a result, the companies were slow to perceive opportunities as well as threats in their changed environment and to develop skills in lobbying and public affairs management.

By the 1970s, the relationship between Washington and Detroit had become tangled and testy. The government had become an active and everyday participant in industry affairs, albeit in a decentralized and uncoordinated way. Interactions between bureaucrats and executives were played out in courts and hearing rooms amid mutual hostility and suspicion. The two parties had little inclination, few occasions, and no forums to discuss their differences, or to consider how their relationship affected the industry's competitive performance. Such circumstances were not conducive to making effective public policy. Indeed, the process of policy formulation led to poor decisions and awkward arrangements for implementation, and tended to reinforce bad feelings on all sides.

The Growth of Government Intervention

Federal involvement in the auto industry developed in three distinct phases. In the first, from the industry's beginnings to the Depression, the government supported the industry by a variety of direct and indirect measures. Second, from the Depression to the 1960s, the government acted in more varied ways, with mixed effects. On the one hand, the Justice Department and congressional committees kept a watchful eye on the industry's behavior, while on the other, federal road-building and energy policies subsidized the industry's growth. During the third period, from the 1960s onward, the government escalated its involvement massively and became a pervasive presence in industry affairs.

Early Involvements

Before the Depression, the government targeted few actions specifically at the automakers. This is not to say that federal action (or the threat of it) had no influence. On the contrary, the government supported the industry in several ways. The nation purchased its first presidential limousine in 1909; in subsequent years, enormous fleet sales to the military, the post office, and other federal agencies accounted for high profits. Federal statutes in 1916 and 1921 also fostered the auto industry's growth by subsidizing state programs to build roads. State and local governments helped out by issuing standards for licensing and registration and enacting traffic laws that encouraged the orderly use of cars.[49]

Early federal support also included a hefty tariff on imported cars. From 1913 to 1922, the government taxed imports at rates between 30 and 45 percent, depending on the price; from 1922 to 1934, at rates between 25 and 50 percent, depending on the country of origin; from 1934 to the 1950s, at 10 percent; and thereafter, as the General Agreement on Tariffs and Trade (GATT) took effect, at lower levels. As a result, between World War I and the late 1950s, foreign penetration of the American market shrank to the negligible share that European luxury cars could claim.[50]

President Franklin Roosevelt's programs to pull the nation out of the Depression marked the beginning of a second phase of government involvement in the auto industry. New Deal recovery programs, the government's aggressive use of macroeconomic policies, and antitrust enforcement all had significant, if mixed, effects on the auto companies.

The National Recovery Administration (NRA) developed guidelines for big manufacturers to stabilize production, prices, and employment. President Roosevelt took a personal interest in the NRA code for the auto industry, which was already the nation's largest industry in terms of sales and employment. The NRA permitted the National Automobile Chamber of Commerce (forerunner of today's Motor Vehicle Manufacturers Association) to draft its own code, which ratified almost all of the industry's existing practices in pricing, dealer and supplier relationships, and model introduction strategy. Although the automakers guaranteed workers a minimum wage, the companies also avoided or evaded for several years provisions in the recovery legislation that encouraged collective bargaining.[51]

Federal management of the economy, which escalated in the Depression's aftermath, also affected the auto companies' behavior and performance. Macroeconomic tools—taxes, interest rates, trade policies—and laws regulating the nation's economic performance were not intended to help or hurt the auto industry more than any other. In practice, however, federal monetary, tax, trade, and energy policies encouraged the auto companies' growth until inflation became a worry in the 1970s. The government intervened more directly in the auto industry during World War II and several times since then by regulating prices and wages. In each period of wage and price controls, however, the automakers continued to earn ample returns.[52]

On a more disturbing note, serious antitrust investigations of the automakers, which began in this period, foreshadowed the coming era of adversarialism between the government and the industry. In the late 1930s, the Department of Justice and the Federal Trade Commission (FTC) examined the automakers' credit policies and their relations with their dealers. The growing power of the manufacturers was a major irritant to dealers, who complained that unwanted cars, parts, and accessories were forced on them and that their franchises could be canceled arbitrarily.[53] An FTC investigation in 1938 produced no changes in federal policy, although public exposure of company practices and subsequent actions led the automakers to modify their distribution practices. In 1942, the FTC ordered GM to cease requiring its dealers to sell GM parts and accessories exclusively. A Justice Department antitrust suit in the same period permitted dealers to seek other sources of credit than the financial subsidiaries of the automakers. Over the years, dealers were also successful in persuading state legislatures to enact "dealer protection laws" limiting the automakers' ability to locate and terminate dealers and to require exclusive contracts.[54]

In later years, antitrust investigations periodically threatened General Motors. In many cases, suits alleged restraint of trade through vertical integration or investments in related businesses. In the 1950s, GM avoided costly settlements with the Justice Department by divesting a number of wholly or partly owned subsidiaries: Bendix, Euclid, North American Aviation, Greyhound Bus Lines, Hertz Drivurself, and National City Lines, a public transportation company in the business of converting trolley and streetcar lines to buses. In 1961, antitrust pressures led GM and the Du Pont chemical company to sever the links that had been critical in saving GM in the early 1920s. Ford, for its part, was also occasionally investigated. In its most significant settlement, Ford divested its electrical components supplier, Auto-Lite, in 1968.

Even though federal antitrust actions and policies defined relations between automakers and dealers and constrained the automakers' ability to acquire suppliers and related businesses, the government eschewed more drastic measures to increase competition. Despite frequent public cries to "break up General Motors" in the 1950s and 1960s, the government did not force GM to spin off one or more of the automotive divisions.[55] Moreover, the government stood by idly while most of the remaining independent automakers, including Kaiser-Frazier and Studebaker-Packard, left the industry between 1953 and 1962. Indeed, by the latter date, American Motors remained the only mass producer of consumer vehicles other than the Big Three.[56] Congress registered frequent protests at the Big Three's market power in the 1950s. Senator Estes Kefauver (D-Tennessee) conducted extensive hearings to investigate the companies' "administered prices" in 1958. But once more, the government decided there was insufficient evidence to justify a major action to increase competition.

In sum, during the second phase of its involvement, the government manifested an ambivalent attitude toward the automakers. On the one hand, the government recognized the industry's economic salience and admired its achievements. On the other hand, some federal officials were suspicious of big business in general and held the threat of antitrust enforcement over managers in large, concentrated industries like autos. These countervailing tensions—admiration for achievement and suspicion of size—have been conspicuous features of federal auto sector policy ever since.

Escalation and Response

In the mid-1960s, federal intervention in the auto industry became qualitatively different. To its functions as antitrust enforcer, industrial relations mediator, and macroeconomic policy maker, the federal government added a fundamentally new role: product regulator. Rather than reacting to industry behavior or circumscribing it in a general way, the government began active, everyday involvement in the automakers' business decisions through "command and control" regulation.

This new federal intervention occurred on a massive scale. In 1966, Congress passed the National Highway and Motor Vehicle Safety Act; in 1970, came the Clean Air Act; in 1975, the Energy Policy and Conservation Act. The first two statutes created new federal agencies—the National Highway Traffic Safety Administration (NHTSA) and the Environmental Protection Agency (EPA)—with wide powers to define and enforce standards.[57] Out of these new federal policies and agencies came hundreds of specific regulations with different timetables for auto company compliance. Federal policy makers, few of them with any experience in automotive engineering, concerned themselves with the details and specifics of product policy, from seat belts to bumpers, from catalytic converters to exhaust systems, from engine specifications to materials characteristics.

As significant as the substantive increase of federal intervention was the crusading spirit behind it as well as the forms it took. In each case—safety, emissions, and fuel economy—congressional legislation superseded the authority of state or federal administrative agencies. New policies were embodied in statutes because Congress believed that executive branch oversight was insufficient to guarantee the public welfare and that the companies could not be trusted to act wisely on their own. Regulation of safety, emissions, and fuel economy followed a similar pattern in each area: state and federal policies developed in a halting manner, followed by public dissatisfaction with inadequate results, followed by congressional action, followed by adversarial proceedings, followed by new policies that were imposed on the auto companies. The substance of these policies, as well as their implementation, reflected a fundamental mistrust of the industry.

The story of safety regulation is a case in point. The issue first surfaced as a public concern in the mid-1950s, when the nation began to worry about the rising toll of highway deaths, then averaging about 50,000 per year. Yet, in the marketplace, consumers continued to prefer convertibles and "muscle cars" to safer, stodgier models. In 1956, Ford offered a safety package option on its cars that included seat belts, energy-absorbing steering wheels, padded dashboards, sun visors, and other features. This experiment was not a success. According to a company survey, only 14 percent of Ford's customers rated safety as their principal criterion in purchasing, and only 11.2 percent ordered seat belts in their cars. When Ford dropped the safety motif in 1957, its sales quickly picked up.[58]

The lesson the automakers drew from Ford's experience was that safety does not sell. For the next decade executives argued that the proper government role in regulating safety, if any, was to encourage the state and local communities to set and enforce strict traffic laws; beyond that, the concern for safety belonged in the marketplace, where consumers could purchase safety options if they wished. Indeed, at the time, many observers agreed that the driver, not the car, was primarily responsible for passenger safety.

At the same time, however, other observers were drawing a different conclusion: The automakers could not be trusted to serve the public interest without federal oversight. Indeed, the growing perception was that the companies were dragging their feet on the safety issue. In 1958, in response to congressional hearings chaired by Congressman Kenneth A. "Seat Belts" Roberts (D-Alabama), the automakers created the Vehicle Equipment Safety Commission (VESC) to develop a voluntary safety program. But such a program failed to materialize. As journalist Elizabeth Drew pointed out, VESC "took four years to set itself up, had no full-time staff until early 1966, and had issued one safety standard related to cars, a standard in 1965 on tires just as a tire bill appeared imminent."[59]

State and federal policy makers reacted to such indolence by taking steps of their own. New York required seat belts to be installed in every car sold in the state after 1962. In 1964, the General Services Administration (GSA) sought to use its purchasing power as an incentive for industry to provide seventeen safety features as standard equipment on every auto bought by the federal government.

Less than two weeks after the publication of the GSA standards, more sensational events transpired. Hearings on automotive safety chaired by Senator Abraham Ribicoff uncovered the industry's inaction. These hearings became a forum for sharp disagreements between politicians and managers. Perhaps the most electric moment came during an exchange between Senator Robert Kennedy and top GM officers Frederic Donner and James Roche.

Kennedy: What was the profit of General Motors last year?

Roche: I don't think that has anything to do . . .

Kennedy: I would like to have that answer if I may. I think that I am entitled to know that figure. I think it has been published. You spend a million and a quarter dollars, as I understand it, on this aspect of safety. I would like to know what the profit is.

Donner: The one aspect we are talking about is safety.

Kennedy: What was the profit of General Motors last year?

Roche: $1,700,000,000.

Kennedy: What?

Donner: About a billion and a half, I think.

Kennedy: One billion?

Donner: $1.7 billion.

Kennedy: And you spent $1 million on this [safety] research.

Donner: In this particular facet we are talking about . . .

Kennedy: The profits of the company are $1.7 billion per year. I
          would think that you could spend more money on
          research, and I think the rest of the auto companies
          could spend more money on research.[60]

The lines of confrontation were being drawn. Subsequent hearings
revealed that GM had hired a detective to look into the private life of
consumer advocate Ralph Nader. Nader, whose book *Unsafe at Any
Speed* had created a sensation by attacking the crashworthiness of
the Chevrolet Corvair, subsequently became a frequent witness before
congressional committees looking into automotive safety. In 1966,
definitive congressional action finally came with the passage of the
National Highway and Motor Vehicle Safety Act and the creation of
the NHTSA. The law itself required the automakers to make standard
features of seat belts, outside rear-view mirrors, padded dashboards,
collapsible steering wheels, safety glass, dual brakes, headrests, stronger fuel tanks, as well as dozens of other minor safety improvements.
The statute also gave the administrators of the NHTSA great latitude
to write and enforce rules on auto safety. Indeed, the NHTSA's
authority to define standards for such features as collapsible bumpers
and air bags—items that present difficult and costly engineering
problems—has been a source of continuing controversy and expense
for decades.

In the safety controversy Congress acted on the belief that the
industry was irresponsible and could not be relied upon to act on its
own. "I don't think that the automobile manufacturers should be a
'sacred cow' industry," charged Senator Ribicoff.

> I like the fact that they are making a lot of money, and a lot of people
> have jobs. But I think a lot of us would be a lot happier if they would
> spend some of their profits on safety features on automobiles. Unless
> there is a huge cry from people who have the responsibility, I don't
> think the manufacturer is going to do it voluntarily.[61]

The politicization of safety caught the automakers unprepared.
The industry's principal trade association, the Motor Vehicle Manufacturers Association (MVMA), was still based in Detroit in 1966. Each
of the Big Three maintained offices in Washington, although the staffs
were small and normally concentrated on defense contracts. "In

general, the Washington offices are outposts," noted one executive, adding that "the people who man them haven't spent a lifetime in the corporation, and they aren't slated for a rise in the corporation. It's hard for them to make themselves heard back in Detroit."[62]

Industry spokesmen protested the government's invasion of the new realm of product specifications but could do little else to defend themselves. Henry Ford II expressed the automakers' point of view in a speech in 1966.

> I question seriously whether they [federal legislators] have considered the economic impact of the kinds of laws they are considering—the economic impact on our industry. Because, if you start by law to fool around with model changes, to tell the industry that it must do this, that, or the other thing to its products within a period of time in which it cannot be done for engineering reasons, for production reasons, or for any other kind of reason, you upset the whole cycle of . . . the most important industry in the economic picture of the United States.[63]

The arguments between political critics of the auto industry as a "sacred cow" and managers who viewed it as "the most important industry in the economic picture of the United States" were replayed in almost identical fashion during the national debates on regulation of air pollution and fuel efficiency in the 1970s. In both cases, regulations were imposed on the industry without regard for their competitive implications. In the era of Earth Day and environmental activism, Congress passed tough standards for controlling emissions and gave the companies a short timetable for compliance. The Justice Department added to the automakers' burdens by forbidding them to pool research and resources in order to meet the new standards.[64] Once again, Henry Ford II voiced the industry's refrain, pleading in vain for time and financial relief.

> Right now [1973] at Ford, we have some 4,200 people working exclusively and full time on the problem of finding ways to meet emission requirements. And a lot of people have made a career of it. Next it takes money—lots of it. By next month Ford Motor Company's obligations just for meeting the 75 standards will reach almost $100 million.[65]

The same arguments surfaced again after the first oil shock in 1973 when Congress debated a federal energy policy.[66] The Energy Policy and Conservation Act of 1975 put the burden of conservation on the auto companies by requiring them to double the fuel efficiency of their entire product lines within a decade. At the same time, however, to protect consumers, the act extended price controls on imported oil and actually rolled back the price of gasoline at the pump. The statute thus whipsawed the companies by forcing them, quickly and at great expense, to build more efficient vehicles, while at the same time taking away market incentives for the public to prefer smaller, lighter cars.

By the mid-1970s, the relations between Washington and Detroit were increasingly testy. Federal officials regarded the automakers as untrustworthy obstructionists, and auto company managers viewed the government as intrusive and ignorant of engineering realities. Such feelings, given expression in adversarial proceedings, thwarted the design and application of sound public policies. The government made little effort to coordinate conflicting policies, and regulation of safety, emissions, and fuel efficiency took little account of cost and competitive impact. The economic effects of the new regulations were staggering. Even conservative estimates of the costs of compliance reached hundreds of dollars added to new car sticker prices and billions paid out by the companies in capital investment. And these were but the direct costs of federal policy. Major indirect costs included addition or retraining of engineering and managerial personnel, the creation of public affairs departments, expansion of Washington offices, and the acquisition of lobbying skills and techniques. Like pattern bargaining, "pattern regulation" affected the weaker automakers disproportionately. Every company experienced trouble in complying with federal standards, but Chrysler and AMC fared the worst.

EPILOGUE: VULNERABILITIES

Before the late 1970s, the relationships between and among the key industrial actors in the American enterprise system were constant for all automakers. The companies, the union, and the government succeeded in achieving their basic goals. The Big Three enjoyed high profits in an extremely bountiful market that was essentially a private preserve. The autoworkers succeeded in taking wages out of competition and earned impressive incomes, benefits, and rights on the shop floor. The government presided over an expanding economy whose engine of growth was located in Detroit.

As it developed, however, the American enterprise system harbored weaknesses along with strengths. As the revolutions in mass production and mass marketing ran their courses, the automakers came to neglect the possibilities of innovation and change. By focusing narrowly on domestic rivalry, the Big Three failed to appreciate new standards of competitiveness emerging in other markets. Moreover, relations between management and labor on the one hand and between the companies and the government on the other became legalistic and formal over time. Adversarial proceedings shaped interactions between the parties and inhibited effective decision making. Authority and responsibility diverged as the UAW and the government made demands and encroached on management and management fought back by insisting on its rights. Institutions grew rigid. All this happened in controlled circumstances, when competitiveness was a secondary value of the key players. With the onslaught of Japanese imports in the late 1970s, the American automakers were not only unprepared but also ill equipped to respond to the new competitive reality.

CHAPTER 4

Auto Competition
in Europe:
A Tale of Two Companies

"Let me tell you about the European auto market," says a senior executive at Ford. "You've got six mass producers, two multinationals—Ford and GM—and four national champions, Fiat, Volkswagen, Renault, and Peugeot. We're all bunched together, each with 11 to 12 percent of the market. There's excess capacity, but it's very difficult to lay anyone off or to close a plant in Europe. What's more, from here on, nobody will go out of business. Governments won't let it happen. Right now [1984] we're one of the two mass producers making money in Europe but believe me, it's not very much. The only good news is that the Japanese share is pretty much limited. The European market is a strategist's nightmare—it's really a bad trip."

The "strategist's nightmare" in Europe is unfolding in a market beset by the same troubles that plague American automakers: a future of low growth, intensified global rivalry, and the need for enormous capital investment. These troubles have exacted a heavy toll in Europe; many producers have merged or left the business in recent decades. In the mid-1980s, each major European market supports only a few automakers that compete in volume production: Volkswagen, Ford, and Opel (a subsidiary of GM) in Germany; Renault and PSA (Peugeot) in France; Fiat and Alfa Romeo in Italy; and BL

57

(formerly British Leyland and now Rover Group), Ford, Vauxhall (GM), and Talbot (PSA) in the United Kingdom. Although a number of well-known specialty producers—Rolls Royce, Porsche, Mercedes, BMW, and Ferrari—are profitable in Western Europe and some European governments have stakes in some small-scale producers such as SEAT, Saab, and Volvo, the number of viable competitors in the mass market remains quite small: Ford and GM, Volkswagen, Renault, PSA, and Fiat.

This chapter looks at the fates of two national champions in Europe, BL in the United Kingdom and Volkswagen in West Germany, to see how they adapted to the forces sweeping the global auto industry. In so doing, we also examine the enterprise systems of the two countries to see how their histories and structures affect the performance of their leading auto manufacturers. In the case of BL, adjustment has been traumatic, requiring fundamental changes in the relationships among business, government, and labor. Volkswagen, one of the strongest competitors in Europe, has also been forced to adapt to the forces driving change in the industry.

In both the United Kingdom and West Germany, as in the United States, the national enterprise system played a major role in the competitive performance of their respective auto industries. In each country, traditions that developed while the domestic market was effectively closed had a major impact on automakers' ability to adapt to global competition. Patterns of competition, industry and union structure, and government policies and institutions all played a role in the competitive outcomes.

THE ORDEALS OF BL

The postwar record of the British motor industry illustrates vividly how enterprise systems affect firms in global industries. Shortly after World War II, the United Kingdom boasted the second-largest auto industry in the world and Europe's strongest. In 1949, British automakers built more cars (about 400,000) than all other European automakers combined. At the time, the United Kingdom was also the leading exporter of cars in the world.[1] Yet within a decade, the British fell behind the Germans in total production, marking the beginning of a long decline. British automakers have performed erratically since the early 1950s. At present, the British industry is the smallest among the major European producers, ranking even below Spain in total production. Imports account for nearly 60 percent of sales in the home market. As for production, foreign-owned companies, Ford and Vauxhall (GM), have captured an increasing share from the once powerful native industry. The lone British-owned mass producer, BL, survives only because of massive government funding in the past decade.

The BL story makes for dramatic reading. At the time of its creation in 1968, the company (then British Leyland) was roughly the size of Volkswagen or Fiat. BL produced more than a million cars and trucks, achieved nearly a billion pounds in revenue, employed about 200,000 workers, and accounted for about 40 percent of sales in the domestic market. By 1985, BL had become a minor automaker in Europe, with a capacity of about a half million cars. Total employment is now under 100,000 and despite massive restructuring (including the sale of its profitable Jaguar division) the company's prospects for sustaining an independent future are dim.

BL's collapse should be seen against a backdrop of an enterprise system riddled with serious flaws. As the motor industry developed into an oligopoly, competition among British automakers, never strongly developed, failed to breed aggressive, adaptive management. Government intervention periodically whipsawed the industry, stifled the development of the home market, and seriously hindered management's long-term plans and investments. Finally, industrial relations in Britain have been among the most contentious in Europe, contributing to frequent work stoppages and low levels of productivity and product quality.

The Abdication of Management

There are striking parallels in the histories of the British and American auto industries. By the 1930s, a handful of automakers, survivors of a competition among hundreds of producers in the early part of the century, dominated the industries in both countries. The forces that pushed consolidation were again similar in both countries: economies of scale in production and distribution, market saturation and the rise of a used-car industry, increasing demand for closed-roof cars, and the Great Depression. All these enabled large, capital-intensive producers to overwhelm their smaller rivals. In general, the dominant Ford modes of production and distribution through small, independent dealerships were similar in the United States and the United Kingdom.

The largest automaker in Britain after the war, Morris (which, in another striking parallel with American automotive history, succeeded Ford as number one in the 1920s when Henry Ford refused to replace the Model T), claimed 20.9 percent of the market in 1947. Morris was followed by Austin (19.2 percent); Ford (15.4 percent); Standard (13.2 percent); Vauxhall, a subsidiary of General Motors after 1928 (11.2 percent); and Rootes (10.9 percent).[2] More than a score of specialty automakers, including such renowned manufacturers as Rolls Royce, Jaguar, Aston-Martin, Lotus, and Rover, vied for the remaining 9.2 percent. Imports accounted for a negligible share of the market after 1915, when the government imposed the McKenna duty, a 33.3 percent tariff on vehicles entering the country.[3]

These similarities between the British and American auto industries obscure some important differences. In the first place, the British market diverged from the American market in important ways. The British market was much smaller, about a tenth the size after the war, and it grew at a much slower rate. General Motors and Ford each built more cars in the United States than the combined output of all six British automakers in the late 1940s. Per capita income in the United Kingdom lagged behind that in the United States, credit was much scarcer, and the public infrastructure of roads and bridges was much less extensive. Fleet sales to companies and public agencies accounted for as much as 40 percent of the market and relatively few people owned cars. Those who did buy autos tended to keep them longer. As a result, British consumers preferred a different sort of car from that sought by Americans. Design, style, and options were subordinate to other buyer criteria. High petrol costs and a government tax on horsepower led consumers in the United Kingdom to prize durability, handling, and fuel efficiency.

Britain also had no equivalent of General Motors, a single dominant firm to set industry patterns in market coverage, pricing, and administration and organization. Professional management and multidivisional organization were unknown in the auto industry until very recently.[4] Indeed, founding entrepreneurs and family owners ran many of the automakers into the 1950s. The loosely federated Morris properties included four nameplates and more than a score of models in the years after the war. There was little communication or cooperation between various parts of the company. Indeed, Morris more closely resembled the GM of Billy Durant than the GM of Alfred Sloan.[5]

The Morris organization suffered a long decline with the aging of its unpredictable founder, William Morris, later Lord Nuffield. From the late 1920s to the early 1950s, according to one commentator, the company's history "illustrates at every step the ravages of an eccentric dictator." Lord Nuffield became "increasingly preoccupied with minor technical details, besides showing a tendency to shun board meetings, exhibiting a predilection for taking decisions without consultation, and apparently embarking on an undeclared policy of pitting the constituent companies within the organization in competition against each other."[6]

Merger between Nuffield and the company of his old nemesis, Austin, in 1952 made little difference in organization and management. Nuffield's successor, Leonard Lord, head of the new British Motor Corporation (BMC), continued to manage Morris and Austin as separate entities. Lord rationalized production of some standardized parts, but, remarks automotive historian Graham Turner, "in other respects unification proceeded at a leisurely pace." Distribution networks remained separate; management teams failed to work together. Recalled one executive, it "was like mixing oil and water." The two companies even retained their own incompatible books and accounts.[7]

Things were little better on the shop floor, where the domestic automakers in effect abandoned control to craft unions and shop stewards. Indeed, Ford techniques of mass production came late to British companies such as Morris and Austin. To begin with, a strong tradition of craft unionism limited the hiring of unskilled workers for assembly-line production and restricted the ways in which they could be organized and managed.[8] Second, during World War I, the government, concerned about the effects of labor unrest on industrial output, further strengthened organized labor's hand by pressuring employers to negotiate a wide range of restrictive work practices with unions and shop stewards. And third, most employers (and the government) believed that piece-rate compensation would be more likely to motivate workers and stimulate productivity than pay based on hours or days worked.[9] Piece-rate compensation, which endured through the 1960s, had two serious drawbacks: it worsened the problem of fragmented work structures in the plants, because individual output is more easily measured under craft organization; and it further reinforced the role of the shop stewards, who were responsible for negotiating the rates and for filing grievances occasioned by the system.

In short, the structure of organized labor, government policy, and the prevalent mode of compensation impeded mass production and modern techniques of shop-floor management. Because the assembly line was less central to production, British factories tended to be smaller and less productive than plants in the United States or on the Continent. As time wore on, moreover, the situation grew worse: the auto companies had few incentives to add new capacity to achieve greater economies of scale and they ran into institutional barriers to adopting labor-saving technology.

The industry structure, market conditions, management policies, and factory organization that emerged in Britain mattered little before the 1950s, however. When markets at home and especially abroad boomed, the automakers earned high profits. Between 1947 and 1956 the motor industry consistently outperformed other manufacturing industries. Return on capital (net profit as a percentage of total assets) averaged more than 20 percent at most of the automakers.[10]

Government intervention never disturbed the competitive dynamics of the British auto industry. Not only were the British producers protected by the McKenna duty, the horsepower tax, and other forms of protection through the 1960s, but there was little government concern about industry structure and company behavior. Indeed, the government approved the merger of the country's two largest producers, Morris and Austin, into the British Motor Corporation (BMC) in 1952, and made no effort to prevent the decline of Standard, a one-time mass producer, in the 1950s.

Yet despite this bright picture, the strengths of the British auto industry in the early postwar years were more apparent than real. Most companies were too small, operated too many small plants, and achieved levels of vertical integration too low to capture the economies of scale that made the U.S. producers so profitable and powerful. The home market turned out to be less promising than it had seemed. British automakers had little capacity to adapt to the keener competition developing on the Continent. In the 1960s, inconsistent government policies and turbulent labor relations exposed fundamental weaknesses in the British enterprise system.

"The Incredibly Deleterious Effect" of Government Intervention

The relationship between business and government in the United Kingdom is quite different from that in the United States. British managers seldom voice the twin American complaints about over-zealous antitrust enforcement and excessive regulation. As has been noted, the British government protected the auto industry from foreign competition and promoted industry concentration. Later, it provided incentives to help the automakers respond to social concerns about safety, emissions, and energy efficiency. All this is not to say that British government policies fostered healthy competition in the industry. On the contrary, the shifting macroeconomic policies and conflicting political and social agendas of Labour and Conservative governments played a major role in the industry's decline.[11]

Government intervention affected the auto industry's development in two important ways. First, shifting macroeconomic policies stunted the growth of the home market. Second, successive governments (especially Labour governments) tended to use the auto industry as an instrument to achieve larger social goals. The government restricted demand in part to stimulate use of the nationalized railroads and public transportation. It used the auto industry as a testing ground for social and political reforms. And in the 1970s, the government, anxious to preserve engineering skills and employment, nationalized the largest domestic producer, BL, and ran it as a publicly managed business.

The recovery of European markets after the war created fantastic opportunities for the British auto industry. Every car built could be sold at home or abroad. The postwar Labour government (1945–1951) was concerned, moreover, with maintaining a favorable balance of trade and did not hesitate to manipulate domestic auto demand as a means of reaching this goal. In 1946, the government rationed the sale of cars in the United Kingdom and used its control of raw materials and the steel supply to encourage the automakers to export 50 percent of their output. This figure was soon raised and by 1950 British producers exported more than 80 percent of the cars built in the United Kingdom. Only mobilization for the Korean War stopped this trend.

The auto industry's rapid growth after 1945, ironically, had a number of adverse effects. To begin with, it was growth without competition, since every car made, no matter the cost or quality, could be sold. As a result, the automakers had few incentives to design new models, improve product quality, or rationalize production. Second, restrictions on the sale of cars in the United Kingdom meant that the automakers could not cultivate domestic demand and consumer loyalty. Although the manufacturers anticipated a boom in sales once rationing was lifted in 1952, the "pent-up" demand failed to materialize as British consumers continued to make do with public transportation and used cars. Finally, since import duties shielded the British home market, the absence of import competition, internal rivalry, and a sellers' market at home combined to reinforce genteel competitive habits. As the industry reconverted from war production after the Korean War it encountered two unpleasant surprises: a low-growth home market and the rising strength of more aggressive continental producers.

Chronic balance-of-payments difficulties beginning in the 1950s and, later, severe inflationary pressures induced the government to rely on an assortment of macroeconomic policies—high taxes, political interventions, monetary adjustments—designed to limit or reduce overall consumer expenditure. Given the sensitivity of auto sales to the level of disposable income, these deflationary policies had a disproportionate impact on the car market, depressing demand and straining the resources of domestic manufacturers. The government manipulated demand by altering the terms for down payments, credit, and repayment periods for car purchases. Brief periods of "stop" policies were punctuated by periods of "go," a pattern that worsened cyclicality in the industry and wreaked havoc with long-term planning. Between 1956 and 1975, the government altered hire-purchase terms for cars more than twenty-five times, with most of the changes coming under the Labour government elected in 1964. On average, the industry experienced a major shift in controls every ten months during the 1960s.

Stop-and-go policies generally improved overall trade balances, but it is difficult to overestimate their disastrous impact on the automakers. In 1964, British demand had topped 1.2 million cars, providing a domestic market second only to that of Germany in Europe. During the next six years, demand stabilized at between 1.0 and 1.1 million cars while the rest of Europe enjoyed continuing rapid growth. This overall stagnation concealed a recurrent cycle of dramatic miniature booms and busts usually lasting only a few months. "It is impossible to convey the unsettling effect, the incredibly deleterious effect, that these shifts in demand had upon our operations," recalled one industry executive. "I'm talking about one-tenth to one-quarter of the entire demand disappearing overnight, or, for that matter, reappearing overnight. Try and deal with growth and contraction of that kind in any sensible, planned way."[12]

Stop-and-go policies also caused severe and expensive under-utilization of capacity, impeded investments, and raised total costs. Periodic layoffs worsened the increasingly troubled relations between labor and management. When the Heath Conservative government finally abolished all credit restrictions in 1971, the British market boomed. Nearly 60 percent more cars were sold in 1972 than a year earlier. Unfortunately, the domestic industry no longer possessed the model range, productive capacity, or continuity of production to satisfy this new demand. Imports, aided by Britain's contemporane-ous entry into the European Economic Community (EEC), accounted for most of the new sales.

Other government actions hindered automakers' efforts to become more competitive. In the 1960s and especially after the formation of the Wilson Labour government in 1964, government intervention increasingly took the form of using the auto industry as a prominent instrument of long-term political and social change. The seeds of this policy were planted by the first postwar Labour government, which had nationalized the railroad and trucking industries. But the Con-servatives shared culpability, not only in carrying on the manage-ment of the nationalized industries but also in promoting investment and employment in underdeveloped regions of the country. In the early 1960s, for example, the Conservative government induced sev-eral automakers and major suppliers to invest in areas of high unem-ployment such as Scotland, Wales, and Merseyside. Government incentives included financial assistance and other subsidies, and lending teeth to these inducements, the Department of Industry refused to issue development certificates for new plants in the Mid-lands. Between 1958 and 1962, manufacturing flowered in unlikely places: Ford, Vauxhall, and Standard opened new plants on the Mersey; BMC and Rootes built in Scotland; and Rover began opera-tions in Wales.

No reliable figures are available on the long-term cost of such regional policies, but the overall impact is clear. Regional policies complicated logistics, raised transportation costs, and subsequently hindered efforts to rationalize production capacity. But the greatest cost of regional policy resulted from the automakers' troubles with an unskilled and untrained labor force in areas of the country that lacked engineering and manufacturing know-how.[13]

Fragmented Structures and Bitter Relationships

Before the late 1970s, relations between labor and management in the British auto industry were the most acrimonious and counterproductive in Europe. Frequent layoffs and strikes, low productivity, high manning levels, restrictive work practices, and angry disputes over the introduction of new machinery consistently plagued the automakers. Between 1969 and 1977, the British auto industry recorded more than ten times the national average for lost working days. [14] Between 1955 and 1976, productivity in the British auto industry, measured by "equivalent" cars produced by employee per year, increased from 4.1 to 5.5. At first sight, this increase does not seem bad, but over the same years output per worker increased from 3.9 to 7.9 cars in West Germany, and from 19.8 to 26.1 cars in the United States.[15]

Labor turmoil in the British auto industry became a serious problem in the 1960s. Before then, a favorable labor market and the automakers' generally good fortunes after World War II had contributed to labor harmony. But several forces were undermining this era of good feelings: cyclical unemployment made worse by the government's stop-and-go policies, labor's resistance to the government's incomes policies, and the general polarization of politics in the 1960s. In addition to these forces, three other factors enlarged the problem: the absence of a definitive body of labor law, multiple unionism overlaid with an independent shop stewards' organization, and ideological and class differences between labor and management.

One expert characterized the British industrial relations system as "largely informal, largely fragmented and largely autonomous."[16] Largely chaotic is a more succinct description. To begin with, Britain has no equivalent to the Wagner Act. A series of statutes and court decisions dating to the early nineteenth century defines the British industrial relations system.[17] Collective bargaining is viewed as a voluntary activity between employers (or federations of employers) and unions representing employees. Labor agreements in the United Kingdom, as in most Western industrialized countries, characteristically include such matters as wage rates, pay incentive schemes, hours of work, shift and overtime working conditions, holiday provisions, and procedures for handling grievances. Contracts, however, do not carry the force of law and may be indefinite in duration. Unions have so-called coercive rights to strike and can legitimately call strikes to modify provisions in an existing contract. The government has no mechanisms for compulsory arbitration or policing of union or employment policies and practices, and there are few restrictions on workers' ability to call strikes.

The organization of national unions is chaotic as well. British unions are organized according to various membership criteria: craft based; trade (industry); general (virtually open membership); and white collar. All four types exist in the auto companies, although craft unions and traditions have dominated most of the industry's history. The two largest unions in the industry are the Amalgamated Union of Engineering Workers (AUEW), a craft union that traces its origins to the 1850s, and the Transport and General Workers Union (TGWU), a general union that quickly organized unskilled workers in the 1940s and 1950s. Although the leaders of the AUEW and TGWU have generally been cordial, relations between the two unions have been acrimonious over the years, especially at the plant level.

Before the late 1970s, moreover, collective bargaining in the auto industry was severely fragmented. The AUEW, TGWU, and scores of others that represented workers in the domestic auto companies negotiated national agreements through the Confederation of Shipbuilding and Engineering Unions (CSEU) and the Engineering Employers Federation (EEF). (Ford and GM had succeeded in establishing companywide bargaining in their British subsidiaries.) The national agreement between the CSEU and the EEF typically was then used as a minimum basis for separate negotiations at the plant level between management and individual unions.

Because most auto plants had more than a dozen unions represented—one Morris plant had thirty-six—and individual bargaining units could be as small as a half dozen people, collective bargaining at the local level had significant economic consequences. Until quite recently, contracts were not negotiated simultaneously. As a result, senior plant managers were involved with collective bargaining throughout the calendar year. In an industry so dependent on an integrated production process, a handful of workers strategically placed could idle an entire plant or company with a wildcat strike. In addition, jurisdictional squabbles between unions were frequent and each union tended to protect itself by negotiating extremely specific work rules. Finally, multiple unionism inhibited the development of pattern bargaining and pattern wages. This meant the persistence of wage differentials not only among companies but also among plants and among workers in each plant. Individual unions used settlements reached by other unions as occasions to renegotiate their own contracts for higher wages and benefits or to call strikes.[18]

Compounding these problems, the leadership and policies of the national unions were often remote from the membership. The structure of collective bargaining tended to emphasize negotiations at the local level. Indeed, the most important bargaining took place at the shop level where shop stewards represented workers' interests. Indeed, since national wage agreements were generally taken as minimums, it was not unusual for some autoworkers to earn twice the national settlement. Although the shop stewards were union members, they frequently acted independently on such matters as setting the local bargaining agenda and calling strikes.[19] Moreover, as we have seen, the prevalence of piece-rate wages in the auto industry contributed to shop stewards' influence. As a result, the stewards had enormous power in the plants and were subject to no other control than the annual votes to elect them. It was they, more often than the unions, who called wildcat strikes or promoted other job actions.

Factors beyond the immediate well-being of shop-floor workers occasionally motivated the stewards. Left-wing ideologues were disproportionately influential as stewards. Perceiving the strategic importance of the role, radical and Trotskyist stewards called strikes or planned disruptions to protest government policies or the capitalist system generally. In the mid-1960s, the government's Department of Employment estimated that more than 90 percent of all strikes were "unofficial," called by stewards or workers without the authorization of the union. These strikes accounted for more than two-thirds of all man-days lost.[20] An official of the Amalgamated Engineers (the predecessor of the AUEW and a conservative craft union), William (later Lord) Carron, attributed such industrial disputes to "subversives" in the plants. Or, as he put it in an article in 1962, "One still finds pockets of militancy which are inspired by motives that cannot be accepted as being based purely upon trade union principles. These motives spring from attempts to change the system of government we have in the United Kingdom and would attempt to replace this system with one that has been rejected . . . by an overwhelming majority of opinion."[21]

Radical shop stewards continued to thrive at least partly because of persisting class distinctions in the United Kingdom. Indeed, an examination of "the bloodymindedness" of British workers in the 1960s settled on

> the worker's sense of the basic unfairness of his position over against the owner, his resentment at toiling to make profits for one whose birth spared him the need to toil. This in turn was linked . . . with the values, perception and expectations of the working class . . . as father handed them down to son . . . . To work harder, it seemed to the wage-earner, meant not getting on in the world but working yourself or your mate out of a job.[22]

A Severe Case of the British Disease

The cumulative effects of the British enterprise system were devastating across the auto industry, especially when the continental producers got back on their feet and competitive rivalry intensified throughout Europe. In 1960, Britain trailed only the United States and West Germany, with a 10.6 percent share of world production; by 1970, the industry had become the sick man of Europe, its production totals surpassed by Italy, France, and Japan, as well as the United States and Germany. In the early 1980s, British producers accounted for only 3.3 percent of world production. Market share plummeted in every country that permitted relatively open competition, including the United Kingdom. Between 1965 and 1982, the percentage of British-made cars in total registrations in the United Kingdom fell from 95.0 percent to 42.7 percent. Decades of mismanagement, inconsistent government policies, and fractious labor relations exacted a heavy toll. A series of public investigations in the 1970s uncovered the grim facts. "The present competitive position of the British car industry is poor" was the understated conclusion that the government's Central Policy Review Staff (CPRS) delivered. [23] The leading British producers operated too many small plants, kept too many models in production for too long, relied on extremely inefficient distribution channels, and acquired a disturbing reputation for building low-quality vehicles.

The inefficient scale of most British factories resulted in severe cost penalties. Chrysler's four assembly plants in the United Kingdom achieved a total volume of about 300,000 cars—roughly the rated capacity of a single plant in the United States or Japan. In 1968, the year of its inception, BL built twice as many models as General Motors, but produced only a fifth of GM's volume. In addition, overcapacity plagued every company. The CPRS estimated that most automakers could build 20 percent to 50 percent more cars than could be sold.[24]

To make matters worse, British factories were full of antiquated machinery and relied too heavily on manual labor. By the mid-1970s, the effects of chronic underinvestment could no longer be disguised. In 1974, according to a government survey, Chrysler U.K., Vauxhall, and British Leyland ranked last among European mass producers in fixed investment per employee. Ford's investment per worker in the United Kingdom stood at half its level in the United States.[25] At the same time, the CPRS calculated that manning levels in British plants were 40 percent to 80 percent higher than on the Continent. Overmanning alarmed even sympathetic politicians. At the Labour party conference in 1966, Prime Minister Harold Wilson agreed to meet with six representatives of BMC shop stewards. When twelve stewards arrived for the meeting, Wilson counted them and said, "Yes, that's one of your problems at BMC, isn't it? You always have twelve men where six would do."[26]

And the product! A quality survey in 1967 found an average of twenty-seven defects in British-made cars. The reputation of British cars was so low that when Ford distributors in Switzerland learned that the company planned to supply them from Germany rather than from the United Kingdom, the distributors took out full-page ads in local papers to announce the "good news." The West German Auto Club presented its Silver Lemon Award for "horrible mechanical faults" to BL for its Austin 1300 in 1975.[27]

Finally, the traditional distribution system matched the traditional production system in disquieting detail. Between 1968 and 1976, the manufacturers terminated nearly 7,000 dealers—and still had about 5,000 left. BL dealers were half the size of and much less profitable and less able to supply quality service than import dealers in the United Kingdom. BL had virtually no presence in the major growth markets outside the United Kingdom. Its foreign sales were concentrated in places like Iran, Portugal, and the remnants of the British Empire.[28]

Cure by Amputation

Hard times brought restructuring in the industry. Leyland, the commercial vehicle manufacturer, absorbed Standard-Triumph in 1961 and Rover in 1965. Daimler merged with Jaguar in 1960; together with Pressed Steel Bodies, Ltd., they joined BMC to create the British

Motor Holding Company (BMHC) in 1965. After much government hemming and hawing, Chrysler acquired increasing amounts of Rootes stock after 1964, assuming complete control (though not complete ownership) by 1968. GM's massive American earnings shielded Vauxhall, but Ford began restructuring its European operations in 1967, putting Ford U.K. and Ford of Germany under one umbrella organization. The granddaddy merger of them all occurred when the Labour government engineered the joining of the conglomerated Leyland and the conglomerated BMHC in 1968 to create British Leyland.

These combinations and investments merely postponed the day of reckoning, however. In the recession that followed the first oil shock, Aston-Martin, Chrysler U.K., and British Leyland approached the government for relief. Aston-Martin eventually declared bankruptcy. Chrysler chairman John Riccardo threatened to liquidate the British subsidiary unless it received public help. The government eventually agreed to cover more than £50 million of the company's losses and to provide an additional £61 million in immediate loans. Facing tremendous financial problems in the United States, Chrysler subsequently sold its British subsidiary in 1978 to the Peugeot group, which appears to be slowly liquidating the properties.[29]

More spectacular was British Leyland's collapse in the mid–1970s. Despite the merger in 1968, the problems of the old BMHC continued to mount. In addition to facing all the troubles of its predecessors, British Leyland had to cope with the formidable tasks of integrating still more disparate organizations and overcoming intercompany rivalries—all this against a backdrop of particularly discordant labor relations and inconsistent government actions. Despite heavy borrowing (the company's debt-to-equity ratio in the early 1970s was nearly one to one), attempts to rationalize and modernize operations, and the slow, painful dislodging of piece-rate incentives, production levels stayed flat, market share declined, and profits, when earned, were razor thin. The recession after the oil shock exposed fundamental weaknesses. When the company applied for additional loans in the fall of 1974, the leading British banks refused to extend them. British Leyland had no recourse but to seek government support.

In December, the minister of industry, Anthony Wedgwood Benn, announced that the government would fund necessary investments in return for an equity share and a say in British Leyland's policies. Benn appointed Sir Don Ryder (later Lord Ryder) to head a team to investigate the company and make appropriate recommendations. The Ryder Report, ready in the spring of 1975, portrayed an alarming situation but emphasized the public interest in supporting the company: "In general . . . vehicle production is the kind of industry which ought to remain an essential part of the UK's economic base. We believe, therefore, that BL should remain a major vehicle producer, although this means that urgent action must be taken to remedy the weaknesses which at present prevent it from competing effectively in world markets."[30] The report went on to propose wholesale changes in the company's organization and its management of labor relations, product policy, marketing, and distribution. After heated partisan debate, Parliament approved Ryder's recommendations that the government buy out existing shareholders (£65 million), subscribe an additional equity stake of £200 million, and be prepared to underwrite another £1.2 billion in investment installments over the next eight years.[31]

British Leyland's misfortunes presented an opportunity to the Labour government and the trade unions to achieve some of their own objectives. For example, the Ryder Report recommended that the company install an elaborate, three-level hierarchy of consultative committees to promote worker participation and industrial democracy. These new arrangements were imposed on British Leyland and had few supporters in the company. Many managers and trade unionists either ignored the new committees or, worse, tried to sabotage them. One consultant recalls the arrangements as

> a stupid system that created a lot of confusion. At the time, industrial democracy on the German model was a fad among intellectuals in the Labour party. The fall of the Heath government in 1974 unleashed all sorts of hairy monsters, among them the people who designed this system. There were an incredible number of committees without much thought given to who should be on them or what they should discuss. A lot of shop stewards simply refused to participate. Many that did found themselves on committees remote from their own shops and the people who elected them.

Pat Lowry, who was in charge of labor relations in the company at the time, was more restrained. "The system wasn't too bad for a year or two but it was too formalized and bureaucratic. The real problem was that it was impossible to reconcile industrial democracy with the company's desperate situation. We simply didn't have time to make it work."

The situation was not much more hopeful on the government front. Nationalization placed the company under the control of the newly created National Enterprise Board (NEB), which was charged to manage state-owned businesses. With Ryder as chairman, the NEB took an active role in BL affairs, monitoring key product decisions and approving all expenditures above £5 million. "The NEB reviewed essentially all our investment programs," recalled one manager.

> In addition, major changes in policy, our annual budget, our corporate plan, and our current monthly performance were subject to close scrutiny. Because he fancied himself an expert on the industry and he had so much at stake, Ryder constantly intervened in the company's management. Key product decisions, such as the design of the Metro [the company's new entrant at the low end of the market], were held up. Ryder's involvement made things very difficult. I wish that he hadn't taken as much interest in British Leyland and had spent more time on the other companies owned by the NEB.[32]

British Leyland continued to suffer heavy losses under the awkward arrangements of nationalization. A process of negotiations at two levels of the corporation (divisional and headquarters) and three in government (the NEB, the Department of Industry [DOI], and Parliament), delayed and complicated major investments. Labor troubles increased as some workers struck to protest government policies as well as the company's. Shop stewards, worried about their own authority in the plants, sabotaged the system of participative management. Other workers, complained one manager, saw "the government as a fairy godmother who would continue to supply funds no matter what happened." Indeed, an early confrontation between Ryder and the unions reinforced this view. In December 1975, less than six months after nationalization, a wave of strikes prompted by government pay policies and management efforts to reform compensation, work rules, and lines of demarcation led Ryder to freeze investments. The company threatened to send workers home if its production targets were not met. Despite such actions and threats, Ryder eventually released the investment, no employees were dismissed, and productivity levels never approached the targets. The stewards effectively called management's bluff.

In 1977, a strike by toolmakers who protested management's plans to unify collective bargaining and standardize wage structures lasted five weeks and idled 40,000 workers. In that year, the company estimated that labor disputes had cost the production of 225,000 vehicles. Productivity was lower than in 1975; total production was down nearly 40 percent; BL's market share in the United Kingdom fell below Ford's, to 23 percent. At this point, the government intervened again. Continued massive losses and ongoing appeals for government aid could no longer be tolerated. In the fall of 1977, Leslie Murphy replaced Lord Ryder at the NEB and appointed a new chairman and chief executive at BL, Michael Edwardes.

Within a week of taking office, Edwardes announced major changes in management and operations. He asked several Ryder-appointed directors to step down from the board. He and his lieutenants restructured the top management of the company, bringing in sixty senior managers from the outside. Other changes followed shortly: a new accounting and control system to standardize cost data; the creation of a formal strategic planning function; decisions to build a test track and technical center. Within months, the company slashed its administrative overhead and began rationalizing its production system and product offerings. Edwardes followed General Motors' policies of decentralizing the car groups to allow decisions to be made at lower levels of the organization and to control corporate overhead. The company plugged a hole in its future product offerings by reaching an agreement with Honda to build the Accord in the United Kingdom, selling it under the Triumph nameplate. In early 1978, the company even changed its name to BL, Ltd., attempting to change the associations in the public's mind that the company was still the disorganized heir of the Morris and Leyland properties.[33]

At the same time, the new management confronted problems embedded in the British enterprise system. Edwardes had made it clear when he accepted the job that he needed a free hand to make dramatic changes in the company. Prime Minister Callaghan and Benn's successor at the Department of Industry, Eric Varley, agreed with Murphy of the NEB that the new management would be allowed to pursue its plans with a minimum of government interference. The new government officials retreated from the activist intervention of Benn and Lord Ryder. The Conservative government of Margaret Thatcher elected in 1979 continued this policy of laissez faire. Indeed, the Thatcher government dismantled the NEB and returned ownership of BL to the Department of Industry in 1981.

At Edwardes's request in August 1979, the DOI stationed a permanent employee in the BL chairman's office to act as a liaison between the company and the government. This arrangement, which helped overcome problems of communication caused by the demise of the NEB, had several other advantages, according to Edwardes. As he put it, for the civil servants involved, "it provided a stimulating challenge as well as the invaluable industrial experience which I believe is so lacking in Whitehall." For BL,

> it provided an internal source of advice on how any particular proposal might look to the Government; plus being an informal supplement to the normal channels through which we dealt with the Government. . . . Information could thus be exchanged or draft letters cleared informally, without establishing precedents or commitments. It also contributed to establishing relationships directly with the other departments that had a voice in decision-making on BL—such as the Treasury, the Central Policy Review Staff, and Number 10 itself.[34]

This is not to say that the company and the government saw eye to eye on every issue. Indeed, BL was a vociferous opponent of Thatcher's stern monetarist policies and suffered greatly from high interest rates and an unfavorable export position created by the strong pound.

Overcoming troubled relations with the company's work force and reestablishing managerial authority in the plants proved more daunting tasks. Edwardes described the problem.

> To regain the management role would mean counteracting shop steward power, which had got out of hand to the point where national union leaders, local union officials, and certainly management, were being treated in a cavalier fashion by some 200 militant stewards who had filled the vacuum left by management. Not to put too fine a point on it, we needed to take on the militants. To do this meant improving communications, and going direct to the shop floor, while keeping national union officials in close touch with our problems and plans.

Edwardes continued:

> The objective of this plan was not to destroy or weaken the unions. On the contrary, it was to rebalance the whole order of things so that together with management national union officials would be able to play a proper role without finding their authority eroded by strong stewards, weak management, and a lack of understanding of what management was trying to achieve.[35]

Edwardes ignored the Ryder-designed machinery of participative management, which he characterized as only producing "a bureaucratic paperchase dissipating management resource and effort."[36] On the other hand, BL management worked diligently with the unions to standardize collective bargaining terms throughout the company. It held the line on granting the traditional, automatic wage increases without corresponding increases in productivity. It determined to fight aggressive wage demands. But the first real test of Edwardes's policies came when the company decided to shut down an assembly plant at Speke in Merseyside in February 1978. This plant, which built the TR7, was less than twenty years old, but slack demand for the model, Speke's geographical isolation (which caused high transportation costs and logistical problems), and frequent work stoppages made it a losing proposition. BL explained the reasons for the decision patiently to employees and offered them liberal severance terms. As a result, when the workers voted on the closure, they accepted it peacefully. The closing of Speke—the first major closing of a British auto factory in decades—was a sign that times had indeed changed.

In his first two years at the helm, Edwardes also faced down strikers at the Bathgate truck assembly works, at a fuels factory at Castle Bromwich, at the Drews Lane transmission plant, and at the old Austin assembly plant at Longbridge. At Longbridge, when management felt that local shop stewards misrepresented the company's policies, the company circumvented the stewards by establishing close communications with local union officials and with the workers themselves. Recalled Edwardes,

> This often meant sending letters to employees' homes (where they could calmly and deliberately consider the situation with their families), the issuing of factory briefing sheets, and posters. When we felt a particular issue had wider significance we used newspaper advertisements and they seemed to be effective, for the militants invariably called "foul." These actions were supplemented by meetings on the shop floor, face to face with managers.[37]

Continued heavy losses in 1978 and 1979 led to more draconian measures and a pivotal confrontation with the stewards. The top management team devised a new recovery program that Edwardes called "probably the most extensive restructuring of a major company that has ever been done in a very short period of time."[38] The Edwardes plan, as it quickly became known, called for heavy new government investments, reducing employment by 25,000, discontinuing the Triumph and MG models, the closing or radical shrinking of thirteen plants, and the restructuring of work rules and compensation practices throughout the company. Management discussed the recovery plan with national union leaders and won reluctant agreement to submit the plan to a vote of all employees in the fall of 1979.

The outcome was a resounding endorsement of management: 80 percent of eligible employees voted; of these, 87.2 percent approved the plan.[39] Some employees who did not endorse the plan continued to work against it, however. One of these, a radical shop steward at Longbridge, Derek Robinson (known as Red Robbo), was dismissed for circulating (and perhaps writing) a pamphlet that called for various measures to thwart the recovery plan.

Robinson's dismissal triggered a strike at Longbridge and other BL locations. Management demanded that the workers return to work immediately; otherwise, they would be let go. The leadership of Robinson's own union, the AUEW, met threat with threat. Terry Duffy, the union's president, announced that he would authorize a companywide strike on December 4. But Edwardes would not back down. At an extraordinarily tense private meeting between BL and AUEW officials on November 27, Edwardes claimed,

[Robinson] is trying to wreck the company. . . . His objectives are synonymous with closing the company. . . . If . . . the men respond to your all-out strike plea . . . that is, if all the men, or a large part of them are out on Tuesday [December 4, the proposed beginning of the official strike], we will write to tell them that they have in effect dismissed themselves. They will have broken their contracts of employment. We will never engage them again.

Later, on national television, Edwardes elaborated on the charges against Robinson. His thirty months at Longbridge "were marked by 523 disputes, with the loss of 62,000 cars and 113,000 engines, worth £200 million."[40]

The AUEW managed to delay the strike by agreeing to conduct their own inquiry into Robinson's behavior. The union's findings, announced in February 1980, criticized Robinson for "serious failings and lack of responsibility," but recommended that the company reinstate him because it had not followed proper procedures in dismissing him. If Robinson were not reinstated, the union would authorize a strike. Once again Edwardes refused to back down. Management persuaded the AUEW to submit the strike to a referendum at Longbridge on February 19. The next day the results were in—the workers voted 14,000 to 600 to accept the dismissal. To management, the outcome represented a watershed. The independent stewards had been dealt a major, possibly permanent, setback. The recovery plan could move forward. Over the next several months BL managers, taking the companywide vote on the Edwardes plan as a mandate, pushed through reforms in the work place. Management continued to ignore the machinery of participation. It demanded and won greater flexibility in moving workers across jobs. And it standardized compensation for similar jobs in different plants, ending the anomalous "customs and practices," the basis of the shop stewards' authority. In Edwardes's view, the two-day period in April 1980 that saw the introduction of the new work practices also saw "arguably the most important industrial relations move since the war . . . 30 years of management concessions (which had made it impossible to manufacture cars competitively) were thrown out of the window, and our car factories found themselves with a fighting chance of becoming competitive."[41]

At the end of 1983, BL announced its first profitable quarter in almost a decade, although the company remains financially troubled. Nonetheless, BL has made rapid improvements in productivity under the new work rules. In 1980, the Longbridge plant had averaged seven cars per man; by 1982, production exceeded twenty-five per man. BL's new, post-Ryder models, the Metro and Maestro, as well as the BL-Honda Triumph Acclaim, were popular in the marketplace. The Land Rover and Jaguar divisions were actually profitable; the sale of the Jaguar division to private investors in 1985 brought BL an added infusion of cash. Yet by middecade the company's share of the domestic market continued to hover around 18 percent, and it had virtually no presence in major markets outside the United Kingdom. Most analysts agreed that unless the company succeeded in establishing itself as a specialty producer, or further cemented ties with Honda, or the electronics revolution radically affected economies of scale, the company would continue to face a troubled future.

THE TRIALS OF VOLKSWAGEN

As recently as a decade ago it was fashionable to look at West Germany as number one. Like the Japan of the early 1980s, Germany boasted an extremely efficient and productive economy featuring a highly educated and stable work force that enjoyed a rising standard of living. From the ashes of the Third Reich arose an apparently model society. The signs of this "economic miracle" *(Wirtschaftswünder)* were conspicuous. Unemployment and inflation stood at insignificant levels. Strikes and other forms of employee unrest were rare, at least in the private sector. Many management experts (though not many managers) praised the system of industrial governance through co-determination for apparently satisfying the trade-offs between efficiency and equity that bedevil every Western industrial nation. The German reputation for quality and engineering was unsurpassed. Adding to its traditional strong bases in heavy industrial goods, coal, steel, and chemicals, the Germans became world leaders in cameras, consumer electronics, and cars.

In recent years, however, the picture has not been as bright. Although the German auto industry remains the strongest in Europe, its market share in Germany and around the world has been under siege. German automakers' share of total world production fell from 15.6 percent in 1970 to 12.9 percent in 1983. Over the same period, their share of exports sent to North America declined from 40 percent to 12 percent. Import penetration of the German market, largely propelled by the Japanese, jumped from 21.1 percent in 1977 to 27.2 percent in 1983. As in the United Kingdom, the foreign multinationals have begun treating their German subsidiaries as parts of an integrated whole. Despite good profits in Germany in the 1970s, Ford and GM added capacity in places like Spain and Austria and retired production in higher-cost areas like Germany and Holland.

Volkswagen (VW), the largest automaker in Germany and for many years the symbol of the nation's economic miracle, has weathered several financial crises in the past decade. In 1974, a loss of 807 million deutschemarks (DM) earned the company temporarily a postwar German record for dismal performance. Subsequent (and smaller) losses followed in 1975, 1982, and 1983. Problems rooted in the company's system of corporate governance—itself a symbol of modern industrial democracy—have complicated VW's efforts to reestablish its premier competitive position among European automakers. Once Europe's low-cost producer, VW is now struggling to control costs, improve quality, and reorganize manufacturing and marketing on a worldwide basis.

VW's trials reflect cracks and strains in the nation's enterprise system as it adapts to new competitive realities. In the past two decades, the same forces that beset the auto industries in the United States and the United Kingdom—slackening demand in the home market, intensified global rivalry, and the need to reinvest heavily in modern techniques of production—have sorely tested the interrelationships between and among business, government, and labor that were once the mainsprings of the German postwar recovery.

Foundations

The German enterprise system offers a sharp contrast to the systems that developed in the United States and the United Kingdom. To begin with, large, capital-intensive, concentrated industries have dominated the German economy through most of the past century. In addition, Germany manifests a strong tradition of industrial democracy: unions and works councils have played an important countervailing role to employers in several different periods of the nation's history. Finally, the central government has intermittently intervened to direct and shape economic growth, especially through infrastructural development and supportive trade policies.

The German system also bears the marks of traumatic and discontinuous evolution. War, defeat, revolution, and the policies of foreign occupiers have given distinctive twists to German industrial institutions and the relationships among them. Although the Americans and British commonly receive credit for rebuilding the German economy after World War II, the German enterprise system reflects more generally the abrupt swings of the nation's history before that: the rise of great industrial cartels and banks before the First World War; the liberal reforms of the Weimar Republic; and the sharp centralization and repression of the Nazi regime.

Two prominent features of the German economy, large-scale, concentrated industries and a distinctive form of corporate governance, appeared with the beginnings of industrialization. Perhaps because the industrial revolution and political union came late to Germany and its leaders felt anxious to catch up to the booming economies of England and the United States, the Germans never developed the suspicion of big business that emerged elsewhere. In the late nineteenth century, large corporate banks and industrial cartels grew together, hand in hand. The German banks played the same role that the stock market did in the United States, suppliers of capital and credit. Over the years, the relationship between banks and large companies grew closer and more interdependent in most industries.

Although the early automakers were small and tended to be free of outside influences, these companies nonetheless operated under corporation laws that reflected financial interests. After 1870, the law mandated a dual form of governance for businesses above a certain size, a supervisory board *(Aufsichtsrat)* representing shareholders (especially the banks) and an executive board *(Vorstand)* consisting of salaried managers charged with running the daily affairs of the business. The supervisory board met several times a year but normally made all key investment decisions and elected the executive board.[42] In this system of governance, control of the supervisory board is critical to control of corporate operations. Since the early part of this century, competing interests—banks, unions, employees, and even the government—have periodically vied for positions on the supervisory boards of large companies.

In the case of the auto industry, such struggles became important first in the 1920s. Before that, the industry—the world's oldest auto industry—developed in a halting fashion under entrepreneurial control. Gottlieb Daimler and Karl Benz, pioneers of the internal combustion engine, had founded the first commercial auto companies in 1890. Despite this early head start, auto production grew slowly. The nation had few roads suitable for motoring and many of these were badly maintained. Factories remained tiny and the automakers were slow to recognize the Ford revolution. As late as 1913, the Germans produced only 23,000 cars, about one-tenth the number that rolled off Henry Ford's new assembly line in Highland Park that year. Daimler, Benz, and other manufacturers concentrated on building luxury vehicles and left the mass market in Europe to the French and later the Americans.

Germany's defeat in World War I and the democratic revolution of 1918 radically worsened German automakers' fortunes. Depressed economic conditions—the burden of reparations, hyperinflation, and low per capita incomes and savings rates—restricted the growth of the market. In 1929, when GM sent a group of managers to evaluate the position of its newly acquired subsidiary, Adam Opel AG, the managers reported back that the German market stood at "about the same level of development as the U.S. in 1911"—before the coming of mass production. Despite Ford's entrance with a modern assembly plant in Berlin in 1926, moreover, most German automotive technology remained backward. Opel had a moving assembly line by 1924, but the company failed to reap full advantages because the process was not designed to accommodate interchangeable parts.[43]

Democratic reforms of the Weimar Republic aimed at circumscribing employers' power and recognizing workers' interests tended to complicate decision making and raise production costs in the plants. National legislation made works councils—committees of workers elected to discuss business affairs and employment policies with management—mandatory in factories with fifty or more employees. After 1920, moreover, employers were obliged to bargain collectively with free and independent unions on a full range of wages, benefits, and working conditions. More than two hundred unions operated throughout the economy. These unions were organized around many principles: skill, occupation, industry, ideology, and religion. Jurisdictional disputes among the unions and between the unions and the works councils were especially rife in the early 1920s, a period of intense ideological ferment in Germany.[44]

The combined effects of a troubled economy, backward technology, and troubled industrial relations were devastating to the auto industry. On the eve of the Depression in 1929, the Germans manufactured only 117,000 cars, slightly more than half the total built in France or England and only 3 percent of the total produced in the United States. By 1932, the German total stood at 44,000. In these circumstances, consolidation was inevitable. Between 1920 and 1936, the number of German automakers plunged from nearly 200 to 13. Ford and the American-owned and -financed Opel became dominant producers, and the German producers merged under bank control or left the business. Daimler joined with Benz in 1926 to become a producer of distinctive cars and a mass producer of commercial vehicles. In 1932, four smaller companies merged into one of the largest mass producers, Auto-Union.[45]

The collapse of the Weimar Republic in the aftermath of the Great Depression changed the competitive position of the German auto industry dramatically. Hitler's Act for the Organization of National Labor (1934) suppressed the unions and works councils and returned control of the work place to management. The head of the Nazi German Labor Front (DAF), Robert Ley, defined his job as "to restore absolute leadership to the natural leader of a factory, that is, the employer. . . . Many employers have for years had to call for the 'master in the house.' Now they are once again to be the 'master in the house.' "[46] Collective bargaining and strikes came to an end.

At the same time, Hitler considered the auto industry a driving force in economic development and the government therefore intervened directly in the automakers' affairs. Encouraged by direct and indirect subsidies, the auto companies rapidly modernized plant and equipment. The government provided a centralized fund for industry research and development, became a large-scale buyer of cars and trucks, and underwrote the construction of Europe's best highway system. Finally, Hitler raised the tariff on imported vehicles to 40 percent (from 20 to 25 percent) and enacted a domestic content law. By 1937, imports fell to 9 percent (from a high of 40 percent in 1928) and total production surpassed a quarter million vehicles.[47]

In 1938, Hitler symbolized the nation's push for increased production by awarding Henry Ford the Grand Cross of the German Eagle for his contributions to modern industry. To cultivate still more growth, the Nazis formulated a mandatory consumer savings plan and enlisted the nation's premier automotive engineer, Dr. Ferdinand Porsche, to design an inexpensive car for the masses. Before this "Volkswagen" could fully gestate, however, Hitler plunged the nation into war and auto production in Germany ceased between 1940 and 1946.

Miracle Growth

The auto industry's performance in the postwar economic miracle rests on an enterprise system built on the legacies of the nation's discontinuous development. In Andrew Shonfeld's elegant phrasing,

> The defeat, division, and chaos which Germany suffered in the 1940s did not wipe out the legacy of the past; it only lifted temporarily the pressure of history. When the Germans began to reconstruct their economy, they built upon the familiar structural foundation and plan, much of it invisible to the naked eye, as if guided by an archaeologist who could pick his way blindfold about some favorite ruin.[48]

From the Weimar era, the Germans inherited an obsessive fear of inflation; from the Nazis, a deep suspicion of centralized government planning. From their Allied occupiers, the Germans acquired a decentralized government in the form of a parliamentary democracy and a constitution that, among other things, guaranteed the rights of free trade unions. The mainsprings of the German recovery were, accordingly, the establishment of a stable currency, a laissez-faire approach to economic development, and a social compact between employers and employees.

In the first months after the Nazi surrender, the victors took steps to ensure that Germany would remain a weak nation. In the language of the time, the nation would be decentralized, deindustrialized, and denazified. Once again, as after the First World War, the victorious Allies intended to make Germany pay. Industrial output would be restricted to 1932 levels. The Allies' first "level of industry plan," for instance, proposed to fix German auto output at 40,000 units per year.[49]

Growing strains in the alliance and the dawn of the cold war, however, forced the Allies to rethink their policies. As Soviet influence spread throughout Central and Eastern Europe, the Western Allies saw the need to create a stable parliamentary democracy in Germany. Creating a stable government required a much greater level of support to help rebuild the economy. As a result, the Allies increased economic assistance through policies such as the Marshall Plan and gradually stopped collecting reparations. At the same time, the Allies halted plans to dismantle German industry. Although the Americans and the British forced the breakup of the most conspicuous cartels that had supported the Nazi war machine, including the largest steel, coal, and chemical companies, many large companies and oligopolistic industries remained intact. Over time, the giant banks even reformed and concentrated their financial holdings as they had before the war.

Next, the Allies turned their attention to the stabilization of the currency. Inflation had been a serious problem after the war with the reichsmark declining in value almost daily. The population resorted to foraging and trading on the black market to supply basic needs. A few American cigarettes were worth thousands of official marks. In June 1948, the Allies finally authorized a new currency, the deutschemark, to replace the old reichsmark. At the changeover, the money supply was contracted more than 90 percent (a ratio of 100 RM to 6.5 DM) and citizens were allowed to exchange only 60 RM to DM at parity. Debts were restructured at a ratio of ten to one as well. To help offset these draconian measures, the government lowered taxes across the board and exempted from any taxes incomes saved and invested. The Allies also lifted price and wage controls in progressive stages. These actions soon took effect: goods reappeared in the shops; industrial production climbed sharply; prices rose moderately, stabilized, and began to fall.

The successful rebuilding of Germany also depended on the creation of a stable government and a broad national consensus on the course of recovery. Late in 1948, the Allies permitted representatives of the eleven *Länder* or states under their control to design the form of the new government. A "parliamentary council" finished the Basic Law of the Federal Republic of Germany in the following spring. The Basic Law created a Western-style parliamentary democracy: a bicameral legislature, a strong central executive and cabinet, an independent judiciary, and extensive powers reserved to the *Länder*. The new parliament elected in the summer of 1949 chose the leader of the conservative Christian Democratic Union (CDU), Konrad Adenauer, as the first chancellor of the new republic.

Although it had no predecessor before the war, the CDU and its ally, the Christian Social Union of Bavaria (CSU), quickly built a strong consensus around its laissez-faire economic policies. Adenauer's minister of economics, Ludwig Erhard, took charge of the economic recovery. Erhard was a disciple of the Freiburg school of economics then developing the notion of a "social market economy" *(Soziale Marktwirtschaft)*. There were four articles in the new creed: competition in the marketplace will produce the most efficient and equitable outcomes; government intervention should be limited; the proper role of the state is to influence (as opposed to control) the workings of the market in the interests of equity; and economic and social policy should be closely linked. The social content of this economic philosophy was not fully developed, although the new government acknowledged the state's responsibilities to the aged, the disabled, and the unemployed as well as employers' obligations to provide their workers security and a measure of participation in decisions that affected the levels and conditions of employment.[50]

The social market economy quickly gained widespread support among the electorate. In part, fortune smiled on the Christian Democrats: the end of vindictive Allied policies and the currency reform benefited them. The nation's eagerness to make a fresh start also helped the new government. But the liberal economic policies had an appeal of their own to citizens who had endured the horrors of the centralized management of the economy under the Nazis. As Erhard himself put it,

> More perhaps than any other economy the German one has had to experience the economic and supra-economic consequences of an economic and trading policy subjected to the extremes of nationalism, autarky and government control. We have learnt the lesson; and if the basic principles of a liberal economic policy are championed . . . with a vigor possibly startling to foreign [observers], the reason must be sought in the special circumstances of our recent history.[5]

The final building block of the recovery, the necessary complement to the establishment of political and economic legitimacy through the currency reform, the Basic Law, and the social market philosophy, was the restructuring of relations between employers and employees.[52] By the early 1950s, the Federal Republic established a system of dual representation with strong echoes of the Weimar period. German workers' interests were represented in two distinct institutions, the unions and the works councils *(Betriebsräte)*. The unions negotiated industrywide agreements on wages, hours, and some benefits with regional employers' associations. The works councils, in contrast, operated at a company level. All employees below the management board *(Vorstand)*—managers as well as hourly workers—elect representatives to the works councils, which meet periodically to discuss company-specific employment policies and general business matters. The labor movement itself was consolidated into sixteen large industrial unions that eschewed traditional distinctions based on skills, crafts, or ideology.

The establishment of dual representation entailed a struggle between employers and unions. As happened in the 1920s, the unions, which sought a stronger presence at the plant and company levels, resented the works councils, and employers resisted labor at every turn. The unions had resurfaced and begun to reorganize at the local and state levels almost immediately after the surrender, but it took them several years to clarify their role and status. For one thing, once the Allies made it clear that German industry would not be nationalized, the unions had to await the refounding of employers' associations before collective bargaining could resume.[53] For another, since the economy was rebuilt along decentralized lines, collective bargaining took place among employers at the regional, rather than at the national, level. Legislation of 1949 further limited the scope of bargaining and prohibited either side from establishing formal ties with political parties or organized religious groups.[54]

The labor movement also had to restore order in its own house. In the late 1940s, few union leaders of the prewar years were still alive. Many of the most militant survivors, moreover, lived in Soviet-occupied territory and had limited influence on the unions in the Western zones. The leading trade unionists in western Germany, including Hans Böckler of the metalworkers, were determined to consolidate the labor movement so as to avoid reliving the confusion of the 1920s. When the unions finally gathered in Munich in 1949 to create a national labor federation, the Deutscher Gewerkschaftsbund (DGB), under Böckler's leadership they reorganized the movement with two broad principles in mind. Unions were organized across industries *(Industriegewerkschaft)*, as opposed to craft, religious, or general lines. Representation in the private sector was confined to sixteen broad industry-based unions. Second, to limit jurisdictional disputes, the DGB decreed that there could be only one union in a single plant or industry *(Einheitsgewerkschaft)*.[55]

Because both tradition and law limited the scope of collective bargaining, the labor movement pursued its broader goals through political means.[56] At its founding congress, the DGB had announced a political and economic program that called for centralized economic planning, full employment, co-determination, the nationalization of key industries, and "the attainment of social justice through the appropriate participation of working people in the total returns of the economy." The key to the entire program was co-determination *(Mitbestimmung)*, an arrangement in which labor and management would have equal representation on supervisory boards. If the unions could win sanction for co-determination, they would be in a strong position to realize the rest of their goals. In 1951 and 1952, the DGB mounted determined campaigns for co-determination in legislative battles. In the early 1950s, co-determination was not a remote ideal; the system was in place in the iron, steel, and mining industries *(Montanindustrie)*. At the end of the war the British occupiers, acting on instructions from the Labour government at home, had accepted Böckler's proposal that workers should comanage these industries in the Ruhr Valley. In the companies affected, employees could elect half of the supervisory board *(Aufsichtsrat)* and earned the right of approval of the labor director *(Arbeitsdirektor)* who serves on the management board *(Vorstand)*. This arrangement continued de facto until the Federal Republic enacted the Co-determination Act of 1951. This statute, passed after violent debate in the Parliament and around the nation and under the threat of massive strikes, was a clear victory for the unions.

The 1951 law, however, proved to be a high-water mark in the struggle for co-determination. The unions and their political allies, the Social Democratic party (SPD), failed to extend the system of the *Montanindustrie* to other industries. Despite the DGB's own reorganization and the forging of close ties with the SPD, the movement's political clout remained limited. At its founding, the DGB unions represented about 85 percent of the organized working class and about 30 percent of all German workers—not enough to carry the day.[57] The Works Constitution Act enacted in 1952 sanctioned the works councils, distinguished their authority from the unions, and established a more limited form of comanagement. In all joint-stock companies *(Aktiengesellschaften)* above a very small size, employees were entitled to elect one-third of the supervisory board but had no further reach into the management board. Works councils were established in all companies, even those privately held, with authority to discuss and approve employment policies and other business matters.

The reorganization of the labor movement and the Works Constitution Act proved to be a stable compact between employers and employees. Although the unions continued to be dissatisfied with the extent of co-determination and the mandate of the works councils at the company level, German managers and workers enjoyed a mutually supportive relationship. Workers enjoyed rising real incomes, job security, and a voice in the management of enterprise. In return, managers enjoyed labor peace and astonishing rates of productivity improvement. The enterprise system was designed to produce growth.

Volkswagen and the Wirtschaftswünder

The economic miracle swept through every sector and all levels of society. Between 1948 and 1952, the gross national product (GNP) rose 67 percent and industrial production 110 percent, and by the latter year private per capita consumption surpassed the prewar high. During the 1950s and early 1960s, GNP growth averaged 7.6 percent per year, nearly twice the rate of other European countries and ranking below only Japan in the world. Exports as a percentage of GNP climbed from 8.5 percent in 1950 to 15.9 percent by 1960. At the same time, productivity improved at a rate of 7 percent per year. Unemployment fell to about 1 percent by the end of the decade, and inflation hovered between 1 percent and 2 percent. Absenteeism was negligible. Strikes and industrial disputes were rare.[58]

The auto industry played a key role in the West German revival. Within two years of the currency reform auto production exceeded the prewar peak. Total output grew in annual leaps of 20 percent to 50 percent until the first serious postwar recession, in the mid-1960s. Germany passed the United Kingdom as Europe's largest auto producer in the mid-1950s, becoming second only to the United States in cars built. The rapid growth of the German market absorbed only part of this output; from the early 1950s onward, exports to Europe and the United States accounted for more than 50 percent of total production.

The dominant German automaker, Volkswagen, was the symbol of the *Wirtschaftswünder.* Ironically, in the early postwar years, the company's independent existence was in doubt. The British occupiers tried several times to persuade Henry Ford II to buy the VW complex in Wolfsburg. Each time the offer was spurned, the last occasion after Ford president Ernest Breech declared that the plant was "not worth a damn."[59] Yet under British-appointed CEO Heinz Nordhoff, VW quickly moved into auto production. In 1946, while Ford, Opel, Mercedes-Benz, and Auto-Union (Audi) were still repairing war damage and assessing the market, Volkswagen built its first Beetles. The 10,020 cars built that year represented more than 99 percent of total German auto production. Though its market position was hardly so commanding in later years, the company has remained the country's largest automaker ever since. As recently as 1970, VW and its affiliates built 43 percent of the cars made in Germany.

Behind this remarkable story lay VW's single-minded determination to build reliable, low-cost vehicles while constantly lowering their cost. There was nothing fancy about it: VW borrowed technological and market strategies in their entirety from the elder Henry Ford. Just as Ford had perfected the Model T, so VW strove, in Nordhoff's words, "to develop one model of car to its highest technical excellence."[60] Although VW subsequently built minivans and offered a small range of larger cars, the vast majority of its business in the 1950s and 1960s revolved around the Beetle. Like Ford in its early years and Toyota in the years to follow, VW developed a logistically simple, regionally concentrated production system. At Wolfsburg and nearby cities, VW established massive operations. Nordhoff insisted on streamlining the manufacturing process and, in a reverse *kanban,* the company maintained big inventories of parts and components but low inventories of finished vehicles. Since the Beetles could be sold as quickly as they were built, this "pressure-vacuum production" required maintaining higher levels of efficiency and output.[61] As volume built up, tremendous scale economies accrued to the company.

Profit margins also reflected an enviable labor market and harmonious labor relations. Refugees from East Germany and later from southern Europe and Turkey provided a labor abundance that served to hold wages down. Workers received rising real incomes, but wages climbed at a rate below increases in productivity. As a publicly owned company—after Ford refused to buy VW the British turned the properties over to the federal government—VW could not belong to a regional employers' federation. It thus maintained separate collective bargaining agreements with its employees. Most VW employees are members of IG Metall and earn wages that are generally higher than those of workers at the other automakers. In addition, VW is said to benefit from the close identification between the company's and the workers' interests. Certainly, labor peace has prevailed in the company; there have been no significant strikes at VW since 1949. The labor market partly explains this; so too does the system of co-determination that allows employees a voice in company policies. VW, in contrast to the other mass producers, carried out the spirit as well as the letter of the co-determination laws. Indeed, Nordhoff built close ties with the work force before the co-determination laws required it. Nordhoff began holding quarterly meetings with employees in the late 1940s to discuss the company's business plans.[62]

The form of industrial governance at VW supported not only labor peace but also manufacturing quality. The two are, of course, related.[63] In an industry in which logistics and manufacturing continuity are crucial to success, labor harmony is indispensable. But the identification between workers and employers at VW nourished the company's growth in particular ways: the formal and informal communication networks partly played the role that quality circles later filled. Collective bargaining, though an adversarial process, was conducted against a backdrop of cooperation—a pointed contrast to the United States or the United Kingdom, where hostile relations were the norm.

Volkswagen's fortunes—and those of the other German automakers—flourished in a favorable macroeconomic environment.[64] As we have seen, the government's economic philosophy proclaimed the virtues of the market. The CDU and CSU governments of the 1950s and 1960s tried to avoid industry-specific interventions and in the case of autos, at least, they succeeded. The embarrassment of VW's public ownership prompted the federal government to transfer some of its interest to the state government of Lower Saxony and to sell 60 percent of the company to private stockholders in the early 1960s. VW and Opel received some incentives to locate facilities along the East German border, but these were minor. In contrast to their counterparts in the United States, German automakers faced few battles with the government over antitrust or regulatory issues. In contrast to their counterparts in the United Kingdom, German automakers experienced no shifting demand management, centralized planning, wage and price controls, or state intervention in contract negotiations. The government indirectly supported the auto industry by promoting exports and encouraging savings and investment. Public investment also underwrote the building of Europe's most extensive highway system.

The relationship of the German enterprise system to the *Wirtschaftswünder* was mutually reinforcing. Rapid growth entailed greater rewards for all parties and obscured the tensions that plagued other national economies. Miracle growth, moreover, occurred in the context of a broadening consensus on economic and social policies in West Germany. The CDU and CSU governments of the 1950s slowly legislated a social program that took the sting out of criticisms from the left. In addition to the co-determination laws, the government enacted national programs for social security and health care. The CDU and CSU even discovered Keynes, resorting to aggregate demand management policies in response to recessions in the late 1950s and early 1960s.[65] Political forces on the left matched the conservatives' move toward the center as well. At Bad Godesberg in 1959, the SPD retreated from socialist ideology and embraced liberal economic theory. The DGB followed suit four years later at its convention in Düsseldorf, where, spectacularly, the federation retreated from Marxist doctrines in favor of Keynesian economic doctrines.

This is not to say that ideology disappeared from politics or collective bargaining or that political disagreements ceased, but the consensus around social market philosophy was genuine. The apotheosis of cooperation between left and right occurred in response to the recession of 1966–1967. From this crisis emerged a coalition government of national unity that included ministerial positions for the CDU and CSU, and the SPD. In 1967, the Grand Coalition formalized the consensus in the Act for the Promotion of Stability and Economic Growth. This statute spelled out the government's four fundamental objectives in economic policy. According to the "four corners of the magic square," government policies should "contribute, in the framework of a market economy, simultaneously to achieving price-level stability, a high degree of employment, and external equilibrium, together with steady and adequate economic growth."

The Fading Miracle

The cooperation and consensus that the Act for the Promotion of Stability and Economic Growth symbolized could not withstand the same forces that transformed the nature of competition elsewhere. The maturity of the large European markets, excess capacity, trade liberalization and globalization of competition, and the energy crises obliged management, labor, and government to adapt and interact in new ways. This process of adaptation exposed rigidities in the German enterprise system. Institutional arrangements that functioned smoothly in an environment of growth worked less well as the pace of growth slowed. In the early 1970s, for the first time since the war, VW faced serious internal problems. And its moment of weakness coincided exactly with the rise of the Japanese auto industry.

The *Wirstschaftswünder* could not easily or indefinitely be sustained as the growth of the overall economy slackened noticeably in the 1970s. Between 1951 and 1960, real GNP had increased at a rate of 8 percent, slowing to 4.7 percent in the next decade. Between 1971 and 1980, real GNP averaged an annual growth of just 2.9 percent. The rates of industrial production and productivity improvement followed similar downward curves. In the early 1970s, the unemployment and inflation rates began to inch up.[66]

In circumstances that required the division of diminishing economic returns, political alliances were bound to shift. In 1969, the Grand Coalition foundered largely on the question of revaluing the deutschemark, which had held a constant value against the dollar for two decades. The Social Democrats advocated revaluation to control inflation and raise the standard of living throughout society; the Christian Democrats, on the other hand, worried about the effects of revaluation on the country's exports. After the ensuing elections, the SPD and the Free Democrats (FDP) formed a parliamentary majority and the revaluation took place. The new government, moreover, proved far more willing than its predecessors to manage the economy actively. The SPD-FDP coalition practiced countercyclical demand management policies, intervened in labor-management negotiations, and employed sector-specific policies to pursue its broad social goals.

The rule of the new government provided occasion for reopening debate on social issues that had lain dormant since the early postwar years. The labor movement unveiled a series of new demands. The unions became more aggressive in collective bargaining, agitated to broaden the rights of employees, and pushed harder to expand the system of co-determination. Rapid recovery from the 1967 recession emboldened the unions to ask for big wage hikes to offset the moderate settlements of earlier years. In the first year of the new government, wage settlements averaged 12 percent higher than the year before, touching off a trend that continued unabated through the mid-1970s. At the same time, to improve working conditions and protect employees against economic and technological rationalization, the unions succeeded in increasing relaxation periods and time off and extended the seniority rights of older workers.[67] By the mid-1970s, the wages of German autoworkers approached those of their American counterparts and German benefits were superior.

The SPD-FDP government also enacted a series of statutes that enlarged the rights of workers. The Protection against Dismissal Act (1969) made involuntary layoffs complex and expensive for employers. Reform of the co-determination laws in 1972 and 1976 broadened the responsibilities of the works councils and increased employee representation on the *Aufsichtsräte*. After 1972, the automakers were required to consult the works councils on such issues as the design of the work place, the pace of work, manpower levels and planning, and training. After the 1976 law took effect, employees could elect half of the supervisory board, and their representatives were given the right to appoint the head of the personnel department (*Arbeitsdirektor*). The employers' associations fought the new legislation bitterly and, in the case of the 1976 co-determination law, succeeded in retaining the tie-breaking vote for management on the supervisory boards.

Polarized political debate and mounting disputes over corporate governance came at an awkward moment for VW. Competition in the West German market had intensified in the late 1960s. After years of steady growth, demand leveled off at about two million units per year. Imports captured an increasing share of the market at 20 percent and continued to climb. VW remained the largest producer, but saw its share of the market slowly decline as Opel, Ford, and foreign imports made aggressive gains. In these circumstances, consolidation was inevitable. Marginal auto producers merged with larger concerns: Audi and VW in 1966; Glas and BMW in 1967; NSU and VW-Audi in 1969. At the same time, German companies that were not direct competitors—VW, Daimler-Benz, and Porsche—jointly sponsored research and development and production operations for major components.

Efforts by the government and the Bundesbank to control inflation worsened the industry's competitive position abroad. Between 1969 and the collapse of the Bretton Woods system in 1973, the value of the deutschemark rose 40 percent against the dollar. This had a devastating impact on leading exporters like Volkswagen. The retail price of the Beetle in the United States jumped 61 percent between 1969 and 1974, from $1,799 to $2,895, just when the Japanese mounted their assault on the small-car market in the United States. In the space of a few years, VW's share of the American market, which still accounted for about a quarter of the company's sales, fell from 7 percent to about 4 percent.

Although increasing competition and the government's macro-economic policies put downward pressure on profit margins, the automakers' costs continued to climb. The darkening environment and the increasing institutional rigidities of the German enterprise system affected all of the auto companies but particularly VW.[68] After 1969, the government representatives on the supervisory board combined with the labor representatives to give the employees a de facto majority voice on company policies. The altered balance of power at VW coincided with the end of an era at the company. Nordhoff's death in April 1968 had deprived the company of a charismatic leader. His immediate successors—Kurt Lotz (1968–1971) and Rudolf Leiding (1972–1974)—found it difficult to manage the shifting coalitions on the supervisory board.

VW's competitive troubles became serious in the early 1970s. Not only did the company rely heavily on the production of a single model and on export markets subject to increasingly fierce competition, it also had to cope with wage increases that far outstripped the rates of inflation or productivity improvement. In 1970, 1971, and 1972, wages rose at annual rates of 17 percent, 8.7 percent, and 9.6 percent, respectively. Benefits, particularly in the form of vacations, holidays, and sick leave, rose rapidly as well. VW executives estimated that its assembly-line employees worked thirty-five to forty fewer days than autoworkers in the United States, themselves the recipients of ample time off.[69] High labor costs, moreover, were geographically concentrated. Although VW had opened assembly plants in South America and South Africa in the 1960s, 80 percent of its total output originated in West Germany.

Structural problems in VW's governance impeded management's efforts to make the company more competitive. VW had trouble settling on a long-range plan and establishing managerial continuity. Lotz, who invested heavily to expand and diversify the product line (perhaps too far), resigned as CEO in 1971 after feuding with IG Metall representatives on the supervisory board who clashed with his designated labor director. Leiding's tenure was even shorter. Though he won agreement to phase out the Beetle, his efforts to control labor costs and expand production capacity outside Germany ran afoul of the labor and government directors. In 1974, after VW posted its record loss of 807 million DM, the federal government pressured Leiding to resign.

The restoration of VW to competitive health required changing the balance of power at the top. Chancellor Helmut Schmidt appointed Hans Birnbaum as chairman of the supervisory board; Birnbaum in turn appointed Toni Schmuecker as CEO. The government representatives on the *Aufsichtsrat* voted with the new management against the union representatives to trim the payroll. By the end of 1975, VW employed 32,000 fewer workers than two years before.[70] Schmuecker and the government directors also persuaded the supervisory board to approve construction of an assembly plant in the United States. The IG Metall directors voted for the plan only after receiving assurances that the investment would not contribute to plant closings or forced layoffs in Germany.

VW returned to prosperity for a fleeting moment during the economic recovery that followed the first oil shock when rationalization plans took hold and the Beetle's successor—the Rabbit—proved initially successful. After the second oil shock, however, the losses returned. As happened in the board rooms of Detroit and Dearborn, executives in Wolfsburg were shocked to discover the magnitude of the Japanese competitive advantage. High wages, liberal benefits, outmoded production techniques, and quality problems produced a cost disadvantage of between $700 and $1,000 per car. Despite the new assembly plant in Pennsylvania, VW's share of the American market continued to tumble, falling below 2 percent in 1983. In that year, the company canceled plans to open a second assembly plant in the United States and replaced the Rabbit in 1984 with the Golf, a larger, upscale model. Indeed, VW no longer competes for customers on price in the American market, but rather on the basis of reliability, performance, and "German engineering."

By the mid-1980s, VW's trials showed signs of continuing into the near future. Although the West Germans reached an informal "agreement" with the Japanese in 1981 to limit exports to 11.4 percent of the German market, by 1985, the Japanese share crept up to 13.3 percent and continued to climb. Despite a rebound of profits in 1985, VW has failed to earn a return on capital above its cost of capital for many years. In 1986, VW acquired SEAT, the Spanish maker of small cars, to fill out the low end of the market. VW also announced plans to export small cars to the United States from Brazil. Because of its cost position, the company will concentrate on building upscale, differentiated cars in its German and American factories.

Although the return to power in 1983 of the CDU-CSU coalition reduced government intervention in the industry, political problems of regulation persist. The Green party targeted the automobile as a source of serious environmental problems. In 1984, the government mandated emissions controls tougher than the standards of the European Community (EC), although the automakers and other members of the EC recently forced a three-year delay in implementation of the policy.

Labor and management remained at an impasse on further rationalization, overseas investment, extending employees' rights, and appropriate measures to curb unemployment.[71] In 1984, IG Metall struck targeted companies in the auto and auto supply industries in an attempt to shorten the workweek to 35.0 hours. The strike lasted seven weeks before a compromise settlement that fixed the workweek at 38.5 hours could be reached.

In sum, Volkswagen has adapted slowly and awkwardly to the new international competition of the 1980s. The enterprise system that fostered the *Wirtschaftswünder* had become, as one manager put it, "so overdeveloped that we can only maintain it with booming growth." Economic contraction has created problems and forced trade-offs between the industrial actors that defy easy solutions no matter how good the relationships and communications networks.

CHAPTER **5**

The Japanese Auto Industry's Rise to Dominance

Japanese producers are the dominant players in today's global auto industry. As recently as two decades ago, the great American and European automakers regarded their rivals in Japan (if they regarded them at all) as insignificant producers of cheap cars that seemed unlikely to capture more than a marginal share of the world auto market. By the early 1980s, however, the Japanese producers had become world leaders in building high-quality cars at low cost. They have set competitive standards that the American and European auto companies are hard pressed to match.

In the mid-1980s, the auto Mecca of the world is no longer Detroit but Japan. From around the world, auto executives, union leaders, government officials and academics make the pilgrimage—to Toyota City and the efficient *kanban* operation; to Nissan's highly automated Zama plant; to Toyo Kogyo's sprawling Ujina complex, the largest integrated auto plant in Japan; to Honda's precision-run Saitama plant.

They come to learn the lessons of the industry's success: the reduction of waste in the flow and handling of materials on a just-in-time basis; the involvement of workers in quality control circles and their commitment to quality and productivity; the integration of automation on the shop floor; and the role of the Japanese govern-

97

ment in contributing to the industry's success. But mostly they travel to Japan to learn because objective evidence told them that the Japanese auto industry had become the measure of competitive excellence in the world. A few simple facts tell the story.

- In 1980, the Japanese auto industry surpassed the United States as the world's leader in the production of motor vehicles, turning out more than eleven million cars, trucks, and buses. Although the United States regained the number one position in 1984, this had less to do with American automakers' efforts than with the economic recovery in the United States and a wave of protectionist sentiment around the world that restrained Japanese production.

- Around the world, Japanese automakers were recognized as industry leaders in both cost and quality. In the area of costs, official estimates in the late 1970s indicated that the Japanese automakers enjoyed a $1,500 landed cost advantage over their American counterparts—that is, the Japanese could assemble, ship, and land in America a subcompact car for $1,500 less than the cost to American manufacturers to build the same car here. Additional analysis to refine the estimated cost advantage yielded a range of numbers from $1,300 to more than $2,000; some industry insiders felt that as better information about Japanese production costs became available, the "real" number would be closer to $3,000.[1]

- As for quality—difficult to measure objectively and precisely— the Japanese-made products consistently outperformed all competitors, according to several industry ratings. For example, one list of the highest-quality cars in the world awarded four of the top five positions to Japanese automakers, based on customer satisfaction polling. In another survey, Japanese-made cars consistently outpolled both American and European products in dependability, problem-free delivery, fuel economy, and value for the money.[2]

- Finally, as an industry, the automakers have assumed a central role in the overall economic performance of Japan. In an economy known for its capacity to produce hardgoods, the auto industry represents the nation's industrial paradigm. The eleven vehicle assemblers provide, directly and indirectly, roughly one out of every ten jobs in the country. Taken together, the Japanese automakers account for 8 percent of the total value added of the country's manufacturing sector and 17 percent of its exports. In

1984, autos ranked as Japan's most lucrative export item, earning more than $29 billion—more than twice the amount gained by the number two export item, steel.[3]

By any standard of measurement, these figures depict an impressive performance. But what makes the accomplishment of the Japanese auto industry even more remarkable is the distance it had to cover in arriving at its position of global dominance—as well as the sureness and swiftness with which it covered the ground. In the first years after World War II, the capacity of Japan to have an auto industry—any domestic auto industry, much less the global leader—was in doubt. What changed this course was the evolution of the Japanese enterprise system and its key role in the industry's steady rise to dominance.

In a series of phases, management, labor, and government first successfully steered their way past the industry's barriers to entry. By forging the beginnings of a coalition of interests based on the mutual benefits of a growing auto industry, the three sides together overcame the initial obstacles. In the first period (1946–1953), they institutionalized the relationships through systems of linking mechanisms that promoted ongoing communication and the exchange of quid pro quos between the three sides. While retaining independence, each recognized the value of shared interests.

In the second phase (1953–1973), these linkups provided the important channels for the implementation of a high-growth strategy for the auto industry, as well as for the efficient resolution of disagreements that could have derailed the strategy. During this phase, the enterprise system continued to evolve as the external environment and each of the three sides evolved. But the focus continued to be on the shared economic and political interests of management, labor, and government and on the negotiation of agreements among all three parties that would acknowledge and promote the interests of all sides.

Finally in the third phase (since 1973), the industry's drive to competitiveness was rewarded with global dominance: the system of relationships overcame a series of worldwide crises that tripped other auto-producing nations. In the turbulent 1970s, the Japanese enterprise system proved its adaptability and flexibility. For the future, the only question facing the industry is whether the relationships that provided the essential underpinnings for its phenomenal growth can continue to adapt to a changing competitive environment, or whether the politics of the world auto competition will disrupt the equilibrium of the relationships between Japanese management, labor, and government.

SOURCES OF COMPETITIVE ADVANTAGE

The country and its natural resources and economic endowments lend little support to an indigenous auto industry. As the Japanese automakers are fond of saying even today, "We are a small island with no natural resources." Behind that clichéd litany is an important economic truth. The lack of natural resources represents a severe handicap for an industry like autos, which relies upon numerous, various, and substantial raw material suppliers. In terms of economic endowments, moreover, Japan did not have the necessary high-quality base of component suppliers, sophisticated technology, or infrastructure to support an auto industry. Capital availability and capital investment were additional limitations: when the Toyota Motor Company was formally established in 1937, its total capitalization amounted to $3.5 million.

If the natural and economic endowments of the country were one impediment to the emergence of an indigenous auto industry, the relationship between workers and managers—heralded today as a source of Japan's advantage—was a second. In the pre–World War II period, Japanese companies gave little indication of the current participatory style of management. Blue-collar workers were strictly second-class citizens, occupying the bottom tier of the enterprise in a status-conscious society.[4] Legalized repression effectively squelched any meaningful role for organized labor: the Peace Preservation Law of 1925 gave the police the power to suppress unions. Between 1920 and 1938, over 60,000 persons suspected of radicalism or communism were arrested; few were actually communists, most were labor leaders and organizers.[5] In 1937, as Japan began to transform itself for war, unions regarded as belonging to the political left wing were summarily abolished; in 1940, all remaining unions were disbanded and the government created an organization for workers in support of the war effort.

Finally, the development of Japan's auto companies in the years shortly before and after World War II gave no indication of future global leadership. Between 1924 and 1934, the Japanese motor vehicle market was totally dominated by Ford and General Motors, both of which used knock-down kit assembly plants to claim a combined

90 percent of the market. Nissan did not begin fully integrated auto production until 1934; Toyota did not even complete its first trial car until 1935—the same year that a government mission traveled to Germany to inspect the Volkswagen development project launched by Adolf Hitler. Finally, having observed the importance of rolling stock in Manchuria in 1931 and having witnessed the benefits of the German auto project, in 1936 the Japanese government moved to support the primitive domestic industry, almost entirely as a matter of national defense and national industrial development. A series of measures enacted by the government in 1936 and 1937 bolstered Japan's would-be automakers and forced Ford and General Motors out of the market entirely by 1939.

Still, the Japanese automakers' development was painfully slow and awkward. Between 1936 and 1941, the entire industry produced fewer than 8,000 passenger cars and only slightly more than 140,000 trucks and buses. Then, in 1942, before the automakers could really become fully developed producers, the government shifted the companies into industrial support of the war effort. When, in 1946, the Japanese government under Prime Minister Yoshida began again to think about national economic development and adopted a policy targeting support for a list of priority industries, the auto industry was not on the list.

Yet within a few decades, the Japanese auto industry not only managed to develop, it also became the dominant force in the global auto industry. From the record of the Japanese industry's triumph emerges a clear lesson of international competition: Competitive advantage can be created through coalition building between management, labor, and government. The building blocks of an industry's competitiveness are the interactions within the national enterprise system. Recognizing and integrating the interests of each constituency is the key to success; any undertaking that does not reflect a consortium of interests is doomed to failure from a competitive point of view. It is a principle explicitly identified by Hideo Sugiura, a top official of Honda, who says, "We have learned from experience that any project we have undertaken simply for ourselves has never turned out well."[6]

Viewed from this perspective, the Japanese enterprise system, though different from that of the United States, is not unique. Rather it represents a highly pragmatic, efficient, outcome-oriented approach to negotiating the same economic and political factors that each auto-producing nation must contend with: large corporations, large unions, and large governments; democratic political ideals; and global competition.[7] What distinguishes the Japanese enterprise system is the explicit acceptance by management, labor, and government that both authority and responsibility for competitiveness must be shared by all three parties; the creation of communication and reward systems to support that understanding; and the negotiation of quid pro quos to carry it out.

This coalition of interests and expectations, of authority and responsibility, was not always there; it evolved over the span of the Japanese auto industry's development. But to begin, it required first and foremost an acceptance of the legitimacy of each party by the others. In the case of the Japanese auto industry, this level of agreement was not automatic or even easy to achieve.

THE MAKINGS OF THE SYSTEM

Mitsuru Tsuchiya, now a managing director of Toyota, remembers distinctly what life was like in Japan in 1946. "We lost everything at the end of World War II," he says. "We had nothing left. There were one hundred million people and they had lost everything. One hundred million people wondering how to live, how to keep body and soul together. Then the Americans came. They told us to purge the industrial circles and to democratize industry. Everyone in the industry thought every day, every minute, every second how to revitalize the Japanese auto industry."[8]

For the Japanese automakers in the chaos of the immediate postwar period, the struggle was to exist. As Toyota's Tsuchiya remembers, the general economic environment was unremittingly harsh. The entire country suffered from severe shortages in consumer goods, fuel, and raw materials. Working-class families endured unbelievable hardships: in April 1946, a government census of the Japanese work force found 4.32 million Japanese working between 8 and 20 days per month; 1.96 million working 7 or fewer days per month; and 1.59 million completely unemployed. In the fall of 1946, government economists estimated that real wages had actually fallen since the year before.

Industrial production was at a virtual standstill: Four years after the war's end, production had only climbed to 60 percent of the 1930–1934 levels, with most of the growth coming from mining, not manufacturing. In this economic environment, currency inflation spiraled out of control. Between August 1945 and November 1948, Bank of Japan notes in circulation rose from ¥30 billion to ¥280 billion.

To bring order to this economic chaos, in 1948 the occupying American forces adopted a harshly deflationary policy called for by Detroit banker Joseph Dodge. His nine point program—the Dodge Line—proved stern medicine: in 1949, a full one-third of Japan's four million small business either merged with other companies or went bankrupt.[9]

Yet in spite of these discouraging general conditions, the management of the auto companies set about the business of making motor vehicles. In 1945, shortly after the end of the war, Nissan, Toyota, and Diesel Motors banded together in a joint group—the Consortium of Auto Manufacturing—seeking access to government-controlled critical resources by developing a case for the establishment of a Japanese auto industry. Two years later, the consortium published a wildly optimistic report, which argued that Japan already had the technological capability to catch up and compete in the auto industry, concluding that "it would not be impossible to equal American standards within a few years." The report went on to point out that transportation, in general, and the auto industry, in particular, were vital to the future economic and industrial development of the country, and the auto industry was being retarded by the nationwide shortage of raw materials. The lack of resources would have to be dealt with if the auto industry were to develop.[10]

In fact, the auto industry faced business problems more severe and more encompassing than just the lack of raw materials. Whether the consortium recognized it or not, the obstacles confronting the automakers represented almost a total barrier to entry: the automakers lacked capital and technology; they lacked a market and sufficient production scale; they lacked the capacity to differentiate their product from the competition; they lacked suppliers and the necessary infrastructure to support the industry; and they were getting a late start on the experience curve.

In the immediate postwar period, labor represented a hostile force, pressing demands and interests in the form of an intensely political unionism. Three factors shaped the Japanese labor movement of the late 1940s and early 1950s. First, the postwar economy was incapable of employing or supporting the work force. In the first five years after World War II, five million people returned to Japan from abroad, further distorting the labor market. These depressed economic conditions sharpened the workers' response to union-organizing drives.

Second, the message of the unions was predominantly political. In 1945, an imperial amnesty released 300,000 prisoners and restored the civil rights of 600,000 others, many of whom were union organizers who had been deprived of their rights and freedom since the prewar crackdown on labor. Their return to Japanese society, particularly at a time of worker deprivation, helped trigger a powerful labor backlash. After years of suffering as the country's political whipping boy, labor had become a potent political force.

Finally, wittingly or unwittingly, the Supreme Commander for the Allied Powers (SCAP) government contributed to labor's political expression. Having won the war, the occupying Americans proceeded to the task of remaking the Japanese system—with the United States as the model and the New Deal the message. In 1946, SCAP framed a new constitution for Japan that went beyond even American boundaries: article 28 of the new document spoke directly and forcefully to the role of organized labor, stating that the right of workers to organize was "eternal and inviolable"—a fundamental human right. Subsequent legislation hewed to the American line: the Trade Union Law, patterned after the Wagner Act, set the terms and conditions of collective bargaining, and the Labor Standards Law defined acceptable working conditions. Thus, SCAP's signal to the Japanese was that organized labor was to enjoy a position of power and influence in a newly democratized system.

The result of these factors was active and antagonistic political unionism. The form of the union was traditional: company or enterprise unions rather than trade or craft unions sprang up as the fastest response to labor's new-found legitimacy. In 1946, for example, union membership in Japan grew by a factor of four. But even though the form was traditional, the power of the unions and their posture toward management was unprecedented. In the economic chaos of the postwar years, unions resorted to bitter strikes and even attempted worker control of production.[11] In 1946, there was an average of 118 labor disputes per month; in 1947, an average of 113; and in 1948, an average of 170 disputes per month.[12]

Labor's agenda behind these disputes tended to focus on three issues. The first two were wages and job security, straightforward responses to the inflation-plagued economy, the glutted job market, and the uncertainty of work. The third issue, however, was more a matter of ideology or philosophy. Labor's third demand was for the "democratization of management"—an imprecise slogan that referred in part to the abolition of the old status system and the class, wage, and benefit distinctions between white- and blue-collar workers. But it also referred in part to an alteration of the traditional relationship between management and labor and the redefinition of management prerogatives.[13] As much as anything, labor's demand for the "democratization of management" was a call for management to accept the legitimacy of labor and recognize the workers as full participants in the operation of the enterprise. It was this demand that proved particularly hard for management to accept. In the areas of wages and job security, there were either preexisting traditions or emerging understandings that could shape the relationship between management and labor: the seniority-based wage system and the promise of "lifetime employment" at the larger firms. But the issue of the democratization of management was a major departure; the best management could do was to begin to discuss the real meaning of the issue, as often as not in no-holds-barred sessions where the issues under attack were traditionally defined as management's rights.[14]

If labor was an angry adversary, the best that could be said of both SCAP and the Japanese government was that they chose to pursue policies of benign neglect toward the auto industry. In 1945, at the close of the war, the entire stock of trucks and buses in Japan totaled only 54,000 vehicles. Consequently, SCAP authorized truck production to proceed at 1,500 vehicles per month and allocated 6,000 tons of imported rubber to be used for tire fabrication. Auto production, however, was not allowed because of the shortage of materials and the view that autos were a consumer luxury. It was not until 1947 that SCAP authorized auto production to begin again and even then strict conditions were imposed: No more than 300 units per year could be produced and engine size was limited to 1,500 cc.

Nor were the Japanese government officials any more supportive of their auto industry. In December 1946, when the Yoshida government issued its first economic policy statement, adopting target industries to receive priority treatment, the auto industry was conspicuous by its absence. In fact, the Japanese government was openly divided on the question of the significance and value of an indigenous auto industry. The Ministry of Commerce and Industry (MCI)—precursor to the Ministry of International Trade and Industry (MITI)—favored the cause of the automakers. As early as 1948, MCI issued the Basic

Counterplan for the Auto Industry, which proposed that the government assist the automakers by buying only Japanese-made cars, using the foreign exchange shortage to keep out foreign-made vehicles, and using licensing agreements to help the automakers replace their obsolete production equipment and obtain access to foreign technology.

MCI's advocacy on behalf of the industry was effectively canceled, however, by the opposition of officials of both the Secretary General and the Bank of Japan, who cited the classical economic theory of comparative advantage to support their position: "Efforts to foster an automobile industry in Japan are meaningless," argued the governor of the Bank of Japan. "This is a period of international specialization. Since America can produce cheap, high-quality cars, should we not depend on America for automobiles?"[15]

As a result of this position, autos were not given favored treatment; indeed, from 1946 to 1950 the Japanese government looked the other way as 22,000 American-made cars were brought into the country, ostensibly for use by the occupation forces. Instead, they were resold for use as taxis, thereby avoiding the 40 percent tariff and the 30 to 50 percent commodity tax that would have applied had they been classified as ordinary auto imports. As late as 1950, the Japanese government showed no compunction in depriving the Japanese automakers of what little domestic demand existed at the time by approving the use of limited foreign exchange for the purchase of 150 used Fords for taxis in Yokosuka.[16]

Faced with labor's hostility and government's indifference, the Japanese automakers chose to go it alone. Their start was inauspicious. Their products were primitive. In 1947, Nissan introduced its first postwar passenger car, with specifications almost identical to a model produced in 1936; when Toyota unveiled its Toyopet car in 1947, it was a passenger car body mounted on a truck chassis. Factories were small and backward: in 1948, a government report found that the annual combined production capacity of Nissan and Toyota was a maximum of 20,000 vehicles—less than the monthly production output of any one of the American Big Three.

Their production facilities were inefficient and their cars costly to produce: at Toyota, the set-up time for machinery for auto assembly was two to three hours; in 1952, a made-in-America Ford had a $167 landed cost advantage over a Toyopet in the Japanese market. Finally, the Japanese automakers were crippled by low domestic demand

and the use of secondhand black-market American cars to fill what little demand existed: as late as 1950, 92 percent of the passenger cars in Japan and 57 percent of the trucks had been in use for more than seven years and 88 percent of the passenger cars had been in use for more than ten years. As far as the use of American cars was concerned, in 1953 almost 4,000 more secondhand American-made cars were sold in Japan than new Japanese-made vehicles.[17] On the basis of simple competitive economics, the attempt of the Japanese automakers to succeed without the support of labor and government seemed doomed to failure.

Then two events—one involving management's relationship with labor, and the other with government—not only rescued the automakers from near-certain bankruptcy but also began the process of coalescing the Japanese enterprise system into a supportive, win-win set of relationships capable of propelling the industry into a strong competitive position.

The first watershed event was a wave of bitter, all-out strikes mounted by labor against management, the high-water mark of Japanese political unionism. The wave struck across most of Japanese industry in the late 1940s and early 1950s. According to Ichiro Shioji, former president of the Japanese Autoworkers Union,

> Most of the unions of the major Japanese industries were communist controlled. While the union bore the name of the trade union, it was really an instrument of the communist party program, a means of achieving the communists' revolutionary purpose. The communists would struggle for the sake of struggle. They didn't mind if the company went bankrupt—that wasn't their concern.[18]

The wave of strikes caught the auto industry, hitting Toyota in 1949 and Nissan in 1953. In both instances the circumstances and the outcome were remarkably parallel. In April 1949, the Toyota union went out on strike, protesting a repeated cycle of delayed payments and 10 percent wage cuts, followed by a call from top management for "voluntary resignations"—a euphemism for coming layoffs. According to one top official of Toyota who remembers the period of the strike, "During this time, Toyota suffered terribly under the poor economic conditions. The company could not pay adequate wages to labor. Toyota's bankers asked Toyota to lay off workers in order to improve the company's desperate financial condition. Faced with the layoffs, the union went on strike. At the same time, Nippendenso, a major supplier in the Toyota family of companies, was also in very great trouble and was forced to make layoffs. All in all, Toyota needed ¥200 million at the end of 1949. However, Toyota could not collect money from most of its dealers for the cars that they had purchased because they were short of cash, which in turn prevented Toyota from paying the interest they owed to the banks."[19]

The workers' strike proved painfully effective. Production dropped dramatically, from a level of 992 vehicles in March 1949, before the strike began, to a level of only 304 vehicles in May 1949. Finally, after a brutal fifteen-month strike, the battle came to an end in a victory for neither side—a lose-lose outcome. Roughly two thousand workers were cut from the Toyota work force; and Kiichiro Toyoda, president and founder of the Toyota Motor Company, and his entire executive staff resigned from the company *en masse*. To rescue the failing company financially, a bail-out was arranged by the Nagoya branch manager of the Bank of Japan, not from concern for Toyota, according to one company official, "but because of his concern for the regional economy and the impact of a Toyota bankruptcy."[20]

Most important, the strike left an indelible mark on both managers and workers. Says Toyota's Tsuchiya, "We learned many lessons from these bitter experiences. Both labor and management learned the lessons. There was no expectation of a better life for the employees unless a stable corporate base could be established."[21] Shirou Umemura, president of the Toyota Motor Workers Union, agrees completely with Tsuchiya. "Today's relationship between labor and management resulted from that experience," he says. "Labor learned two lessons. First, do not repeat those miserable conditions again. Second, to maintain employment, workers must see to it that the proper volume of work is maintained for that company."[22]

The strike at Nissan three years later replicated the Toyota experience in important ways.[23] According to Ichiro Shioji, who became president of the Nissan union after the strike, "The direct cause was a wage negotiation. The union wanted a raise to cover the cost of living. Most of the workers backed the union leaders because of the severe conditions, the dire want of food, shelter, and clothing. Nissan at the time was making fewer than one thousand units per month, mostly trucks. The company was on the brink of total collapse. It proposed to lay off 2,000 of its 7,000 workers."[24]

After four months of the strike, a group of 500 workers split off from the union and formed a new union, willing to return to work. Gradually the new union won membership from the old, replacing the more ideological, political leadership with more cooperative, economic leadership. As the new union took form, Katsuji Kawamata, formerly a top official of the Industrial Bank of Japan and, since 1947, Nissan's chief financial officer, became increasingly active in running the company. On both sides, new leadership sought to begin a new relationship. Says Shioji,

> We learned a lesson from that bitter struggle. We learned that both sides benefit, not from conflict and adversarial relations, but through common objectives and cooperation with each other. In those days, the relationship between management and labor was characterized by hate and mutual distrust. We learned that cooperation and mutual trust were more beneficial for both. We gradually built up a system of consultative practices that led to the creation of a new labor-management relationship. The key to the stability of the labor-management relationship is trust. It can't be achieved just by talking. It has to be built up by practice and experience.[25]

The climactic strikes and their resolution proved to be the end of one era and the beginning of the next in Japanese labor-management relations. For the auto unions it meant the end of the political unions that had characterized the initial postwar years. After the strikes, the unions accepted an economic relationship, negotiating over wages and benefits—but without any specific political ideology. The political views had been replaced by a pragmatic acceptance of the economic interdependence of labor and management: improvement of the workers' standard of living and the prosperity of the firm were comparable to "the right and left wheels of the vehicle. Both wheels are required for the vehicle to move, and they move synchronously whichever direction the vehicle is headed for."[26] Out of the strike came the recognition by the workers and the union that they shared responsibility for the economic performance of the company.

Management of the auto companies arrived at a comparable understanding from the strikes. Ironically, though labor moved away from its political agenda, one of the basic changes brought about by the strikes was, in fact, political: the workers had established their legitimacy as an integral part of the enterprise. Management had been democratized; power would be shared, consultation would be carried out. Says Tsuchiya, "Management realized that cooperation between management and labor was essential to get industry back on track."[27]

The two sides had, in effect, crossbred. Labor accepted the imperative of growth for the company and accepted, as well, its share of responsibility for producing growth. Management accepted the requirement of workers for a rising wage and job security, as well as their legitimate participation in the operation of the company. From the lose-lose experience of the strikes, both sides emerged determined to make future transactions win-win.

This compact did more than avert economic ruin for the automakers. It also put into place the first positive link in the enterprise system and made an important contribution toward overcoming several of the barriers to entry that had thwarted the industry's progress. As a result of a supportive relationship with the workers, the companies could begin to move more quickly along the experience curve. Improved quality and productivity could begin to flow from an involved, committed work force. And if the other barriers could also be overcome—capital, technology, scale, suppliers, and infrastructure—the automakers would be in a position to grow.

The resolution of the relationship between the automakers and the government proved to be the catalyst. In June 1950, the Korean War broke out, changing first SCAP's appreciation of the Japanese automakers and then the appreciation of the Japanese government. In 1950 and 1951, the United States military purchased almost 12,000 trucks from Toyota, Nissan, and Isuzu as part of the war effort, expenditures totaling ¥9.8 billion. As a result of the purchases, Toyota's net income more than tripled.

Even more important in the eyes of the Japanese government, the military purchases catapulted Toyota and Nissan into first and second place in dollar earnings. Overnight, the auto industry had become the nation's leading source of foreign exchange, the lifeblood of the Japanese economy. Foreign exchange—"real" American dollars—meant that there was a currency on hand with international value, unlike the postwar Japanese yen, currency that could be used to purchase all of the raw materials needed by the resource-poor Japanese economy. For that reason, exports were critical, and suddenly the auto industry produced the country's highest-value export commodity.

On the strength of the industry's performance, in 1952 MITI finally carried its case within the councils of government: the auto industry was recognized as a national strategic industry. The period of benign neglect was over.

The year before, in anticipation of the strategic designation, MITI had surveyed the automakers to find out what the companies thought their own needs were. In response, the automakers had identified a public policy agenda for government assistance they said they needed: ¥300 million and one year to be able to mass-produce small cars; capital support from the Japan Development Bank; help from the government in importing technology, production equipment, and auto parts; a tax structure favoring small cars over large ones and Japanese-produced cars over imports; and government measures to prevent the resale of the used foreign cars that were taking up the domestic market.[28]

In 1952, with the auto industry officially designated a strategic industry, MITI began to promote its auto policy. MITI's first measure was designed to help the automakers modernize and upgrade their production facilities. The Law of Promotion for Rationalization of Enterprises gave automakers and other strategic industries an accelerated rate of depreciation—a 43 percent write-off in the first year. The reaction of the automakers to the government incentive was instantaneous: in 1952 auto industry modernization investments doubled over 1951; in 1953 investments were two-and-one-half times the level of 1952.

MITI's second measures were designed both to protect the Japanese industry from overaggressive foreign investment and to attract badly needed foreign technology. To accomplish these objectives MITI first announced its Basic Policy regarding Technical Contracts, strengthening government control of such contracts on the grounds of deteriorating foreign reserves. Then in its Guidelines regarding Foreign Technology and Assembly Contracts for Passenger Car Production, MITI spelled out the conditions under which Japanese automakers could gain access to foreign technology. Specifically, MITI ruled out both foreign investment in the auto sales sector and the simple assembly of knock-down kits sent into Japan by foreign automakers. Foreign investment in production facilities or technology contracts would be approved only if they were deemed by the government to be supportive of the development of the Japanese auto industry.

Following this policy announcement MITI granted approval to four automakers seeking five-to-seven-year technical tie-ups with foreign producers: Nissan tied up with Austin, Isuzu with Rootes Motors, Hino with Renault, and Shin-Mitsubishi with Willys-Overland. In each case, the contracts stipulated that the Japanese producers would develop the capability to produce the joint vehicle independently by the end of the agreement. Two companies, Fuji and Nichiei, applied for foreign linkups and were turned down by MITI; as a result they were driven from the auto industry.

Finally, in 1953, MITI announced one more auto policy of this embryonic period of the new government-management relationship, and management's response helped define the realistic limits of the relationship. The Plan for the Rationalization of the Auto Industry was a bold, sweeping plan for strong government direction of the fledgling industry. Its announced purposes were to consolidate the industry and thereby lower prices, improve quality, and strengthen the automakers' international competitiveness.

To accomplish these purposes, MITI laid out a comprehensive set of proposals—in effect, an offer to the automakers with both vinegar and honey. Government responsibility for the auto industry would be centralized in one production administration. The industry would voluntarily form a cartel—or, if they were unwilling, the government would form it for them. Those companies left out of the cartel would be compensated; those companies included would be supervised by the government. To achieve higher quality and lower costs, all materials and parts would be standardized and all orders for materials and parts would have to go through the cartel. MITI also proposed to undertake research and development through an institute and to support market demand growth through a centralized auto finance bank that would promote auto sales.

The automakers flatly rejected the proposal, sending MITI the clear message that the companies did not consider themselves subservient to the government. It was an important message, for it contributed to defining the terms and conditions of the management-government relationship—just as the stress of the strikes had helped to define the limits of the labor-management relationship.

With the failure of MITI's rationalization plan, it was clear that the two sides needed each other. The government was prepared to invest in the automakers and even assume responsibility for their competitive performance—too much responsibility in the eyes of management. Management was prepared to acknowledge a legitimate national interest in the economic performance of the companies and was even prepared to accept a government auto policy that structured choices for them to make and cushioned the risks of failure. But outright government control of the entrepreneurial companies was out of the question. The relationship would work on the basis of quid pro quos:

in exchange for incentives, protection, or other public policy posi-tions that would help them grow and prosper, the automakers would recognize the legitimacy of the government's hand in the auto com-petition. But the system worked best when the government consulted the automakers to determine their needs and preferences and then, operating from the companies' agenda, constructed a menu of oppor-tunities and incentives from which the companies could choose as they wanted.

The resolution of the terms of the relationship between govern-ment and the auto industry not only created the basis for an ongoing exchange between the two parties over the long run. Over the short run, it also provided the means for the companies to overcome the remaining barriers to entry. MITI's tax and technology policies went a long way toward answering the companies' needs in those areas. Issues of market demand and production scale would be met as MITI clamped down on foreign imports, responding to the 1951 survey. And in the next phase of development, as the enterprise system began to develop, the automakers could look forward to critical government assistance in building up the infrastructure and supplier network needed for a competitive auto industry.

THE SYSTEM TAKES ROOT, 1953–1973

In the two decades after the Nissan strike in 1953 the Japanese enterprise system focused its collective energies on two goals: growth and exports. To achieve those goals meant first reinforcing the devel-oping relationships among management, labor, and government through quid pro quos and linking institutions, and, second, gearing up the production system to allow the industry to reach sufficient scale to become a low-cost, high-quality producer.

The trade-offs within the system, though never explicitly identi-fied, took concrete form during this period; looking back, it is clear what each of the three sides stood to gain by its contribution to the auto industry's growth.

For the workers in the companies and their company union, the system promised to deliver constantly rising real income and sub-stantial benefits; job security; power sharing and consultation on the job; social status in the community as an employee of a national strategic industry; and though labor-management cooperation was continually stressed, the right to protest or raise issues within the consultative system.

For the government, the growth of the auto industry represented a vehicle for the realization of national goals: employment for the work force; a positive balance of trade; a rising standard of living; and an engine for national economic development that could bring along a wide range of other industries.

Finally, management of the companies, upon whose success the realization of the other promises would depend, collected on all of the trade-offs of labor and government: a cooperative work force, with no strikes, no absenteeism, no grievances; production flexibility and the capacity to introduce new technology with the full support of the work force; and the conditions required for high productivity and high quality. They were also able to call on the government for low-cost capital; a guaranteed domestic market and demand-side economic measures to help stimulate growth; and the development of a high-quality supply industry to contribute to the automakers' competitiveness.

As the auto industry geared up for growth, then, the Japanese enterprise system proved a source of tremendous competitive advantage. And the system itself continued to adapt. Bilateral mechanisms and linkups gradually evolved that would improve and increase the flow of information among management, labor, and government, control and resolve disputes efficiently, and highlight the shared fortunes of all sides.

For example, the nature of the labor-management relationship led to a complex reward system that directly contributed to the feeling that the fates of the two sides were linked. For workers at the larger automakers, this reward system came to include permanent employment, seniority-based wages, twice-a-year bonuses based on the company's performance, and an elaborate array of company-provided benefits, such as subsidized housing and health care and, eventually, athletic facilities and food cooperatives. This system was not a culturally determined throwback to the days before World War II or a preplanned set of policies. Rather, the specific elements of the economic bargain between labor and management gradually emerged through lengthy negotiations in response to particular needs on both sides. And, importantly, they emerged with both sides mindful of the larger quid pro quos to which they were mutually committed.

Thus, seniority-based wages tended to reinforce the loyalty of workers who stayed with the company. Twice-a-year bonuses stimulated the workers, reminding them that their economic well-being was linked with that of the company; at the same time, it represented a convenient system of forced savings. And the commitment of permanent employment and the off-the-job benefits represented a binding relationship for both workers and management, expressing an economic and psychological tie.

In addition to the reward system, in the early 1950s labor and management worked out an extensive joint consultative system that promoted communication and problem solving up and down the two organizations. Management-labor committees formed at every level, from the shop floor to the board room, aligning the two institutions in separate but parallel hierarchies.[29] Consultations covered virtually every aspect of the company: the company's current status, investments, plant location and relocation, technology, personnel administration, working conditions, and even social concerns.[30] Although the same topics would be discussed at every level of the twin hierarchies, the specifics under consideration would reflect the capacity of the people at that level to do something about the problem. For example, in personnel administration, top union and management officials might meet to discuss overall future labor needs of the company and approaches to meet those needs; middle union and management staff would discuss current companywide personnel practices; plant-level union and management representatives would discuss the specific performance of the factory; and work-station workers and supervisors would discuss the particular needs of the people at that station.

In the evolution of this joint consultation system, there were four important developments. First, the distinction between management prerogatives and negotiable issues became blurred. The consultation system both reflected and reinforced the larger concept that the long-term interests of labor and management would converge. In the short term, the consultation system represented a sharing of power and responsibility between labor and management, with both sides responsible for running the company.

Second, the consultation system stressed information sharing at all levels. The underlying assumption was, not that secrets could not be kept, but that secrets were antithetical to the company's health: they would undermine the trust necessary for labor-management cooperation. Moreover, information sharing was essential if workers and managers were to make sound decisions for which they could be held responsible—and not only at the top. One Toyota official says, "The most important thing is to have a channel at the midlevel between midlevel managers and midlevel union officials. This is the most important channel because these are the people who most frequently have to make the operating decisions and have to implement the operating decisions."[31]

Third, the system worked as an efficient mechanism for the resolution of disputes. Problems and disagreements could surface, and be discussed and resolved at the lowest appropriate level and with the least delay. Consequently, even though the problems that would occur were the same as those in any enterprise system, in Japan they were contained and controlled in a structured fashion.

Finally, the joint consultation system represented a clear and distinct channel, separate from collective bargaining. Indeed, the existence of the two different channels served to underline the two different elements in the overall labor-management relationship. The consultation system was to promote cooperative problem solving to help the company prosper and grow. Collective bargaining was to divide the fruits of that growth. One was to help bake the pie; the other, to cut it up.

A parallel system of information sharing and joint problem solving also developed between management and government over this twenty-year period. Channeled largely through MITI's structure of consultative committees, the system provided for a continuous flow of general information between the individual automakers and MITI officials on both a formal and informal basis. According to one company official, "The informal committees are more important than the formal committees. Generally speaking, the committee members will be hard on the issues but not hard with each other."[32]

MITI bureaucrats also used the consultative committees to test and refine the proposals that became the government's auto policy over this period. The proposals did not always find favor with the automakers; indeed, during the 1950s and 1960s the relationship between the government and the automakers was frequently stormy as MITI sought both to nurture and, on occasion, to direct the independent-minded companies. But the consultative committees had the important benefit of controlling the disagreements, in part by preparing both sides in advance and in private for what would later take place in public.

These trade-offs, linkups, and mechanisms were important to the building of the Japanese enterprise system in three ways. First, they embodied the larger national effort to find a way to construct a postwar, economically competitive Japan through the creation of a Japanese system. In a very real way, the work of all elements in the country was a painful trial-and-error process seeking a set of economic and political relationships capable of producing competitiveness and sustained growth. The process was neither simple nor fast. The people who were involved from each side borrowed freely from other countries. They adapted their own practices of the past and the practices of others. Some conventional wisdom they took more seriously and religiously than did its sources: the concept of Toyota City is borrowed from Henry Ford's totally integrated River Rouge production facility completed in the 1920s; within the halls of Toyota's sales operation Alfred Sloan's *My Years with General Motors* is regarded as the last word on auto marketing.

But just as often, they turned conventional wisdom on its head. The notions of an involved, committed, and multiskilled work force and of a negotiated strategy with government defy the laws of Frederick Winslow Taylor and Adam Smith. The result was a unique amalgam—Japan's late entry into the competing national enterprise systems. Indeed, the real competitive advantage provided Japan by its loss of World War II was not the opportunity to rebuild the country's physical infrastructure with modern plant and equipment. Rather, it was the chance to rebuild the country's enterprise system, learning from the mistakes and best practices of other competitor nations around the world.

Second, the evolution of the system over this period resulted in mechanisms and practices that were internally consistent. Although not by design, in application the process allowed for experimentation by management, labor, and government within the framework of the larger understanding spawned in the early 1950s. Experiments that worked were kept, broadened, and expanded. Experiments that failed were rejected. The result was an internally consistent and self-reinforcing set of relationships between management, labor, and government and a dynamic process of testing and adapting to keep the relationships flexible.

Third, the internal dynamic of the system provided a sturdy institutional skeleton that could support the policy of rapid growth that was the major goal of the industry during this period. The relationships were not the substance; they were, however, the process that enabled the substantive policies to develop and be implemented. They provided the channels of communication, the forums for nego-

tiation within which the policies could be shaped. And they provided
the basis for trust and understanding that permitted the policies to
be implemented. Finally, they reflected the thrust of the policies—
that global competitiveness and growth were in the best interests of
all.

Beginning in 1954, the year before the Liberal Democratic Party
started its three decades of uninterrupted dominance of the Japanese
government, the automakers and government focused on a two-part
agenda for the industry's future: steps for growth and preparation
for globalization. In 1954, Japanese car production stood at nearly
14,500; total auto registrations were 138,500. In comparison, in the
United States in that year production and registrations reached
5,507,417 and 5,535,464, respectively. Clearly, if they wished to compete, the Japanese would have to grow, and they therefore developed a strategy of protectionism, concentration of the suppliers, and
public-private investment.

The first concern, one that had surfaced in MITI's 1951 survey of
the automakers, was the need for a supportive trade policy. Specifically, the Japanese market continued to be picked to pieces by
American used cars and European imports. Moreover, nothing constructive had been done to prepare for Japanese auto exports—the
ultimate aim of the competitive strategy. In 1954, the government
went to work on both sides of the trade policy agenda.

In a series of moves, the government sought systematically to
exclude foreign-made cars from the Japanese market. MITI began by
implementing a stringent "buy Japan" program covering all minis-
tries in the federal government as well as local authorities. New
regulations cracked down on the resale of American-made cars by
American armed forces. At the same time, MITI slashed the amount
of foreign exchange that was available for European auto imports,
cutting it from $13.7 million in 1953 to $0.9 million in 1955. These
measures had a dramatic effect in closing off the Japanese market: by
1957, the import of foreign parts and knock-down kits had ended; by
1958, all passenger car assembly in Japan was using only Japanese-
made parts. Even more dramatic was the effect the measures had in
preserving the Japanese market for Japanese producers. In 1954,
when Japanese automakers produced 14,500 cars, imports amounted
to 80 percent of domestic production. In 1960, with domestic production at more than 165,000 cars, imports were a paltry 2.1 percent.

By 1971, with domestic production at more than 3.7 million units, imports represented only 0.5 percent. Growth in the domestic market belonged to the domestic automakers.

At the same time, the government and the auto industry began to think about exports in a preliminary fashion. In 1954, the government institutionalized its support for exports through the establishment of the Supreme Export Council and the Industrial Export Council. A series of other measures strengthened the private sector trading companies, simplified export insurance, set up quality inspectors, and offered companies an 80 percent tax deduction of net export earnings as an incentive to export. The Japanese automakers responded, perhaps before they were really ready. In 1957, both Toyota and Nissan opened offices in Thailand; Nissan signed a licensing agreement with a Taiwanese company. In 1958, the same year that the government created the Japanese External Trade Organization to scan the foreign environment, Toyota opened a Brazilian auto plant and attempted to penetrate the U.S. market for the first time with the odd-looking Crown model, a car totally ill suited to the demands of the American motorists and the American highways. Although the exporting effort proved a dismal commercial failure, it was a successful experiment, providing important information and worthwhile lessons for the next attempt.

The second major element in the growth strategy was the government-led effort to integrate the parts suppliers into the network of competitive relationships. According to one Japanese auto expert, in the mid-1950s the government decided that "a strong parts industry was necessary to build a strong auto industry; that parts were the real basis for the auto industry."[33] As a consequence, the government launched a series of initiatives designed both to upgrade the suppliers and to replicate the labor-management relationship in the supplier-management relationship—a mutually dependent, mutually advantageous economic deal, a sum-sum game.

The effort began in 1956 with MITI's formation of an ad hoc Auto Parts Committee to study the situation and design and implement a plan. Typically, the committee was drawn from the interested parties, including MITI officials from the Heavy Industry Bureau, the presidents of auto parts companies, and officials of the auto industry association representing the major automakers. The committee's report indicated that there were too many financially weak companies in the supplier sector operating on too small a scale. The results were predictable: inadequate capital prevented the introduction of modern production techniques and inadequate economies of scale drove costs too high. The suppliers were locked into a self-defeating cycle, with severe problems that only reinforced each other. More-over, the high cost and questionable quality of parts were being passed on to the automakers, undermining their drive for competi-tiveness. To break this cycle, the committee proposed a series of five-year plans, focusing first on the smaller suppliers, then on the primary ones.

MITI's initial tool was inexpensive capital. Using the Japan Devel-opment Bank and Small Business Finance Corporation, MITI chan-neled $50 million in low-interest loans to selected suppliers. The amount of the loans was not so substantial as to accomplish the modernization of the part manufacturers' facilities: Over the first ten years of the effort, the $50 million represented slightly more than 13 percent of the total capital investment in the supplier sector. In fact, the real power of the money came from its relative scarcity. Only a small number of the suppliers got any MITI money at all. Those that did could go to their banks and leverage the government loan into a substantial private loan—using as security the recognition that they were among MITI's chosen few. Those who did not get MITI loans could either try to survive on their own or choose the wiser course and merge with one of the bankable suppliers. To add to the incen-tives, in 1956 MITI extended favorable tax treatment to the auto parts suppliers, permitting 43.5 percent depreciation of new capital invest-ments in the first year. The message was clear: Those suppliers with access to capital would be the ones making new investments, getting the tax deduction, becoming more competitive, gaining new markets. The rest would not survive.

The result was the first wave of consolidations and mergers among the suppliers, concentrating production among fewer producers in forty-five categories of parts, and the first round of modernization in the suppliers' plant and equipment. The second round began in 1961; MITI amended the Law concerning Provisional Measures for Devel-opment of the Machine Industry, originally enacted in 1956, so that it would include auto parts, machine tools for auto production, engines, and vehicles for industrial use. As had been the case in 1956, MITI was seeking further concentration among the suppliers, better coor-dination of research and development, and lower prices through simplified design and production. The 1961 plan for the suppliers identified as its goal a 25 percent cost reduction in parts for small and medium-sized cars by 1963. In fact, between 1960 and 1965, costs of parts declined by 30 percent per year.

The third and final effort by MITI came in 1966 when the government sought to consolidate more than seven thousand supplier companies in the areas of lighting parts, brakes, electrical parts, oil seals, and wheels. By this time, however, MITI's previous phases had resulted in the merger of most of the small and medium-sized companies. Those left at this point were large and strong enough to resist MITI's program and the supplier plan diminished. But it had accomplished its goal of upgrading the cost and quality position of the suppliers. Even more important, in the process MITI's efforts had succeeded in promoting a working compact between each of the major automakers and a family of its suppliers.

The relationship between the suppliers and automakers followed the pattern of the labor-management relationship. For each of the major automakers, a group of suppliers became an attached "family," dedicating all or nearly all of its production to the auto company. The quid pro quos gave both sides an economic benefit. For the suppliers there was a guaranteed customer, protection from the ups and downs of the business cycle, a source of capital and able workers, and, for as long as the auto company grew and prospered, the promise of rising profits. For the companies there was the guarantee of high-quality parts, delivered on time and at a price established by the automaker rather than negotiated in the open market.

In the case of both Nissan and Toyota, the system delivered associations of suppliers, tied so closely to the automakers as to constitute a virtual subsidiary. Nissan's suppliers, for example, were divided into the Takawakai, roughly 110 small and medium-sized companies that relied heavily on sales to Nissan, and the Shohakai, 50 of Japan's largest parts companies that sold to all automakers. Almost 40 percent of all Nissan's parts were purchased from the heavily dependent Takawakai, 30 percent were produced within Nissan, 20 percent came from the more independent Shohakai, and the rest came from unassociated parts companies.

In the case of Toyota, the relationships between the automaker and its suppliers grew even closer. Toyota's suppliers came to be grouped into three associations: the Kyohokai, the Association of Toyota Parts Makers, consisting of 226 companies; the Seihokai, the Association of Toyota Mold Gage and Jig Makers, consisting of 21 companies; and the Eihokei, the Association of Toyota Construction and Equipment Manufacturers, consisting of 37 companies. Each association was tied to the Toyota "family"; each participated in familywide studies of ways to improve quality, reduce cost, and advance innovation. These close and strong relationships allowed Toyota to implement the just-in-time production system, which depended on zero defects from the suppliers. In 1962, Toyota applied the just-in-time system in all of its plants; in 1970, 60 percent of the suppliers were operating on the just-in-time system in their plants as well. The overall result of the supplier-automaker relationship was another strong link in the emerging Japanese enterprise system. Because of the government's intervention, the automakers could begin to depend on domestic production of low-cost, high-quality dependable parts. The suppliers could count on expanding economic prospects. And Japan could expect to capture more of the value-added chain as its auto industry grew toward global competitiveness.

The third element of the growth strategy was a double-barreled investment program: by the automakers to boost supply and by the government to stimulate demand. Supported by MITI's commitment that the auto industry had national strategic importance, in the mid-1950s the companies went on an industrywide investment binge. By 1960, Nissan, Toyota, Hino, Prince, and Isuzu had all made major financial commitments to expand and upgrade their production facilities. Across the industry, capital investment took off on an exponential growth curve: in 1951, investment came to ¥1 billion; in 1957, ¥14.8 billion; in 1961, ¥70 billion; and in 1965, ¥112.8 billion.

At the same time that investment was pouring into new capital equipment, substantial amounts of money were diverted toward research and development, so that by 1960 the auto industry ranked second in R&D spending, trailing only the chemical industry. Significantly, the burden of the investment was shared by the companies and the government, with a substantial portion of the money coming from MITI through the Motor Vehicle Technology Institute and from the Ministry of Transport through the Technical Research Laboratory. Other sources of funding for research and development were the Small Motor Vehicle Industry Association, the Motor Vehicle Parts Association, the Body Industry Association, and the Production Technology Center. The funds were applied to a variety of issues as far ranging as the sources: parts standardization, performance studies for export cars, safety issues, engine size reduction, and manufacturing simplification.

The companies' investments had three results over the twenty-year period. First, production capacity grew along a strong and steady course. In 1953, the Japanese automakers turned out fewer than 9,000 cars. Two years later, they produced more than 20,000 cars. In 1960, production went over the 165,000 mark and in 1965 it topped 696,000 units. By 1970, the Japanese industry was producing more than 3,178,000 cars and in 1972 Japanese automakers produced more than 4,000,000 cars.

Second, the expanding investment and growing production allowed the Japanese automakers to develop into full-line producers in a gradual evolution. Toyota, for example, deliberately patterned itself after General Motors, opening a series of five distribution channels to handle five different car lines. Similarly, Nissan began to experiment with different car lines and to market its products to a more discriminating and sophisticated consumer.

Finally, the industry's investments paid off in steady and impressive productivity gains. Between 1960 and 1970, productivity improved by 11 to 14 percent per year across the industry. Just as the government had contributed to the industry's success, so did the industry share its success with the workers: wage gains over the period were roughly 11 to 12 percent per year, slightly lower than the rate of productivity improvement. In effect, the enterprise system was working as it was supposed to, in support of the production system.

While the automakers were working to increase and improve the supply of Japanese-made cars, the government was using its policies and programs to stimulate demand. In 1954, for example, the government lowered the commodity tax on small cars by 5 percent, a signal to both consumers and producers. Beginning in the mid-1950s, to support increased auto usage the Japanese government embarked on an infrastructure investment program that kept pace with the industry's own investments. Between 1955 and 1960, the Japanese nearly doubled the kilometers of paved national roads; between 1960 and 1965, paved municipal roads tripled, prefectural roads doubled, national roads doubled. In 1960 Japan had no superhighways. Five years later, the government had constructed 181 kilometers of superhighways and five years after that the figure had reached 649 kilometers.

The combination of supply-side investments by business and

demand-side investments by government produced the desired results. Between 1958 and 1963, auto registration in Japan grew by 475 percent. In the decade of the 1960s, moreover, the sales of the Japanese automakers increased at an incredible pace: from about 410,000 in 1960 to a staggering 4,100,000 in 1970. The first goal of the system, growth, had been achieved.

In fact, it had almost been achieved too well. With protection from foreign competition and demand-side stimulation provided by government, cooperation and productivity by labor, high-quality and low-cost components by suppliers, and booming demand in a high-growth economy by consumers, the 1950s and 1960s seemed the time to be in the auto industry in Japan. And so more and more companies entered the business. Between 1958 and 1963, when Honda became the last entrant with a 600 cc sports car, the number of car companies in Japan grew from five to eleven.

These new entrants challenged the market share domination that had effectively been established by Toyota and Nissan. In the short two-year span between 1960 and 1962, the two companies' combined market share dropped from 75 percent to less than 50 percent. In 1961 alone, Toyota and Nissan lost 11 percent of their market share—and still saw sales revenues grow by 38 percent in the booming market. By the mid-1960s, the domestic market was a fiercely competitive hodgepodge of scrappy companies fighting for a niche in the growing market: eight firms had at least 5 percent of total production.

But the automakers' surging growth presented the government with a new problem. By the early 1960s, MITI had already turned to the second element of the growth strategy, the drive to export. MITI's concern was that the auto industry's global competitiveness would be retarded by excessive fragmentation and excessive competition in the domestic market.

In 1960 such a concern may have seemed premature. The U.S. market, a major target for Japanese exports, had laughingly rejected Toyota's 1958 offering; Japanese exports to the United States in 1960 amounted to a hundredth of a percent of American car sales from the Big Three. Worldwide auto exports accounted for only 4.2 percent of the Japanese automakers' total production.

But MITI's concerns lay not only with the capabilities of the Japanese automakers but also with the changing global environment in which those automakers had to compete. Its interests and responsibilities required it to scan the external environment for important changes and then to bridge the distance between the outside world and the Japanese industry with policies that would anticipate change.

Around the world the booming Japanese economy had been noticed. Between 1955 and 1960, the Japanese gross national product had nearly doubled; other countries had been deeply affected by the "Japanese economic miracle" and its first wave of exports. Pressure was beginning to build for Japan to renounce its special status as an economic orphan and rejoin the rest of the world—and in particular to remove the protectionist tarriffs and trade barriers that had gone up in the aftermath of World War II. Other countries, including the United States, were beginning to press for the chance to sell products to the Japanese, as well as buy from them. These demands raised two concerns for the future of the Japanese auto industry: first, that opening the Japanese market would permit foreign companies to enter and not only sell cars but, far more threatening, buy Japanese automakers; and second, that the opening of the market and the globalization of the industry would take place before the fragmented and underscaled Japanese automakers could be made ready to compete.

MITI's general concerns were given a definite time line when, in June 1960, the Japanese government announced that it would remove exchange restrictions on commodity imports to accept article 7 status in the International Monetary Fund and that it would join the Organization for Economic Cooperation and Development in 1964. MITI responded in 1961 by setting up two groups to devise recommendations for the auto industry: a Passenger Car Subcommittee within the Heavy Industry Section of the Industrial Structure Council and a Special Subcommittee on Passenger Car Policy, composed of bankers, auto executives, and academics.

The plans recommended by the two groups called for the rationalization of the automakers, the prevention of any new entrants, the reduction of the number of models, and the consolidation of the sales system. Although no agreement was reached on which firms should exit, the goal of the plan was the establishment of a Japanese "Big Three," divided along product lines with a single dominant company in passenger cars, minicars, and specialty cars.

This plan would have benefited Toyota and Nissan, but the small and medium-sized automakers—Toyo Kogyo, Mitsubishi, Fuji, and Daihatsu, which together held about 30 percent of the market—protested MITI's proposal loudly and effectively. Both the 1961 plan and a 1963 Measure for the Promotion of Specific Industries, which would have given MITI the power to direct the structure, product lines, and investments of the industry, were thwarted by the companies' opposition.

In spite of the automakers' resistance, international politics continued to force the issue. In 1965, MITI was pushed to eliminate the formal quantitative restrictions on auto imports, a further indication that the government safety net was beginning to fray. Unable to force a consolidation of the industry by law, MITI turned to incentives: the Japan Development Bank made capital available to help consummate mergers and MITI formulated a special tax deduction to reduce automakers' liability after a merger. The carrot—and the growing financial stake required to stay in the globalizing competition—worked where the stick had previously failed. Toyota negotiated linkups with Hino and Daihatsu in 1966 and 1967; Mitsubishi joined forces with Subaru and Isuzu in 1967; and Prince was totally absorbed by Nissan in 1967.

In 1967, as well, the end of the Kennedy round of international trade negotiations brought renewed calls for the dropping of trade barriers around the world. MITI's response was to play a double game. To the outside world, the Japanese government continued to plead for prolonged protection on behalf of the automakers, insisting that high tariffs, high commodity taxes, and a semiannual auto tax levied by the prefectures should not be dismantled. MITI even went so far as to preserve a secret quota on the import of auto engines for use by the Japanese companies.[34]

To the inside world of the Japanese auto industry, MITI continued to press for consolidation and rationalization, strengthening the industry against the inevitable day when the demands of the foreigners for access could no longer be denied. In 1967, MITI advanced another plan for grouping the automakers under three leading companies—Toyota, Mitsubishi, and Nissan—and when that failed, in 1968 tried yet another proposal with just two groups headed by Nissan and Toyota.

By this time the pressures on the auto industry were becoming too numerous and too powerful; to advance, the system needed some kind of resolution. From the United States were coming threats of reprisals against Japanese protectionism: an import surcharge or quotas on industrial commodities. Among the automakers there was no consensus on how to respond. Nissan counseled compromise.

Toyota remained adamant in its opposition to giving in to foreign pressure. To make sure the company's position was not lost on MITI, Toyota amended its articles of incorporation to prevent foreigners from sitting on its board of directors. Said board chairman Ishida, "The defense of our own castle is the first prerequisite for service to the state."[35] MITI seemed locked into a solution that required some of the independent-minded companies to sacrifice themselves for the good of the industry and the country. At the same time, American companies were discreetly holding out the offer of capital assistance to Japanese automakers through international tie-ups.

This last prospect was MITI's worst fear: that the rich and powerful American automakers would use their financial resources to pluck the Japanese companies that MITI had so carefully sought to nurture. To guard against this outcome, in 1968 MITI and the automakers negotiated an agreement that the industry should develop as a "national industry," that is, without foreign capital tie-ups. At the same time, MITI announced to the United States that 1972 would mark the beginning of meaningful auto trade liberalization and pushed once more for the industry to coalesce behind its two leaders.

The pressure proved to be too much; the automakers finally heeded their own self-interest. Without prior consultation with MITI, Mitsubishi announced that Chrysler would purchase a 35 percent share of the company, Mitsubishi would send its Colt model to the United States, and Chrysler would send knock-down kits to Japan. To MITI the announcement of the deal came as "cold water in the ear while sleeping."[36] It protested that the industry was still not prepared for global competition, arguing that "the actual situation of our country's automobile industry is weak when compared with the mammoth enterprises of the U.S. and Europe."[37]

But most important, the deadlock had been broken. The Chrysler-Mitsubishi link was approved to begin in 1971; Ford followed with an agreement with Toyo Kogyo, and General Motors with Isuzu. In fact, the outcome finally served the overall interests of the Japanese enterprise system. The automakers demonstrated their operational independence from the government and once again illustrated their notion of a proper working relationship: government incentives but not government control. The companies also succeeded in finding a new source of capital for their continued expansion in the face of coming globalization. Moreover, because of the participation of MITI in the process, the companies not only had time to prepare for the new competitive environment but also were able to obtain capital from the Big Three on terms dictated by Japan. Both the level and pace of foreign participation were controlled by MITI, limiting the potency of the U.S. companies in the Japanese market and their hold on the Japanese companies.

Finally, by the end of the period, both goals had been achieved; there was growth and exports. Production had gone from roughly 20,000 autos in 1955 with two passenger-car exports to over 4.0 million cars in 1972 and more than 1.4 million exports. The Japanese auto industry had achieved competitiveness; it was ready to challenge for dominance.

THE SYSTEM ADAPTS

In the 1970s, the Japanese auto industry shifted into overdrive. In 1973, Japanese automakers enjoyed record high domestic sales of 3.05 million units. Over the entire decade both production and exports soared. Between 1970 and 1980, production doubled to more than 11 million units; exports increased by more than five times to 6 million units. Moreover, the ratio of exports to production demonstrated that both goals of growth and exports were being met. In 1970, exports were 20 percent of production; in 1973, 29 percent; in 1980, 54 percent.

A major factor in this explosive growth was the industry's continuing high rate of productivity, made possible by the close relationship between management and workers. In 1979, for example, Toyota had only thirty more workers than the year before, but production increased by 140,000 vehicles; overall output per worker had gone from 49 cars per worker ten years earlier to 66 cars per worker in 1979.[38] In the early 1970s, an article in the Toyota company publication outlined the task before management and workers: "In order to shake off the desperate pursuit of other auto companies and catch up with the two biggest companies in the world, each one of us must always try to surpass the others in every single section of the company. Toyota demands that every worker constantly offer all his abilities and exert himself to promote productivity. We must always try to improve ourselves so we can contribute more and function better."[39]

The industry took on a frenzied pace of overtime production. Workers put in eleven-hour days, for example, working from 5:00 A.M. to 4:00 P.M. with 45 minutes rest. On the transmission assembly line, one transmission would arrive every 80 seconds spaced at five-foot intervals. Eight workers would produce one finished transmission every 80 seconds, or 46 finished transmissions each hour. The daily quota for the two shifts amounted to 715 transmissions. One Toyota employee wrote of this work experience, "Toyota has designed this job so that a worker can only keep up with the line by always exerting the utmost effort at top speed."[40]

By the end of the decade, the effort had paid off. In 1980, for the first time, the combined output of the Japanese automakers surpassed that of the American automakers. At the same time that the Japanese automakers first overtook the Americans in volume, research indicated that they had also succeeded in establishing new yardsticks for cost and quality in the automotive competition. The concept that the Japanese auto companies had created a "landed cost advantage"—could build a small car in Japan and ship it to the United States for less than it cost to build the same car in America—was also identified and was used to describe a simple fact: Over the decade of the 1970s, the Japanese had moved from merely competing in the world auto industry to dominating it. The American automakers—and the automakers in the rest of the world—were in a catch-up position. And the tight integration of the Japanese enterprise system, the massive production base that it had created, and the vast financial resources it had produced all made the future competition, not a game for competitive parity, but a game for competitive survival.

What is most significant about the rise to dominance of the Japanese automakers is that it took more than just "business as usual" for them to accomplish it. The twenty-year span from 1953 to 1973 was, largely, a period of economic and political stability, a period during which the automakers, the workers, and the government could concentrate on solidifying their relationships and promoting the industry's growth. But the 1970s were years of crisis in the auto industry not only in Japan but around the world, bringing new environmental regulation, the energy shock, and changes in trade policy.

The key to the Japanese industry's emergence as world leader was the way in which the Japanese enterprise system responded to each of these tests; where other nations—notably, the United States—tripped over tangled lines of communication and policy between management, labor, and government, the Japanese system responded with adaptability, flexibility, and purposefulness, not only passing the three tests but, in the process, surpassing the competition.

Auto Emissions

By the end of the 1960s, it was becoming clear to the Japanese that increasingly high social and environmental costs were the price of rapid economic growth. In 1971, to coordinate a response to the problem, the Japanese government created the Environmental Agency; stimulated by dramatic episodes of air pollution in Tokyo in 1970 and 1971 and by the adoption in the United States of the Clean Air Act, the agency moved quickly to examine the issue of automobile emissions. As a logical starting point, the agency considered simply adopting the U.S. legislation—the Muskie Act—as its own, including the stringent standards for carbon monoxide, hydrocarbons, and nitrous oxides, as well as the 1975 and 1976 timetable for compliance.

From the point of view of the automakers, the new governmental intrusion into the industry was unwarranted, unwelcome, and uncompetitive. Says one Toyota spokesman, "Toyota expressed its belief that it wasn't possible to meet the standards recommended by the Environmental Agency in the time permitted. We expressed our belief that, with so many models, it would be very difficult to make all of the necessary adjustments in time. Our greatest concern was that such adjustments would upset the mass production philosophy. We just didn't know whether we would be able to mass-produce the technology involved."[41]

At the same time, the automakers felt that the government was not approaching the issue with the proper economic perspective. "The way the initial government intervention in this area occurred was not well structured and contributed to the controversy," says one industry executive. "The original committee on emissions had as its mandate the determination of the quality of life in Japan with respect to pollution. It did not examine in any way the questions of whether or not the auto industry could absorb the costs of achieving cleaner air. The mandate thus hurt the government's ability to judge issues like cost and resulted in a one-sided approach to the issue."[42]

Moreover, the automakers felt themselves caught in a national political drama in which they were cast as the villains. In 1969, Japan experienced its version of the student rebellion that was sweeping the world; environmentalism was a centerpiece of the students' politics. Interestingly, the Japanese companies felt that their Ameri-

can competition would gain the advantage by these political developments. As one executive puts it, "In the United States, the government
was interested in issues like cost-benefit analyses, technological feasibility, and necessity. But in Japan, at that time, enterprises were
regarded as being evil and people didn't trust them. People believed
that we always lied and so even our technological feasibility studies
were ignored."[43]

Finally, in 1973, in spite of the united opposition of the automakers
and their industry association, the agency adopted the standards and
timetable of the Muskie Act—known as Japan's Little Muskie Act. The
response of the automakers was to launch another attack, focusing
on the 1976 nitrous oxide emission standards in particular, an attack
bolstered by the 1973 energy shock and its powerful negative effect
on the entire Japanese economy. A new government review of the
standards conducted by a committee of experts concluded in 1975
that although the industry did, in fact, have the technology needed
to meet the 1976 standards, the 1976 nitrous oxides requirement
should be relaxed both because the industry had been given inadequate lead time and because the cleaner cars were significantly less
fuel efficient, an overriding consideration in light of the energy
crisis.[44]

At the same time that the government responded to the industry's
concerns by relaxing the 1976 standard, it took two other significant
steps. First, it formed a Study Group on Nitrous Oxides Emissions
Control to begin work on the 1978 standard, creating a carefully
designed forum where the debate could be managed well in advance
of the deadline. Second, it implemented a demand-side tax policy,
designed to use market incentives to encourage the automakers to
hasten their compliance with the government's standards. Specifically, the government reduced commodity and motor vehicle acquisition taxes for cars meeting the 1975, 1976, and 1978 emission
standards and it reduced the auto ownership taxes between 1976 and
1977 to encourage consumers to switch to cleaner cars.

The combination of the government's three steps produced a major
change in the debate over emissions. By reducing the 1976 standard,
the government had demonstrated its willingness to bargain with the
industry on the issue; the recognition of the change in the competitive environment caused by the 1973 oil shock once again renewed
the sense of shared interests between the government and the
automakers. At the same time, the creation of the formal study group

gave the two sides a place to bargain and indicated that in return for the government's reasonable stand on the 1976 standard, a similar accommodation would be expected from the automakers; it was their turn to give something back in the ongoing relationship of trade-offs. Finally, by relying on tax incentives to stimulate demand for cleaner cars, the government used the competitiveness of the Japanese automakers and the market to advance the cause of clean air.

The tax incentives, in particular, succeeded in shattering the automakers' opposition to the standards. A Toyota official explains, "Originally the auto manufacturers' association wanted a united front in opposing the emission controls. But then the united front was broken up because Honda wanted to use this situation to its own commercial advantage. As far as Toyota was concerned, the greatest threat to a leader in any industry is the introduction of new technology. For any leader it is the best policy for today to be the same as tomorrow. Change can only threaten the leadership position. We recognized that technological change could make Honda a threat. Honda had always had a very weak position in the domestic market and they were very eager to increase their domestic market share. They saw in this environmental issue a new opportunity to increase their market share."[45]

In 1976, while the study group was still considering the 1978 standards, Honda broke with the other automakers, announcing that it had a new technology that would allow it to meet the strict 1978 nitrous oxides standards under consideration. Shortly thereafter, several of the other small and medium-sized companies made similar announcements, followed by Nissan—isolating Toyota as the major holdout. By August 1976, a majority of the Japanese automakers reported that they could meet the 1978 standard and in October 1976, the study group indicated to the Environmental Agency that the standard was technically and economically feasible. The agency adopted it in December 1976, and Toyota, at last, rescinded its request for a two-year extension and signed on.[46]

Over a five-year period, the Japanese enterprise system had successfully negotiated a potentially divisive and explosive issue, one that continues to gnaw at the relationship between the government and the automakers in the United States. The Japanese worked out the problem by eliciting a commitment from both sides to an ongoing dialogue; by a willingness to compromise over several rounds of debate; by an overriding faith in the operation of the market rather than a dogmatic assertion of standards; and by a clear understanding of the continuing interests that joined the two sides over the long run.

The Oil Shock of 1973

The oil shock of 1973 changed the debate over air quality and tested the Japanese enterprise system in a more direct and profound way. U.S. analysts, accustomed to looking at the world through American lenses, tend to focus on the effects of the oil embargo as if it had been directed only against America. Some auto industry analysts even consider the embargo the watershed event in the current auto competition, the source of Detroit's problems; they single out federal energy policy as the critical weak spot in the American industry's competition with Japan. Every other nation in the world, and in particular Japan, is pictured as being much better prepared and much less threatened by the 1973 oil shock.

But the facts are otherwise.[47] The OPEC oil embargo was a global tidal wave that washed across all shores. What differentiated Japan and the Japanese auto industry was not better preparation or less vulnerability; rather, the adaptability of the enterprise system allowed Japan to absorb the shock and respond quickly and effectively.

The 1973 oil shock represented a direct threat to the Japanese economy; moreover, it was the kind of massive external environmental change that could have upset the negotiated equilibrium between management, labor, and government. In the early 1970s, Japan was more dependent on OPEC than any other advanced nation in the world. Seventy-five percent of Japan's energy needs were met by oil; more than 99 percent of that oil was imported, more than 80 percent of it from OPEC nations. Iran, by itself, was the source for more than 37 percent of Japan's imported oil.

Just as important as the source of the oil was its end use. In Japan, 46 percent of the oil went to power industrial production, the highest concentration in productive end use of any of the major industrialized nations. The United States, by comparison, used only 14 percent of its oil for production but consumed about 52 percent for transportation, most of that to fuel automobiles.

The difference is striking. In America, the oil embargo may have caused impatient drivers to wait in gas lines. In Japan, it imperiled the economy by threatening to undermine the production base. The 250 percent increase in the price of OPEC oil triggered a massive inflationary spurt that drove commodity prices up by 24 percent and completely upset Japan's balance of payments. In 1972, Japan registered a $6.6 billion trade surplus; in 1974, it recorded a $4.7 billion trade deficit.

The oil embargo also threatened to dismantle the carefully constructed enterprise system. For the decade preceding the embargo, the Japanese auto industry had enjoyed booming and constant growth. Sales within the domestic market had climbed an average of 19 percent per year. The oil shock brought a sudden end to that record of growth.

In response to rampaging inflation, the government implemented severe economic measures. Auto-related taxes were increased. Gasoline taxes, which were higher than the rate in the United States but lower than those in most of Europe, were raised dramatically in late 1973 and again in 1976. A tough credit squeeze was implemented. Together, the measures took a stark toll on the automakers, their workers, and suppliers. In 1974, domestic demand dropped by more than 30 percent. The next year domestic sales increased by 50,000 units but still remained 30,000 units below the 1973 level. To respond to the new situation, adjustments had to be made across the enterprise system. Some companies turned to exports as a new source of growth. But the real test of the enterprise system came with the crisis at Toyo Kogyo.

By 1973 Toyo Kogyo (TK), the maker of Mazda vehicles (and since renamed Mazda Motors, Inc.), had grown to become the third-largest-selling automaker in Japan. Led by its president, Kohei Matsuda, whose grandfather had founded the company, TK had used the popularity of its rotary engine to capture more than 10 percent of the Japanese market. In America, the rotary-powered Mazda was named Car of the Year in 1971. The engine was relatively pollution-free; moreover, it was technologically distinctive and thus a legitimate way for the company to differentiate itself. Between 1970 and 1973, TK more than doubled its production of cars, reaching 465,700 units in 1973; in the same year, its total production of cars, trucks, and buses reached 739,100 units, up from only 429,800 three years earlier. Auto exports had also taken off: from 59,300 autos in 1970 to more than 236,800 cars in 1973. Total exports of cars, trucks, and buses climbed from 94,100 units in 1970 to almost 343,800 in 1973.

Employment had grown with production and exports, climbing from 26,500 workers in 1970 to 36,900 in 1973. By 1973 almost 5 percent of the working population of Hiroshima was employed directly by TK and another 20 percent was employed by suppliers to the automaker. With production and exports taking off, TK President Matsuda had begun plans for new investments to expand the company's capacity to one million units. A 1973 magazine article commented on the company's enviable position.

> If the rotary age is indeed at hand, Toyo Kogyo . . . is sitting comfortably in the catbird seat. . . . Toyo Kogyo won a big press at home when Mazda won the "Car of the Year" accolade in 1971, and President Matsuda intends to get all the mileage he can out of such promotional propaganda. "We want to establish an image of technical innovation and quality," he allows. "Our popularity abroad is certainly helping us in this effort."
> Even Toyo Kogyo's massive auto plant on the shores of the Inland Sea fits in with Matsuda's vision. Says he: "By having everything here in one spot, we can achieve production efficiencies and economies not available to other automotive manufacturers. It reflects the image of high quality and advanced technology that our company is trying to project."[48]

Then the oil shock hit. The enormous increase in the cost of gasoline revealed the one major flaw in the rotary engine Mazda—its poor fuel efficiency, under eleven miles per gallon in city driving, the worst rating in its weight class according to the Environmental Protection Agency.

Stubbornly unwilling to reduce his company's reliance on the rotary engine or even to cut back on production, Matsuda watched in 1974 as sales in Japan plummeted by 40 percent. In the United States, between 1973 and 1975, sales dropped by 70 percent. Bound by its agreements with workers and suppliers, TK watched its condition worsen rapidly: overall corporate indebtedness increased 50 percent in the first ten months of 1974 and by January 1975 neared $1.25 billion.

With the support and encouragement of MITI, the Sumitomo Bank, TK's major creditor and lead bank, stepped in to rescue the company. Matsuda was stripped of his responsibilities as head of TK and replaced by Tsutomu Murai from the bank, who, along with almost a dozen other bank executives, began an emergency restructuring of the company. Production was scaled back; plans for the expansion were dropped. Most important, after freezing their own pay, managers approached workers for concessions to help keep the company afloat.

The negotiations proved a severe test of the management-labor relationship. The economic deal that was struck was a mild blow to the workers: base pay was left untouched but workers' bonuses were reduced by 0.1 percent for one year. More significant were the shifts in employment. The production cutback had left TK with 10,000 redundant workers, roughly the growth since 1970. In keeping with the concept of job security, none of the 10,000 workers were fired or permanently laid off. But 5,000 of the workers agreed to "retire" and the other 5,000 were reassigned to become auto salesmen rather than auto assemblers. Many were forced to leave the area to take up their new sales jobs.

In spite of the hardship and the stress of the trade-offs that had been negotiated, the management-labor relationship did not break. In 1975, TK workers voiced their dissatisfaction by voting out of office the union leader who had negotiated the concessions. In his place, a communist was elected to the position of vice-president; during his one-year term, management, in turn, reduced its consultation with the union and closed its books to workers to keep economic information from getting into the wrong hands. But there was no return to the strikes and confrontations of the early 1950s; the concessions were produced by private negotiations between management and workers with both sides keeping a clear eye on their joint longer-term interests.

Over the next few years, the commitment to shared interests worked out. With the support of MITI, the Sumitomo Bank, and local government and business leaders, Toyo Kogyo regained its competitive balance. By 1980 auto production had reached 736,500 units, total vehicle production more than 1,120,000 units, and exports more than 500,000 units. The company was again profitable and in 1983 a Mazda was once again named Car of the Year. More than anything, the crisis had demonstrated the efficiency and adaptability of the Japanese enterprise system. There had been no extended philosophical debate over whether or not a rescue effort would violate the principles of the free market. The public had not been treated to the spectacle of daily stories in the newspapers commenting on the likely bankruptcy of the automaker. Instead, the enterprise system had responded to change in a way that supported the renewed competitiveness of the company as the ultimate goal.

Trade Policy

If the oil shock of 1973 tested the Japanese enterprise system against a violent environmental change, it also brought the full globalization of the auto competition to the rest of the world, a development for which the Japanese had been preparing since the 1960s. Distinctions between markets and products that had been eroding gradually around the world were abruptly and permanently erased. The markets of Europe and, most important, of the United States were unconditionally open for business to the Japanese automakers, initially because of their vehicles' fuel efficiency, then because of their low cost and high quality.

The opportunity could not have come at a better time for the Japanese auto industry. Domestic demand, which had been meteoric in the miracle years of the 1960s, had begun to stabilize as the market matured. In 1973, there were 2.9 million new auto registrations in Japan and a total of 4.9 million new vehicle registrations. In 1980, the new registrations totaled 2.85 million for cars and 5.0 million for cars, trucks, and buses. Although their home market still belonged exclusively to the Japanese automakers, the flattening demand curve meant the industry would have to look elsewhere for the new growth needed to keep the promise to each party in the enterprise system.

In the second half of the 1970s, the growth came from exports. In 1975, the Japanese automakers produced 4.5 million cars and a total of 6.9 million vehicles; they exported 1.8 million cars and 2.7 million vehicles. In 1980, auto production was up to the 7.0 million mark and motor vehicle production reached slightly more than 11.0 million; auto exports were 3.9 million and total exports were 5.9 million. In five years auto production had increased by 2.5 million units and auto exports had grown by 2.1 million units; total production was up by 4.1 million and total exports were up by 3.2 million motor vehicles. Not only was the rest of the world buying more than 50 percent of the industry's output; even more remarkable, it was buying almost 80 percent of the industry's growth.

By 1984 the numbers were even more astronomical. The Japanese automakers exported nearly 4 million cars and another 2 million trucks and buses, or roughly 50 percent of total automotive production. On a company-by-company basis, Toyota exported 50 percent of its automotive production; the comparable numbers for Nissan and Mazda were 50 percent and 72 percent, respectively. Auto exports were the leading source of export earnings for Japan, bringing in $29 billion, 17 percent of the country's total earnings.

In response to this Japanese onslaught, the governments of the other auto-producing nations began, in 1975 and 1976, to voice protests. At first both the United States and the European Economic Community focused on the inability of their automakers to penetrate the Japanese market, rather than on the need to reduce Japanese access to their markets. The Americans and Europeans complained to MITI in March 1976 about nontariff barriers—discriminatory inspection practices, auto taxes, and distribution facilities—which, they claimed, accounted for an import penetration level in Japan of one percent. In May 1976, MITI responded by promising to eliminate the nontariff barriers and set a target of 8 to 9 percent for imports by 1980. In fact, by 1978 the tariff barriers to the Japanese market were eliminated entirely, and yet by 1980 auto imports into Japan had declined to less than one percent of total registrations.

As frustration as well as trade deficits and unemployment grew, the other auto-producing nations began to erect trade barriers of their own, protecting their markets from the Japanese automakers. The French established an informal 3 percent limit on Japanese imports. The Italians invoked the provisions of an old treaty to limit imports to 2,200 cars. In the United Kingdom, a gentlemen's agreement between British and Japanese automakers set the limit first at 9 percent of the market, later at 11 percent.

But the biggest market and the biggest political problem for the Japanese government and the Japanese automakers was the United States. When, in 1979, the Iranian revolution touched off a new surge of fuel-efficient imports and a recession killed demand for American-made cars, the government, the UAW, and some of the U.S. automakers appealed to the Japanese to restrain imports. The auto trade issue between the United States and Japan not only threatened to disrupt the bilateral relationship between the two countries but also placed enormous stress on the relationship between the Japanese government, which felt the need to do something to respond to the American request, and the Japanese automakers, who were eager to take full advantage of their hard-won economic opportunity.

Although the U.S. International Trade Commission declined to intervene and Congress failed to enact protectionist legislation, MITI recognized that the problem was not going to go away. If the U.S. government came to consider the General Agreement on Tariffs and Trade (GATT) ineffective, it could resort to stronger legislative measures. According to Naohiro Amaya, who was vice-minister of MITI in the early 1980s,

> Legally speaking, GATT has rules to settle trade disputes in accordance with the spirit of free trade. Therefore, as far as Japan observes GATT rules strictly, it is allowed to export to the United States 1.8 million cars or even 2 million a year or as many as it can to meet demand there. That is the principle of free trade. But practically speaking, if Japan exports in such a way, it is very likely that the Danforth-Bentsen bill will be passed by the U.S. Congress.[49]

Although the Reagan administration picked up the call for the Japanese government to restrain exports and threats from Congress intensified, according to Yoshiyasu Nao, deputy director of MITI's automobile division, the real debate occurred, not between Japan and the United States, but between MITI and the Japanese automakers. Both sides agreed on the long-term importance of exports to the United States. But they disagreed on short-term tactics, on what steps to take and when to take them in order to gain the greatest advantage and make the smallest sacrifice in responding to the U.S. demands for restraint. "The difference was MITI's assessment of the economic strength of the U.S. auto industry," says Nao. "The Japanese auto companies said that the U.S. industry would recover in the second half of 1981. So the longer we waited, the less pressure we would be under to act. MITI judged that the auto industry would continue to deteriorate. We judged that the longer Japan waited, the less favorable the terms would be."[50]

Throughout the auto trade discussions MITI maintained constant communications with the automakers, both as an industry and on a company-by-company basis. The voluntary restraint agreement that was finally reached in May 1981 was bitterly denounced by the Japanese automakers. But neither the timing nor the terms of the agreement came as a surprise. Because of the consultative system, they had ample warning and time to prepare for the new trade rules and their impact on the auto competition. Indeed, when the voluntary agreement expired in 1985, the automakers and the government agreed to continue informal restraints to head off continuing threats of protectionism in the United States.

FUTURE IMPLICATIONS

In the mid-1980s, as a result of such protectionist measures and threats, more than 70 percent of Japan's auto trade is controlled, limited by voluntary restraint agreements, local content requirements, or other constraints on free trade. This pervasive change in the environment raises unanswered questions about the future of the Japanese enterprise system. Since it flourished in a period of rapid growth, will it adapt smoothly as the pace of growth slows? Will the new environment disrupt the negotiated quid pro quos that created the system's equilibrium?

Although the answers are far from conclusive, the system, led by the companies, has already begun to adapt. First, the major automakers have responded to the formal restraint agreement with the United States by changing the product mix in their exports, moving up from the small subcompact cars that first penetrated the American market into the compact, intermediate, and sporty car segments. They have also loaded their exports with expensive options and commanded a premium price on the volume-restricted cars.

The results have been both economically and strategically rewarding. In 1984–1985, Toyota's net income soared by 29 percent over the year before, even though sales increased by only 11 percent. Mazda's sales showed no increase over 1983, but its net income rose by 19 percent. Even more valuable for the future, the shift into the larger-car segment of the market has allowed the Japanese automakers to begin to challenge the Big Three in an area that has traditionally been the American automakers' meal ticket.

At the same time, the Japanese automakers have begun to diversify as a hedge against a future of limited growth in autos. They have moved into such industries as lawn mowers, marine products, and textile machinery. Nissan has expanded its commitment to the aerospace and defense business; Mazda has experimented with kitchenware and clothing; Toyota has increased its investment in a division of the company that manufactures prefabricated housing.

But the greatest change—and the one with the most far-reaching implications for the enterprise system—has been the growing willingness of the automakers to accede to the political demands of the other auto-producing nations by investing in foreign production facilities and signing joint production agreements with foreign automakers. Since the rise of global protectionism in the early 1980s, the pace and scope of these foreign agreements have been extraordinary. Nissan has struck agreements with Motor Iberica of Spain and Alfa Romeo of Italy, invested in a Tennessee production plant, and committed itself to building another in the United Kingdom. Honda has agreed to build a car with British Leyland, opened an Ohio plant, and announced plans for a Canadian plant. Mazda and Mitsubishi will follow with production in the North American market. Toyota has struck a deal with General Motors to build a car in California, invested in an assembly plant of its own in Kentucky, and announced its intentions to build 300,000 cars a year in Taiwan. All in all, the Japanese automakers expect to produce an estimated 3.7 million vehicles overseas by 1988.

These moves could disrupt the system of close communication and joint consultation and the negotiation of joint gains that has propelled the industry from obscurity to dominance. For the suppliers and the autoworkers still in Japan, it could mean a future of less work, fewer profits, and less predictability of economic gain. The Japanese autoworkers' union, for example, vigorously opposed Nissan's British investment. Other signs of discontent have already surfaced among workers. "Today in the auto industry, workers are concerned about the loss of jobs," says Jouji Kato, chief of industrial relations at the Japan Productivity Center. Worried about the "isolation that comes from automation," Kato says, "labor feels an urgent need to come up with standards to limit the introduction of robots."[51] Indeed, Nissan workers won from company management a new policy on automation promising that, in the future, no workers would lose their jobs because of the introduction of new technology.

Some observers worry that the fabled relationship between the companies and their work force will founder as the automakers manufacture more abroad. Says a top official of the Keidanren, the Federation of Economic Organizations, "In an era of low growth, quality circles are in trouble. A number of workers are simply going through the motions to get management off their backs. Increasingly, workers want to be paid for their participation."[52] Among the suppliers, as well, there are problems developing as a result of the automakers' move away from Japan. Many are looking for new ventures that will reduce their future dependency on the automakers. "Today," says a leading business analyst in Tokyo, "suppliers are eager to establish their own business identities, independent of the automakers. They can't afford to think of themselves as just a cog in

Toyota's machine. For them, the world can only get worse."[53] For the government, the change would mean a reduced role in influencing the future course of the industry. And if the industry falters or fails to maintain domestic employment, it could require a significant change in national economic policy.

In the mid-1980s, however, these worries seem distant. The Japanese competitive advantage in building small cars remains constant and perhaps is even increasing. The dramatic increase in the value of the yen is a source of concern as Japanese automakers are forced to sacrifice profit margins to keep their export prices as low as possible. Nevertheless, workers' wages and benefits are rising, and protectionist policies and new technologies have not led to layoffs. And the Japanese economy continues to benefit from a massive trade surplus. In short, the Japanese enterprise system shows every sign of adapting to the straitened conditions of global competition in autos in the 1980s and 1990s.

PART III

The United States Auto Industry Today

CHAPTER **6**

The Big Three
Struggling for Renewed Competitiveness

At one of the low points of the 1980-1982 auto crisis, Robert D. Lund, GM's vice-president for sales and marketing and a thirty-six-year veteran of the industry, commented, "We're a provincial industry, and always have been."[1]

During the previous four decades, the myopia of the industry hardly seemed to matter. Plentiful and inexpensive gasoline meant that the American auto industry and its customers lived behind a kind of tariff wall for years and did not know it. Foreign cars designed for fuel efficiency were not a serious threat to U.S. automakers in their home market. In such a sheltered market, running the auto industry involved perfecting a proven, profitable formula. Once GM and then Ford had implemented Alfred Sloan's revolutionary marketing concepts and had formally recognized the United Auto Workers (UAW), the greatest challenge lay in finance and engineering: to organize and operate the complicated mechanics of the business in as efficient a way as possible.

Today, much of the provincialism and myopia of the industry has disappeared. The traditional bases of auto competition have shifted dramatically. The old skills and attitudes that sustained U.S. automakers are now either inadequate for or unsatisfactory in maintaining competitiveness. As a result, U.S. automakers have been forced to look

145

beyond their own history and consider new strategies and adminis-trative practices.

With revenues of $96 billion in 1985, General Motors is making a big effort and substantial progress in redefining how it is to compete as the world's largest automaker. Not since Sloan's efforts in the 1920s has GM reorganized itself on a comparable scale. Interestingly, GM has pursued diversification in a way that either builds upon its existing skills or serves its high-technology agenda. It has also aggres-sively developed coalitions with Japanese and Korean automakers to supply low-cost vehicles and major components for 15 percent of its U.S. product line. Finally, with the cooperation of the UAW, it has recently created a new corporation that will design and produce a new small car at home by 1990.

Ford, with $53 billion in worldwide revenues, is also working hard to reform itself. Since it is considerably less vertically integrated than GM, Ford has, until recently, forgone the cost advantages associated with new outsourcing and Japanese supply relationships and has instead concentrated on improving product quality and labor rela-tions at home. Now Ford, too, is forging a new international coproduction and importing strategy.

Chrysler, less than one-fifth the size of GM and operating with a diminishing labor cost advantage, has continued to spin off new models from its aging, compact-car platform while it tries to cement ties with its Japanese supplier, from which it already imports 14 percent of its total unit sales (and almost 50 percent of its subcompact sales). Despite a remarkable recovery from a brush with bankruptcy, Chrysler has, more or less permanently, become a "narrow line" domestic manufacturer and an importer of small cars—and thus, a scaled-down version of its former self.

Even though the Big Three have acted decisively during the past five years to forge more competitive strategies, they have not been able to recapture the share of the small-car market lost to the Japa-nese. Of the 11 million cars sold in 1985, for example, about 20 percent were classified as small cars, and the Japanese captured 45 percent of this market from their offshore production base.[2] By 1990, it is likely that the Big Three will be forced by their Asian competitors to abandon most of their domestic small-car manufacturing capacity in a free trade environment. To make matters worse, it is by no means clear that the Big Three can successfully defend the midsize-car market from Japanese inroads at the bottom of the price range and

European inroads at the top. About 25 percent of the cars sold in 1985 fell into this segment. Offshore Japanese producers captured 23 percent of this segment, and another 5 percent was captured by Honda's U.S. assembly operation. Although traditional U.S. automakers held on to 65 percent of the market for midsize cars, new product announcements by Japanese automakers indicate a clear strategy of further invading this segment—along with European automakers. Thus, despite record profits in 1983–1984 and a robust year in 1985, it does not appear that a revitalized Big Three will be able to restore their competitiveness as full-line, domestic producers by relying upon traditional competitive strategies and relationships with labor and government.

The following account elaborates on this picture of the U.S. auto industry. First, the sea change that has taken place in auto competition and the initial responses and results of the Big Three will be reviewed. Next, the current automotive strategies of each of the Big Three will be examined. Finally, the Big Three's prospects, including estimated use of manufacturing capacity and employment in 1990, will be discussed in the context of the industry's future risks and uncertainties.

THE NEW BASES OF AUTO COMPETITION

Even under the most benign industry conditions, auto competition is a game of high costs and engineering complexity, complicated by cyclical industry sales. It is an industry dominated by economies of scale, where decisions to increase or decrease production must be made in increments of thousands of units and millions of dollars. For automakers, the smallest decision can involve the expenditure of vast sums of money programmed over an extended period of time, requiring the coordination of dispersed corporate divisions, thousands of outside suppliers, and hundreds of thousands of workers. As recently as 1981, the U.S. auto industry directly operated 325 prime manufacturing plants in North America, shared in the output of over 45,000 direct supplier plants, and accounted for almost 1.5 million jobs. To retool a single engine or transmission line can cost an automaker anywhere from $150 million to $500 million. A single new car line can cost as much as $4 billion and take five years to move from concept to production: two years to design and test prototypes, and three years to acquire tooling and train workers to produce the new line of cars. In addition, a single project can require the participation of as many as 30,000 suppliers and service companies before a new car can be displayed in a dealer's showroom. These characteristics of the auto industry constitute enormous economic and political barriers to fundamental changes in corporate strategy and administrative practice.

Rapid globalization of the auto industry, however, has forced U.S. automakers to reconsider their conservative ways. In less time than it takes to bring a new model from concept to the showroom, U.S. automakers found themselves confronted by a challenge to the guiding assumptions that had shaped almost sixty years of industry attitudes and business policy. The Iranian revolution of 1979 not only brought the return of gas lines and high prices at the pump; it also brought an end to the protected market in the United States. Overnight, the industry faced the removal of a subsidy that had favored cars averaging twelve to fifteen miles per gallon. In just two years— between 1978 and 1980—fuel-efficient, small cars of the kind produced in Europe and Japan increased from almost 39 percent of the market to 50 percent. At the same time, larger "standard" models, long the bread and butter of U.S. producers, declined from almost 55 percent of the market to only 44 percent.

This change in market mix brought with it a change in the competitive balance between U.S. and foreign-based automakers. The smaller, more fuel efficient autos of the European and Japanese producers met the demand of the U.S. market, thus giving foreign-based automakers an advantage over their U.S. competitors. By 1982, every 100 vehicles in American showrooms faced competition from 30 Japanese vehicles. In the late 1960s, they had faced only 5.

Outside America, other economic and noneconomic forces were also at work forcing the auto industry to transform itself from one of national competitors operating primarily in domestic markets into one of international firms competing in a world market. Increased intermarket homogenization, declining trade barriers and transportation costs, and increased opportunities to take advantage of lower wages and higher market growth rates in different parts of the world were some of the most important forces at work. As marketing, production, product design, and finance became subject to worldwide economies of scale, competition in national markets increased, eroding the dominance of many national producers. Although some specific consumer preferences and government policies constituted continuing barriers to globalization, by the mid-1970s the manufacturing and assembly operations of major automakers were spread around the world. As a result, the share of total passenger car production exported and the absolute number of motor vehicles involved in foreign trade became an unmistakable trend. A similar pattern was emerging for such large components as drive trains, power steering mechanisms, and engine blocks.

The push toward globalization forced U.S. automakers to face the obsolescence of a substantial portion of their domestic production base. In addition, the capacity of Japanese automakers to produce fuel-efficient cars at a consistently low cost with high quality also called into question the management and labor practices of American automakers. U.S. automakers, who always had prided themselves on strong manufacturing controls, were introduced to foreign manufacturing systems that produced greater efficiencies through even tighter operating practices. Vertical integration, which formerly was considered to give a competitive advantage, came to be regarded as a disadvantage in the new international competition, since it locked U.S. producers into high and ever-escalating UAW labor costs: By 1980, UAW employees boasted an hourly compensation 65 percent above that of the average American manufacturing worker. Labor costs and labor relations, long a stable part of the U.S. competitive equation, suddenly required urgent reevaluation in light of the Japanese challenge. For the first time, U.S. automakers found themselves no longer the standard of world comparison and found themselves, as well, having to respond to the initiatives of others in order to compete.

INITIAL RESPONSES AND RESULTS

The initial responses of the Big Three advanced along four major lines, each of which carried with it significant implications for organized labor, for auto-dependent communities concentrated in the industrialized Midwest and Northeast, and for state and local governments. First, pressured by rising foreign competition and a depressed home market, U.S. automakers began an extensive capital cost-cutting exercise, closing obsolete plants and eliminating excess capacity. From 1979 to 1985 U.S. producers closed, sold, or announced the closing of over forty plants. Second, within the operating plants, automakers sought to implement a series of programs designed to meet the Japanese challenges of cost and quality. Focusing on productivity, U.S. producers acted to reduce the number of man-hours required to make a vehicle, from the average 225 to 285 hours per vehicle needed in the mid-1970s to 150 to 200 hours per vehicle in 1985. In a dramatic and unprecedented series of negotiations in 1982, U.S. automakers used the pressure of current and future plant closures to win wage and benefit concessions from the UAW. Other efficiency moves by the Big Three entailed cutting back on white-collar staff, improved inventory control, more economical transportation arrangements, and increased attention to quality control. One indicator of the early progress in efficiency is that the number of new car sales required for the industry as a whole to break even declined from over 12 million in 1979 to well under 9 million in 1983.

Third, U.S. automakers were forced to make unprecedented capital investments in new equipment and facilities at the same time that they stressed cost consciousness and productivity improvements. In spite of four consecutive years of deteriorating sales, the Big Three spent over $10 billion to downsize their fleets, convert them to front-wheel drive, and improve fuel performance. Fourth, in concert with these massive investments in new production facilities, U.S. automakers sought to resolve a basic dilemma: efficiency may favor production of a minimum number of basic components in large volumes, but consumer tastes demand differentiated models and power trains. The automakers' solution was to purchase more parts from abroad ("international outsourcing") and to enter into coalitions with foreign automakers to share the costs and risks of developing and producing both components and fully assembled vehicles. For example, by early 1982, international outsourcing had grown to include 2.5 million engines and 1.8 million transmissions.[3] In addition, U.S. automakers began looking to Japanese producers to provide finished automobiles that could be sold under American nameplates. In 1982, GM said that it was planning to outsource 50 percent of the bottom 25 percent of its fleet—that is, of the smallest cars sold in the United States by GM, a full one-half of their parts would come from a foreign source.[4]

These initial responses by U.S. producers to the new global competition and the deep economic downturn that followed the second oil shock were far-reaching in scale and scope—a conversion massive enough to represent the largest peacetime shift in technological, human, and capital resources in U.S. history. It was an effort that also had massive repercussions for workers, suppliers, communities, and, ultimately, state and local governments. According to the U.S. Department of Transportation, closing plants and improving productivity and efficiency cost over 250,000 hourly autoworkers their jobs; 40,000 white-collar autoworkers were also laid off.[5] In addition, the combination of production changes, vehicle design changes, outsourcing, reduced sales, and the prolonged recession resulted in the closure of more than 1,000 supplier plants and the loss of 400,000 to 500,000 jobs in supplier industries.[6]

The impact of plant closures and joblessness was magnified by the geographical concentration of the auto industry: 90 percent of total employment was located in ten states. For the most part, the painful transformation of the auto industry and its suppliers was visited disproportionately on the cities and towns of the industrial Midwest and Northeast: Detroit, Flint, Saginaw, Pontiac, Lansing, Cleveland, Dayton, Toledo, St. Louis, Indianapolis, Anderson, Kokomo, and Muncie. The problems of these communities became, in turn, a government problem because of the decrease in revenues resulting from the economic contraction, the increase in expenditures prompted by growing social demands, and the demand of unemployed workers that government "do something" to fix the problem. In 1983, for example, the state of Michigan faced a $900 million budget deficit, almost exclusively because of slumping auto sales and rising social service costs.

These social costs, as well as the competitive status of the industry, have been disguised by record profits and the recall of many of the 270,000 autoworkers laid off as of January 1983. The apparent recovery, however, stimulated by a decline in interest rates and energy prices, a cyclical upswing in consumer spending, and four years of trade protection under Japan's "voluntary" export restraint program, is largely illusory. The competitive advantage of Japanese automakers, reflected in their increasing shares of the small and midsize-car markets, has not been overcome.

U.S. consumers are attracted to Japanese cars for good reasons. Despite massive investments by the Big Three in high technology and wage concessions by the UAW, Japanese automakers continue to make cars more efficiently than do American automakers. Thus, for comparable models the Japanese have a substantial cost advantage over American automakers. At the beginning of the 1970s, Detroit could deliver a compact car on the West Coast for less than an equivalent Japanese model; by the end of the decade, however, the American automakers were at a 20 to 40 percent cost disadvantage, depending on the model. Today, Japan's delivered cost advantage for a subcompact or compact car is currently between $2,000 and $2,500. In the midsize-car class, Japanese car makers hold a $3,100 advantage; in the sports-car market, a $4,000 advantage. The strengthening of the yen relative to the U.S. dollar during 1985 and 1986 has only narrowed this cost gap by about $600. Thus, even if a dramatic strengthening of the yen continues, U.S. automakers will continue to find themselves competing against lower-cost Japanese products.[7]

In addition, a relative disadvantage in product quality continues to affect consumer preferences and the competitive status of the U.S. automakers. Again, the Japanese provide the base line for comparison. Consumer surveys conducted by J. D. Powers and Associates, as recently as August 1983, found that 50 percent of cars made in the United States had problems on delivery, and 56 percent had mechanical problems after delivery. The comparative figures for Japanese cars were 36 and 39 percent. The percentage of respondents in this survey who rated U.S. cars as giving "excellent" or "very good" value for the money actually decreased from 1979 to 1983; the percentage of respondents who so rated Japanese cars increased. A more recent Powers customer satisfaction index (1984) revealed that seven of the ten highest-ranked producers were foreign.

GM'S NEW STRATEGIC LOGIC

The illusion of current profitability has not escaped the top management of General Motors. They know that the small-car segments of the domestic market will continue to be an important source of revenues, despite the recent decline in oil prices, and that the company needs help to supply this demand profitably. According to GM's classification system, subcompact sales tripled from 1970 to 1983; however, GM's own share of the subcompact group slipped from a peak of about 27 percent in 1976 to 19 percent in the 1983 model year. Robert T. O'Connell, GM's vice-president for marketing and product planning, estimates that the subcompact share of the total domestic car market in 1990 could be as large as 40 percent, if oil prices return to their 1984 levels.[8] Thus, a central competitive issue facing GM is how to regain its lost share of the small-car market while working to protect its highly profitable midsize, large, prestige, and sports car business from Japanese and European inroads.

GM can regain share in the small-car market only by fielding a line of products that at least matches current Japanese products on delivered cost, product quality, and performance. There are two ways to do so. First, GM could design and manufacture a competitive small car at home. This would require a coordinated effort by managers, technical and support personnel, and production employees. (In the absence of increased production volume, it might also require government to grease the wheels of change by placing a stronger security net under production employees whose jobs would be threatened or eliminated by automation and changes in work roles.) Second, large portions of the product line or major components could be manufactured in low-cost Japan or in such low-wage areas as Brazil, Korea, and Mexico, and then imported into the United States.

GM's top management appears to have opted for a combination of these two basic strategies. A brief review of GM's product programs and manufacturing initiatives, recent organizational changes, and labor policies provides clues to how GM is planning to play this complicated competitive game.

In 1983, General Motors produced worldwide just under 7.8 million cars, trucks, and buses. U.S. factory sales accounted for just under 5 million units, of which about 4 million were cars and slightly over 1 million were trucks and buses. In the U.S. passenger car business, GM's product mix has been oriented toward developing and producing vehicles for the larger-car market segments, in which it is relatively strong, while relying increasingly on imports to supply it with low-cost products for the highly competitive small-car segments. In 1984, GM marketed thirty-five models in the five principal passenger-car segments: small (subcompact), midsize (compact), large, prestige, and sporty. Twenty-nine out of these models fell in the midsize, large, and prestige car segments. Four other models were sports cars. Only two models, the Chevette and its twin, Pontiac T-1000, fell into the small-car segment. After GM launched the so-called J-cars in the midsize segment in 1981, most of its product development money went into large, prestige, and sports cars—and for good reasons, too. Although GM faced twenty-four competitive Japanese models in the small and midsize segments of the market, there were no Japanese competitors at all in the large and prestige segments. Although GM competed against twenty-one European models (along with three Ford and two Chrysler models) in the prestige-car segment, the imports could only garner 300,000 units out of 1.1 million units sold in this segment in 1983.[9]

At middecade, GM is in the midst of a $6 billion per year program to redesign or replace nearly all of the company's midsize, large, and prestige cars. Through this investment, GM hopes to blanket these segments with at least two entries while its rivals only offer a single car line. Equally significant, the automaker plans to blanket the low-priced end of the market with Japanese and Korean imports. This plan is the key to understanding GM's strategy.

General Motors put the first piece of its Japanese small-car strategy in place by announcing in March 1982 that it would not build a replacement for the subcompact Chevette and that it would invest another $200 million in Isuzu Motors, its 34 percent-owned Japanese affiliate. Isuzu applied this additional capital, along with the proceeds of a convertible debenture offering, to the design and production of new subcompact vehicles that GM planned to import into the United States at the rate of 200,000 a year starting in 1984 and 1985. The first shipment of Isuzu Spectrums wearing Chevrolet "bow ties" appeared in showrooms in November 1984.

GM and Suzuki Motor Company also announced in 1982 a supply and distribution agreement involving both vehicles and components. As many as 84,000 subcompacts were to be available for sale through GM dealers in the United States. According to the agreement, GM was to purchase an approximate 5 percent interest in Suzuki, and, in a separate agreement, Suzuki and Isuzu were to exchange about 2 to 3 percent equity interest. Thus, the three companies took preliminary steps toward a potential mutual assistance pact. Whereas GM would obtain access to new, low-cost products, its small Japanese partners would receive design and financial assistance from the U.S. giant, as well as the chance to achieve new benefits of scale. The first shipment of Suzuki Sprints wearing the Chevrolet nameplate reached dealers' showrooms in May 1984.

In addition, GM entered into a 1983 agreement with Toyota to coproduce 250,000 small (subcompact) cars a year for up to twelve years. The cars are assembled at the site of GM's former Fremont, California, plant but were designed in Japan. High-value-added components, such as engines and transaxles, are also manufactured in Japan. The new cars are distributed and serviced by Chevrolet's dealers throughout the United States. The arrangement was planned to give GM another subcompact to broaden its line, and GM's top officers hoped to demonstrate to both GM managers and UAW members that a competitive small car could be made in the United States. Chairman Roger Smith initially described the joint venture as "a short-term thing for us . . . it's a one-shot deal. I call it two ships passing in the night. We had an empty plant and they had an empty car, you might say, and we put the two together and provided 12,000 jobs."[10]

Finally, in March 1984, GM announced a tentative agreement with Daewoo Corporation of Korea to have their joint venture produce a small, GM-designed passenger car near Seoul, Korea. Up to half of the 167,000 vehicles manufactured under this venture—toward which GM would contribute $100 million—would be available to GM's Pontiac division for import to the United States starting in 1987.

Despite claims that GM's importing and coventuring arrangements are temporary, the scheduling of the new coalitions signals a major shift in corporate strategy. GM coalitions with various Japanese and Korean competitors, which on paper involve the coproduction and importation of as many as 600,000 units, offer the company multiple opportunities. In addition to restoring its market share, GM's strategy will enable the company to broaden its product line in response to increased market segmentation, to give the look-alike car divisions some basis for differentiation in small cars, and to prepare GM to become an assembler and distributor of small cars in the United States if the experiments in cost reduction and quality enhancement fail to increase competitiveness to global standards. Although Japan's voluntary export restraint limits GM to importing only 29,500 cars per year from Isuzu and 17,000 from Suzuki, the structure is in place for a large-scale, joint assault on the U.S. small-car market if the restraints expire or are relaxed. Significantly, the 1984 labor agreement did not preclude GM from increasing its level of outsourcing under certain conditions.

Even though increased importing and outsourcing is GM's dominant manufacturing strategy for its small-car business during the 1980s, the corporation is also pursuing a parallel strategy at home. In January 1985, GM announced the creation of Saturn Corporation, a wholly owned subsidiary, which intends to make a high-quality, cost-competitive small car at home by increasing emphasis on applying new technologies to product development and manufacturing.

Conceived in June 1982 and first unveiled to the public as a large-scale research and development project in November 1983, the Saturn project was set up as a "clean sheet" systems approach to building a subcompact car. The project team was not given a deadline for introduction of the Saturn car. Rather, their primary challenge was to figure out how to build small cars in the United States by applying new technologies to product development and manufacturing. The product was to be not only cost competitive with small foreign cars but also a leap ahead in safety, quality, and performance.

The new Saturn Corporation brings this car into its commercialization stage. The venture is initially capitalized at $150 million and may eventually have assets of $5 billion, making it more than twice the current size of American Motors Corporation. The goal is to introduce both two-door and four-door family subcompacts by 1989. Although original plans to build 400,000 to 500,000 vehicles a year have been scaled back, Saturn will have the potential of producing nearly twice the volume of traditional plants with fewer workers assembling the vehicles than in traditional plants. During 1984 some 10 percent of GM's total research and development budget was committed to this project.

Commenting on the project's expected innovations, C. Reid Rundell, executive vice-president of Saturn Corporation and former director of the Saturn project, said that between $1,400 and $2,500 in cost reductions per vehicle could be achieved through better coordination of design, engineering, and manufacturing, fewer labor hours per vehicle from increased automation, and less expensive manufacturing facilities. Rundell also stressed that the extensive use of modular assembly could dramatically change assembly plant size and design, how jobs are organized, and how materials or subassembled modules are delivered to workers.[11]

Given the sensitive labor issues involved, participation of the work force was deemed crucial from the very beginning of the Saturn project. Thus, in December 1983, plans for a joint study center devoted to exploring how best to build the Saturn car were announced by UAW vice-president Donald F. Ephlin, who directed the union's General Motors department, and Alfred S. Warren, Jr., vice-president in charge of GM's industrial relations staff. In their joint announcement, Ephlin and Warren committed themselves to paying special attention to the entire labor-management relationship in the work environment. "The intent," they said, "is to address any issue or item that has an impact on this relationship either directly or indirectly, and to make recommendations for new approaches that will contribute to the ability to produce a quality competitive product, and enhance the job security of the UAW-GM workers who build it."[12]

The joint study center was directed by a steering committee that gave equal representation to the UAW and GM.

One of the results of the 1984 labor agreement was management's commitment to build the new small car in the United States rather than in Canada, as previously rumored. The UAW apparently saw Saturn as a source of continuing employment in light of GM's parallel "Asian strategy," even though a Saturn plant would employ as many as 50 percent fewer production employees than a normal GM plant.[13]

As a complement to GM's strategy of importing and coproducing small cars, the new Saturn Corporation serves several important functions: it holds out the possibility of developing a profitable, American-made small car by the end of the decade; it gives the corporation a defense against claims that it is leaving U.S. small-car manufacturing; by creating a separate corporation with freedom to develop its own systems and practices, GM separates somewhat its labor relations and negotiations over wages, benefits, and work rules from the traditional GM-UAW bureaucracy; it gives the UAW hope that joint approaches to innovative production systems might be able to take about $2,000 of costs out of small-car production and thereby keep some small-car production in the United States; and finally, even if $2,000 of costs cannot be squeezed out of the manufacture of small cars, whatever innovations emerge from the effort can find their way into the production of other GM vehicles. This last possibility is particularly noteworthy. The challenge of Saturn is not only to produce small cars profitably in the United States but also to serve as a seed bed for innovations that can be adopted in car production throughout the entire corporation. Thus, within GM, Saturn is considered as much a center for new ideas and a source of corporatewide technological innovation as a specific, small-car program.

In addition to GM's coalition strategy with Japanese and Korean automakers and its domestically based Saturn venture, recent organizational changes at GM provide another clue to top management's thinking about the small-car business. In 1984, General Motors announced its first major organizational change since 1921, when the foundations of the modern GM were put into place by Alfred Sloan. The new GM structure established two car groups that were designed to function as self-contained business units: a "small" car group comprising Chevrolet, Pontiac, and GM of Canada and focused on the entry-level and under thirty-five-year-old market segment; and a "large" car group comprising Buick, Oldsmobile, and Cadillac. Each is totally responsible for its products, including engineering, manufacturing, assembly, and marketing, and each is accountable for its quality, performance, and profitability. The five car divisions were continued within the two car groups. Each car division shares responsibilities for product planning, marketing, advertising, sales, and service with a corporate marketing and product planning staff. A consolidated product engineering staff in each car group is responsible for total product engineering, including body, chassis, power train, and advanced concepts. An operations activity within each group has responsibility for sourcing and for the manufacturing and assembly plants. There is a program management team for each new platform developed by the car groups. Finally, each car group has its own financial and personnel functions, a move consistent with the autonomy that the new car groups will have.

The new car group structure provides increased flexibility in the manufacturing and marketing of small and large cars. More specifically, the new structure gives GM the possibility of pursuing several different product designs, plus different production and marketing strategies with minimum disruption to the corporation as a whole. For example, all of the outsourcing, importation, and coproduction agreements are centered in the so-called Chevrolet-Pontiac-Canada (CPC) Group, and the Buick-Oldsmobile-Cadillac Group retains a more self-contained American-based operation. The new Saturn subsidiary will pursue a third strategy despite its reporting relationship to the CPC Group. Thus, although the new structure increases the corporation's responsiveness to market trends and promotes organizational efficiencies, its major significance in light of GM's evolving product policy is that it allows at least three different business strategies to be pursued simultaneously under the same corporate roof. The reorganization around major market segments may also allow GM to pursue multiple labor relations strategies within the corporation, a major departure from industry practice. GM's new organizational framework facilitates a shift in management-labor relations away from so-called pattern bargaining to relations based more directly on market forces, which tend to vary from market segment to market segment.

GM's current domestic labor policies both complement its current domestic manufacturing strategy and pose long-term problems for the corporation. In recent years GM has taken several tracks to reduce labor costs and increase employee attention to product quality. The first track has led to a growing commitment to quality of work life (QWL) programs, where production employees who participate in quality circles are able to influence decisions in the work place. F. James McDonald, GM's president, gives QWL programs high priority and, as a result, spends a good deal of his time reinforcing and participating in QWL sessions throughout the corporation and at the UAW's retreat, Black Lake Lodge. In addition, the industrial relations staff is working to broaden the agenda of QWL groups and other management-labor committees to include cost reduction as well as quality enhancement. At Buick City, the Buick division's large integrated and assembly operation in southeastern Michigan, a joint management-labor study team initiated work on a total overhaul of that operation with the objectives of trimming hourly costs by one-third and salaried labor expenses by over 50 percent, cutting inbound freight cost by as much as 50 percent, reducing inventory by two-thirds, and lowering first-year warranty costs.

A second track has led to labor cost reduction through wage concessions in the 1982 national labor contract and wage restraint in the 1984 contract. Meanwhile, a third track involves heavy investments in automation, including the installation of about 20,000 new robots by 1990. Similar efforts over the next few years will go a long way toward completely automating for all practical purposes what car and truck production remains in the United States. The implications for automotive employment are clear. Says Alex C. Mair, GM's former vice-president and group executive for technical staffs, "We'll be selling more vehicles in the future, and we hope to call back more workers, but there just won't be as many jobs as there once were in the industry."[14] In an October 1983 presentation to GM's personnel directors, Alfred S. Warren, Jr., GM's vice-president of industrial relations, noted that GM's hourly work force would decline by almost 30 percent, from 370,000 to 270,000, during the next three years, assuming aggressive productivity improvements of 8.5 percent per year at constant volumes. In a private interview, Mr. Warren put work force reduction in a broader policy context. Echoing the conclusions of Alex Mair, he said, "Our greatest dilemma is figuring out how to give employment security while at the same time reducing the size of the work force."[15]

GM figured out how to do the latter before the former. By the fourth quarter of 1983, GM was making vehicles with far fewer workers than ever before. In the fourth quarter, 137 man-hours were used in each vehicle in contrast to 141 during the first quarter of 1983 and 142 in 1978, the most recent year of peak sales. At an annualized rate, GM was producing 5.6 million vehicles with 369,000 employees. In 1972 when GM produced a comparable number of vehicles (5.7 million), it employed 413,000 workers. These figures show that a permanent reduction in the work force of somewhere between 50,000 and 75,000 was well under way as GM moved into 1984, a year of record profits for the corporation.[16]

GM's desire to reduce the size of its work force through automation, importing, outsourcing, and coproduction initiatives reflects a basic conflict of values between the corporation and the UAW. To begin with, management's notion of what constitutes competitiveness differs radically from that of labor. Management's concept appears to be producing and selling automotive products, comparable in delivered cost and quality to those of their domestic and foreign competitors, *without prejudice to the location of manufacture.* In other words, the concept of competitiveness held by GM's leadership is not solely geared to the performance of U.S. facilities, but rather to product characteristics independent of their place of manufacture. This, they argue, is consistent with the realities of trying to compete in an industry undergoing rapid globalization. As one GM executive said, "To our way of thinking, a satisfied consumer comes first. Everything else—job security, profitability, dividends—follows from this." Another executive put it even more bluntly, "Either we're going to compete or not."

The UAW and their political supporters appear to define competitiveness somewhat differently: producing and selling automotive products, comparable in cost and quality to those of foreign automakers, *with U.S. labor,* aided, if need be, by local content legislation requiring foreign automakers to locate in the United States. Quite apart from the wisdom of the strategy of either the UAW or GM, these definitions of competitiveness are clearly far apart from each other. This lack of congruence reflects not only GM's status as a large multinational corporation that is struggling for renewed competitiveness, and does not want to be positioned as too much of a national actor, but also fundamentally different views on what constitutes the rights and responsibilities of U.S. labor in the auto industry. It also constitutes a potential barrier to successful implementation of GM's domestic corporate strategy. How can joint gains in the

United States be credible when the definitions of what constitutes a "gain" are so different? How can the trade-offs required to produce competitive cars in the United States (such as a revision of work rules in exchange for some form of job security) be made when quid pro quos (such as job security) are not perceived as credible?

These differences are further reinforced by continuing conflicts over what constitutes "equality of sacrifice," a principle that formed the basis for labor's concessions in the 1982 contract. When executive salaries and bonuses jump the million-dollar barrier by a large margin and when the annual direct compensation of executives is buttressed by stock option gains worth additional millions of dollars, the cleavage between management and labor inevitably increases. (This conflict is also at work at Ford, and to a lesser extent, Chrysler.)

The principles embedded in the 1984 labor settlement have the potential of bridging many of the conflicts between management and labor. These include, on management's side, recognition of labor's interest in job security as a legitimate long-term concern and the willingness to give organized labor a say in decisions related to job security, training and retraining, and job creation in a variety of joint labor-management committees. These principles were most notably represented in GM's creation of a jointly managed $1 billion fund—known as the JOBS Bank—from which wages will be paid to workers laid off because of improvements in technology and production through the introduction of further automation or through increased purchases of components from outside suppliers. On labor's side, the principles of wage restraint in economic gains and the encouragement and support of efforts at the plant level to improve operational efficiencies through such innovations as work rules changes—even if they require requests to waive, modify, or change the national agreement—were also underscored. Although these principles constitute an important step forward in GM-UAW relationships, the less-than-overwhelming 57 to 43 percent ratification vote by the UAW rank and file reveals considerable employee mistrust of GM's intentions.

There are additional aspects of GM's strategy that could be described—how GM's coalitions with Asian automakers relate to plans for increased market success in the Pacific basin; how GM's investing of $1 billion a year in its European operations helps to exploit world-scale economies and to keep Ford from subsidizing

domestic operations with overseas profits; how the $2.5 billion acqui-
sition of Electronic Data Systems and $5 billion acquisition of Hughes
Aircraft can exploit existing capabilities in large systems engineering
and electronics and push GM further into high-technology areas. But
the broad outlines of the strategy described above provide sufficient
information to assess the impact of GM's moves on its own long-term
financial and competitive position, and its relations with the UAW
and the communities where GM has historically been a major
employer.

Viewed from the perspective of its financial and commercial interests, the evolving product strategy of General Motors is astute. By
forging coalitions with Japanese and Korean automakers in the production of small cars, GM is neutralizing its competitive disadvantage
in this segment and protecting its access to first-time buyers while
effectively "liberating" resources for the more profitable, upscale car
business that has been targeted for attack by both Japanese and
European competitors.

In addition, there can be little doubt that GM is making great
progress and will continue to make progress in improving the relative cost and quality of American-produced vehicles. But the corporation is still a long way from profitably producing small cars in the
United States. Although Saturn Corporation may produce a small car
that is both profitable and competitive with Japanese models in terms
of cost and quality, GM's decision to source 600,000 fully or partially
assembled small cars from abroad reflects limited expectations for
this project over the near term. The future profitability of GM's small-
car business is, therefore, largely dependent upon its Asian strategy.

GM's production employees view this strategy with great concern.
To GM's work force, the company's Asian strategy means that most
small-car labor content is being moved offshore. Furthermore, they
view such importing and outsourcing arrangements as a clear signal
to the UAW that unless it cooperates in installing new labor-saving
technologies, increasing productivity, and reducing overall labor
costs, large-scale production of small cars will leave U.S. shores for
good. The prospect of permanently moving all small-car labor offshore and introducing automation and productivity programs at
home has created deep undercurrents of alarm within GM's domestic
work force and the UAW.

Job security was the UAW's number one collective bargaining
concern expressed at a special convention called in March 1984 to

vote on a resolution that would guide upcoming contract negotiations with GM and other domestic producers.[17] What the rank and file seemed to have heard was that GM management had not seen the need to design a strategy that appealed to labor's interests. In commenting on GM's earlier efforts to seek out suppliers and partners in low-wage areas, Lawrence (Red) Connor, president of the UAW local at GM's Wilmington, Delaware, assembly plant, said, "They have no loyalty to any country or anybody."[18] Interviewed in September 1982 after the Isuzu deal had been announced, President Douglas Fraser of the union said, "The perception of our members—and perception is what counts—was, 'They're using our money to make an investment that undercuts our job security.' "[19] These perceptions, realistic or not, must be recognized as a continuing problem, particularly when employee involvement is critical to improving on-the-job effectiveness in an industry where a 40 percent random defect rate is accepted as a norm—that is, where close to every other car built has something wrong with it that has to be fixed or fine tuned.[20]

As GM continues to pursue the importing and outsourcing element of its new small-car strategy, it will jeopardize efforts to create and maintain a broad commitment to QWL programs and other human resource initiatives essential to increase in-plant cooperation, product quality, and productivity. Since the risks of job loss will inevitably increase as the corporation responds to global competition by bringing in more foreign-made components and vehicles, the incentives for many autoworkers to participate in QWL and innovative policy-sharing experiments will tend to decline. Labor-management cooperation and massive revisions in work practices will seem "beside the point" in facilities perceived to be vulnerable to permanent closure, unless guarantees of employment in other accessible GM facilities is assured.

Without the support and cooperation of labor, GM risks being caught up in a vicious circle. High labor costs may well drive GM further toward outsourcing major components and importing small cars from abroad, despite its parallel strategy of corporatewide technological innovation aimed at reducing labor and product costs and preserving its domestic manufacturing base. In the meantime, GM's capacity to maintain its competitiveness as a domestic producer may erode further, since many of the benefits of manufacturing both small and large cars in the same company would be lost. As the production of small cars and major components continues to move offshore, it would only be a matter of time before selected portions of GM's larger-car business began to follow suit. Naturally, Ford and Chrysler would face similar pressures as GM in its search for less costly components and fully assembled products, and it is to this possibility—and its inevitable impact on the utilization of domestic manufacturing capacity and employment—that we now turn.

FORD'S RESPONSE TO NEW COMPETITIVE CONDITIONS

The success of Japanese automakers in the U.S. market and GM's subsequent decision to move aggressively in forging low-cost supply links with Japanese and Korean partners left Ford with two options: to pursue its own coalitions with Japanese, Taiwanese, and Korean automakers, thereby jeopardizing relations with labor, which have been critical for improving product quality and costs; or to cut back its importation of major components and plans for importing small cars from the Far East and Mexico, thereby serving labor's interests but losing competitive ground to GM and Chrysler, who are tapping lower-cost sources of supply. Strategic logic points toward the first option; so, too, do Ford's recent actions.

Although Ford is the nation's fifth-largest industrial firm in terms of sales revenues, it is greatly affected by the moves of GM, the nation's second-largest firm. Ford is a considerably smaller giant than GM, especially in the United States, where it produces only about one-half as many vehicles as GM. Additionally, Ford's production has been weighted toward the small-car market, where margins are lower and where GM's Asian strategy is focused. Small (subcompact) cars represent almost one-third of Ford's U.S. output but less than 8 percent of GM's production. Meanwhile, Ford's overall share of the U.S. passenger car market has declined from a traditional 25 percent to 19 percent during the past decade, while GM's share has eroded to a still-commanding 41 percent. Finally, Ford has less financial slack than GM, despite its recent surge in profitability. Ford's losses of $1.5 billion in 1980 were the second largest in U.S. industrial history, and another $1.7 billion was lost in 1981–1982. Between 1980 and 1982, Ford's credit rating was downgraded three times. Although Ford reported a profit in 1983, and was able to recoup all of its 1980–1982 losses by June 1984, debt made up almost 30 percent of Ford's total capitalization in contrast to only 20 percent for GM in 1985. This meant that Ford had a somewhat heavier burden of interest payments and less absorption power for economic shock than GM.

Ford faces tough competition from GM's small car imports in the North American market because of its cost position. Although the Escort had become the country's best-selling car by 1982, its variable profit margin was not sufficient to cover Ford's overhead and fund the development of its replacement, according to Harold A. (Red) Poling, Ford's new president and former executive vice-president for North American automotive operations.[21] Studies by various Wall Street analysts indicated that Ford was failing to recover fully allocated costs by as much as $300 to $400 on each Escort/Lynx subcompact produced in the United States during 1982 and 1983.

In market segments other than subcompacts, Ford also earned less variable profit per unit than either GM or Chrysler during the early 1980s. To reduce overhead, Ford permanently closed eight domestic plants (including three assembly plants) and has cut hourly and salaried employees by close to 45 percent and 24 percent since 1979, respectively. As a result of this massive cost reduction program, Ford has lowered its break-even point—that is, the sales volume required to cover its costs—by more than one-third since 1979. In the cost reduction race, however, GM was close behind, and Ford's best-selling car—the Escort—still appeared unprofitable on a fully allocated cost basis by the mid-1980s.

A similar picture of Ford's competitiveness emerges from an examination of its product revolution. From the end of the 1977 model year through 1982, Ford introduced seventeen new cars and six new trucks, representing an investment of nearly $10 billion. By early 1984, the new Tempo/Topaz line of compacts was making money on an accounted basis. According to Ford's customer surveys, the quality of Ford's cars improved an average of 59 percent from 1980 to 1982. And in 1985, readers of *Consumer's Digest* voted Ford the top U.S. car maker with fewer defects than either GM or Chrysler. Many of Ford's new products, however, were launched into market segments where GM traditionally held the dominant position and where the Japanese were introducing many of their new, upgraded models. Even though the new midsize Taurus/Sable line was launched with notable success in early 1986, GM plans to outspend Ford two to one on new products and plants for the rest of the decade.

Overseas, Ford is under pressure from GM, especially in the United Kingdom, where GM is undercutting Ford in the fleet business, which constitutes 70 percent of new car sales. Ford's European operations have historically been one of its strengths, and they generated excess cash flow and loans to carry North American automotive operations through their worst years, in 1981 and 1982. During the 1960s and 1970s, a well-conceived European strategy won Ford a leading market position in Europe. After reorganizing production to serve the European continent more efficiently, Ford gambled $1.1 billion on a new front-wheel-drive car to be built in an untried facility in Spain. The gamble paid off, and the Fiesta soon recorded the highest unit sales of any new European car in history. The launch of the European Escort in 1981 was also a great success. The new Escort won for Ford the prestigious Car of the Year Award. By 1983 Ford ranked number two (behind Regie Renault) among European automakers; but during the first quarter of 1984, GM's investments and substantial marketing support began to pay off as it edged ahead of Ford. Although Ford managed to beat out GM by 75,000 units in the first half of 1984 and to take over as Europe's number one sales leader by the end of the year, GM's competitive threat was becoming increasingly dangerous. Although GM was not profitable in Europe, its plan to invest over $1 billion a year in its European business through 1986–1987 will intensify the battle for market share among the six leading European competitors and exacerbate the problem of substantial excess production capacity in the European auto industry. Thus, Ford's fight to preserve its market position and shore up eroding margins has only begun.

Fortunately for Ford, it has been able to run a profitable operation in Europe, whereas GM and several other major competitors were operating in the red. None of the leading European competitors, however, including Ford, was able to earn its cost of capital.

Although the difficult competitive situations at home and abroad would seem to dictate improving cost position by sourcing components and vehicles for the U.S. market from offshore, Ford has been slow to do so. Until 1985, Ford limited itself to importing manual transaxles from Mazda, its Japanese affiliate, and plans to import some four-cylinder engines and a low number of subcompacts from Mexico. This initial reticence to increase its reliance on low-cost sources of supply can be explained not only by Ford's low level of vertical integration relative to GM but also by the company's emphasis on improving relationships with organized labor during the early 1980s. "The outsourcing issue is key to Ford's relationship with the

UAW," said Peter J. Pestillo, Ford's vice-president for labor relations in 1982. He added:

A simple economic analysis might say to bring in the top of the line from Europe (say, the Granada from Germany) and the bottom of the line from Japan. But we can't pursue a maximization strategy. My position is to back off from the economics and face the trade-offs, because you cannot implement a pure economic strategy. We must search for some equipoise—some compromise position to keep a strike from happening.[22]

The company also made significant efforts to respond to labor's concerns about working conditions and job security as the auto crisis deepened after the second oil shock. In 1979, Ford and the United Auto Workers agreed to a joint employee involvement (EI) program designed to let workers participate more fully in the work environment (GM's QWL program was launched six years earlier). By the end of 1982, more than 10,000 employees were active in a thousand voluntary EI problem-solving groups in sixty-eight plants. Furthermore, Ford agreed to restrict plant closings resulting from outsourcing for the life of the 1982 contract, thereby setting the pattern for GM. Ford continued this guarantee against plant closings in its 1984 labor contract; General Motors did not.

In addition to curtailing Ford's international outsourcing option, the 1982 and 1984 labor agreements codified a new standard of behavior for Ford management. The contract language was open to wide ranges of interpretation and various degrees of compliance by both parties, so the success of this new relationship depended entirely upon cooperative attitudes and continued good will between the parties. In speaking about new attitudes, Pestillo said:

We've got to stop talking about rights and to start talking of interests. Whose interests are affected? If it's the union's, then their voice should be heard. An outsourcing strategy doesn't serve our interests because it doesn't serve the UAW's interests. We have to accommodate interests and build a new political alliance. . . . My goals are to retain the good will that has been built up and to prevent conflict over outsourcing.[23]

Overall, the company chose in the 1982 contract to begin a process leading to increased competitiveness through improved labor relations, rather than to go for a quick fix of draconian wage cuts. As Pestillo said, "We bet that deep wage cuts wouldn't survive adversity."[24] As a result of this approach to contract talks, the new master agreement stressed joint problem resolution outside the normal collective bargaining process, as well as concepts of job protection and income security, profit sharing, and employee development and training. For example, the parties agreed to establish a training center that would administer a new program designed to provide counseling, training, retraining, and developmental opportunities for both active employees and employees displaced by new production techniques, shifts in customer product preferences, or facility closings. By the end of 1984, over 11,000 employees had gone through these programs. In addition, Ford and the UAW agreed to establish mutual growth forums, to meet periodically at the local and national levels as a new adjunct to the collective bargaining process. The role of the local forums, operating in about 65 percent of Ford's facilities by the end of 1983, was to explore ways of improving two-way communications and to discuss a plant's general operations, the quality of its products, and methods of enhancing competitiveness and improving job security. Both the local and national forums began to share formerly confidential business-related and other information. As part of the forum process, a UAW officer was invited to address the Ford board of directors semiannually.

Many of these concepts and innovative practices were carried over in the 1984 contract. This time, however, the employee-retraining and job security package basically followed the pattern set by GM (the so-called JOBS program).

Until recently, Ford's response to GM's small-car strategy has been largely shaped by its evolving labor relations policies, specifically, its promises not to close any plants because of the outsourcing of components or the importing of cars built abroad. Other restraining forces include Ford's need to recover previous small-car investments in the United States and federal corporate average fuel economy (CAFE) regulations.

Today, however, the power of these forces to shape Ford's strategy is weakening. In the eyes of Ford, General Motors is now in a position to field a broad mix of relatively low-cost small cars. Depending on how Japanese automakers and GM eventually set their prices in the United States, Ford is concerned that its competitors may reinvest large "trading profits" from their small cars in another round of small (and large) car development programs. Thus, unless Ford plays its international outsourcing and importing cards to match the delivered cost of its competitors' small cars, it may not be able to earn sufficient profit to finance required investments in the next round of new product programs. Ford's fears are well founded: underinvestment relative to competition is a direct form of market share liquidation that is unsustainable for very long. If Ford were to continue its largely self-imposed constraint on additional outsourcing, then its only option would be "segment retreat" into a fewer number of market segments where Ford retains a competitive advantage. But since volume, economies of scale, and commonality of parts are keys to success in this industry, segment retreat would exacerbate Ford's cost problem and lead to further strategic decay.

Significantly, Ford's international resource base is capable of responding to GM's small-car game plan. In the Far East, Ford has already embarked on several joint ventures with Mazda, in which it acquired a 25 percent interest in 1979. Today, Ford is assembling a modified Mazda car in seven Asia-Pacific nations and distributing it in thirty-five countries. In addition, Ford announced that its joint venture partner in Taiwan, Ford Lio Ho Motor Company, plans to expand its subcompact-car capacity, manufacture a new model designed cooperatively by Mazda and Ford, and export about 30,000 vehicles a year. Ford declines to say which export markets it has in mind, but does not rule out the United States. Finally, Ford and Mazda have cooperated in developing the Festiva, a small car to be built by Kia Motors in South Korea and sold by Ford dealers in the United States in the late 1980s.

In Latin America, Ford maintains major operations in Argentina, where it is the market leader, and in Brazil and Mexico. Four-cylinder engines for Ford's North American assembly operations have been manufactured in Brazil since the mid-1970s. In 1982, the company announced plans to build a $365 million plant in Mexico that would produce engines for the United States as well as the Mexican market. In January 1984, Ford announced a $500 million investment in another Mexican plant that would assemble a Mazda-designed, sporty subcompact, using major components imported from Japan. Although Ford has said the venture is the result of a Mexican decree that in effect forces automakers there to build new plants and to expand their exports, the labor cost of less than four dollars per hour in Mexico probably played a role in Ford's decision.

Clearly, these resources and international relationships offer Ford many offshore options. The link with Mazda gives Ford a chance to bring partially or fully assembled small cars into the United States with attractive profit margins, since it takes Mazda 25 percent fewer labor hours than Ford to build a subcompact and at significantly lower wage rates. Like GM, Ford can use its Japanese and Taiwanese connections to develop new car models for worldwide sales, thereby spreading engineering and design costs over a larger number of units, hedging marketing risks, and reducing component costs by using global designs. Even for cars assembled in the United States, Ford can benefit economically from purchasing more components from Japan and Taiwan (at present, only 5 percent of total manufacturing costs). This is a card that Ford, until recently, has chosen not to play as aggressively as GM, even though then-chairman Philip Caldwell told shareholders at the 1982 annual meeting that Ford must seek more economic supply sources or "we won't be around to compete."

Caldwell does not stand alone on this issue. Some Ford executives, such as David N. McCammon, Ford's vice-president and controller, think that increased outsourcing is a requirement for staying in business.[25] Without profits the company cannot expect to raise new money for future car programs; therefore, they argue, Ford should not tie up its capital in plant and equipment, which the competition can render obsolete. In November 1983, Donald E. Peterson, then-president of Ford and now its chairman, lent public support to this argument by saying that the company had been negotiating with its Japanese affiliate about importing small cars under the Ford nameplate.[26] In November 1984, Mazda announced that it would assemble fancy compact cars in an idle Ford plant. Ford expected to buy cars from the new Mazda plant and sell them under its own nameplate. This announcement appeared to confirm rumors that Mazda may produce Ford's new Mustang at a domestic Ford plant using Mazda designs and major components.[27] It also lent credibility to an *Automotive News* report that "nearly half of Ford's U.S. new car programs between now [1984] and 1990, including several luxury models, will be done wholly or in part overseas."[28] Finally, in December 1985, Ford president Harold Poling said that Ford could import about 350,000 cars a year by 1989.[29] If the Escort replacement, currently scheduled for 1991, is sourced overseas, that would raise the total of Ford cars coming from multinational ventures to about one-half of Ford's current annual U.S. sales.

By the mid-1980s, Ford made it clear that it had the capacity and the will to implement a GM-style importing and outsourcing strategy—one that could result in six to seven models being developed and at least partially sourced from both Ford Europe and the Far East, along with a coproduction arrangement with Mazda in the United States. Although the future outlines of Ford's small-car program are still unclear, as is the precise number of vehicles involved, it appears that Ford has been either inspired or alarmed by GM's Asian strategy.

CHRYSLER'S GAME PLAN AND PROSPECTS

Like Ford, Chrysler made a dramatic return to profitability that masks enduring competitive problems. Indeed, the company's public policy proposals and antitrust lawsuits accurately reveal its anxiety about its competitive position.

In 1983 and 1984, Chrysler showed the largest percent increase of the Big Three in car and truck sales. The once failing firm also posted record net earnings, boosted in part by tax credits stemming from unused operating loss carry-forwards. As a result, Chrysler was able to repay $1.2 billion of federally guaranteed loans years earlier than planned as well as launch new automotive products, such as the first American-built front-wheel-drive sports cars, new minivans, a new front-wheel-drive sedan, and a new Mitsubishi import. By July 1984, Chrysler was sufficiently creditworthy that it could line up a $1.1 billion credit line with fifty-seven U.S. and foreign banks, the first it was able to arrange since 1977. Another $300 million was added to this credit line by the end of the year. The company also began adding new capacity to produce an extra 700,000 cars and trucks a year.

Chrysler added over $1.4 billion of debt in 1985, roughly half of which was raised by selling the largest single issue of thirty-year, fixed rate debentures ever by an industrial company. Although Chrysler claimed that the funds were raised at an opportune time to guard against potential recession and acquisitions, some of the funds were available for the company's program to buy back almost half of the fifty-seven million shares of common stock issued during its restructuring. Chrysler officials also believed that such a repurchase program was another important step in cleaning up the remnants— in this case, the dilution of common stock values—of its earlier financial distress.

The turnaround in Chrysler's performance and the emergence of Lee Iacocca as a national celebrity create the impression that the company can prosper as an independent, *wide-line* automaker. The truth of this, however, is still in doubt. To be sure, Chrysler, with fewer plants to retool, can expect to pay less for completely new platforms or model lines than the $2 billion to $3 billion that Ford has spent on its new subcompact program. Nevertheless, between 1985 and 1987, Chrysler will have to launch new small and midsize car lines, costing close to $2 billion, and develop new platforms to replace Chrysler's aging entries in the large and prestige car segments. (Chrysler's large and prestige cars were based either on old, rear-wheel-drive designs or on stretched versions of the relatively newer compact-car platform, called the K-body.) Taking this conservative estimate of $2 billion for both the subcompact and compact replacements and then adding sufficient funds to cover incremental additions to capacity, plus adding dividends on newly issued preferred stock and the repayment of over $300 million in debt due by 1986 and also the repurchase of common stock, Chrysler will need to pay out nearly $5 billion over the next few years to finance new product development and to meet its financial commitments. This conservative estimate is significantly below the $9.5 billion capital investment program between 1984 and 1988 announced by Chrysler, and several billion dollars a year below the planned investments of GM and Ford in their modernization and new product programs.[30]

It will take several years of back-to-back, *after-tax* earnings of $2 billion per year, or a 200 percent increase over the 1983 *tax-free* results, to finance Chrysler's minimum-level program. During this time, Chrysler will begin paying taxes as it uses up its remaining operating loss carry-forwards and its competitors will of course be refurbishing their product lines (GM at the rate of $5 billion to $6 billion per year). Japanese automakers will also provide increased competition as voluntary export restraints are relaxed. Thus, even assuming a smashing success for Chrysler's newly introduced and future models, its financial position remains uncertain. For example, the company's profits *after tax* declined in 1985 by 33 percent to $1.6 billion, despite a modest increase in unit volume. In addition, with Chrysler's cash flow in 1985 only about 40 percent of estimated capital spending and a total debt-to-equity ratio of 63 percent—in comparison with 20 percent for GM and 28 percent for Ford—Chrysler has a more limited capacity to withstand an unexpected competitive or economic shock than do its two domestic rivals.[31]

Given Chrysler's enormous cash needs and financial uncertainties, it shares with its stronger domestic competitors a serious problem in balancing the interest of labor with the dictates of production economics. Beginning in the early 1970s, Chrysler pursued a series of "fix or fold" strategies built around concepts of domestic contraction, disintegration, and international outsourcing. Jobs have, in essence, been traded for a run at corporate revival.

There is a special twist to the Chrysler case, though. When the company was shrinking its operations, the government pressured the UAW to make wage concessions on two different occasions as part of a loan guarantee process designed by Congress to preserve jobs. The irony is that jobs were not preserved because of the company's need to close down obsolete facilities, retire excess manufacturing capacity, and so slim down the salaried work force. In fact, Chrysler now employs less than one-half the number of employees it did when the Chrysler Loan Guarantee Act of 1979 was passed by Congress. Many of those employees who remained at Chrysler are antagonistic to management. The best indicators of this antagonism are the razor thin approval of the 1979 labor contract, the wholesale rejection of the September version of the 1982 contract, and the demand for up-front cash rather than profit sharing in the 1983 contract extension. Chrysler's employees are also committed to regaining and preserving wage parity with the employees at Ford and GM, even though this could destroy a significant competitive advantage for their employer.

To complicate matters further, the emerging small-car strategies of General Motors and Ford, coupled with the expiration of auto import quotas, will inevitably force Chrysler to expand its current reliance on assembled cars and major components imported from Japan, thereby threatening domestic job security. Since Chrysler already imports 14 percent of its unit sales from Japan, additional importing does not require a significant change in either corporate policy or practice.

It is therefore doubtful that Chrysler will finish the decade with either a broad line, an advantageous labor cost position, or the capacity to withstand unforeseen economic shocks. If the "new Chrysler Corporation" does remain an independent automaker, it will be as a small U.S. producer whose narrow product line will need to be buttressed by imported vehicles designed and produced by others. Whether it be independent or merged into another company, Chrysler will remain a shadow of its former self.

Showing the optimism of a successful turnaround manager, Harold

K. Sperlich, Chrysler's president, has explained that by closing twenty plants and cutting the work force in half, the company is now able to break even at a volume of 1.1 million units. Sperlich calculates Chrysler will have to maintain at least a 10 percent share of the market to cover its fixed costs of $3.5 billion. Here is his explanation of how Chrysler plans to maintain its share:

> We've got to give away the top 10 percent of the market—that is, the biggest cars and medium and heavy trucks. As for the bottom 20 to 25 percent, here you're up against the best of Japan with a $2,000 cost advantage.
>
> You're out of your mind to try to beat the Japanese on price, but we do need product representation for our dealers and customers. We use cars imported from Mitsubishi to cover this segment. We have a $800 a car variable margin here.
>
> As for the remaining 65 to 70 percent of the market, the question is how to get our desired share while minimizing our investment. The trick is to stay lean and get some scale economies similar to those enjoyed by GM by keeping things *simple*. *Focus* is also a key word for us. We are focusing on front-wheel-drive cars with high fuel efficiency. We are giving up the V8 engine, for example, to invest in four-cylinder engines. We're focusing on vans, too. Finally, while we will manufacture some trucks for ourselves, we will import small trucks from Japan. We are trying to make our approach to this part of the market unique in terms of our quality and warranties.[32]

Sperlich also explains that at a break-even volume of 1.1 million units, Chrysler's fixed costs represent $3,000 of the price of each vehicle. He estimates that if the company could increase its volume 50 percent, each unit would only have to contribute $2,000 to fixed costs, thereby "releasing" a $1,000 for-profit margin.

Tom Denomme, Chrysler's vice-president for strategic planning, is less sanguine than Sperlich about the company's long-term prospects as an independent automaker. In his view, the United States can only afford two large domestic auto manufacturers: "If we concede an import share of 30 to 35 percent and a 45 percent share to GM, then there is only room for one other firm to be economically viable. Ford and Chrysler cannot coexist as majors."[33]

Understandably, Denomme argues that the "new Chrysler" needs a merger or additional joint ventures to help it develop its product line. A senior manufacturing official echoes Denomme's opinion and concedes that Chrysler needs an overseas partner in the bottom quarter of the market. "At current volumes," he explained, "self-manufacture is vastly more expensive than purchasing components from suppliers who operate on a larger scale."[34] This is why Chrysler is deepening its relationship with Mitsubishi and other partners.

In addition to the 140,000 assembled cars and trucks supplied by Mitsubishi, Chrysler's Japanese partner supplied 2.6 liter engines and other components in 1985. Chrysler also purchased engines from VW and Peugeot (in which Chrysler holds a 15 percent stake), CV joints for front-wheel-drive cars from Peugeot, and a variety of parts for a wide array of domestic and overseas suppliers.

As for the future, Chrysler announced plans in 1985 to form a joint venture in Bloomington, Indiana, with Mitsubishi to coproduce 180,000 cars by 1988. In addition, Chrysler is planning to set up a joint venture with Korea's Sansung Group to supply 80,000 to 100,000 fully assembled units per year. Chrysler's evolving "coalition strategy" has the effect of both lowering the amount of so-called local components and providing less job security for its employees.

Chrysler's work force can hardly be said to be cooperative. Given the company's record of losses and near bankruptcy, one might expect production employees to be understanding of Chrysler's financial and competitive position. But this has not been the case. The wage concessions required by the Chrysler Loan Guarantee Act were approved by a bare 51 percent of those voting in 1979. The initial 1982 labor contract was defeated by a margin of more than two to one. By then, job security had become a major issue for the union. The UAW-represented work force at Chrysler had shrunk to about 45,000 (down from 125,000 in 1978), and the union was naturally concerned about plant closings. Production employees also wanted to recoup some of the wage concessions made during the last three contracts. The average Chrysler assembly-line employee received hourly wages of $9.07 in 1982, compared with $11.76 for GM employees. Finally, Chrysler autoworkers wanted to preserve their hard-won medical and pension benefits, which were costing Chrysler $325 million per year, or about $300 per vehicle.

Although the tentative agreement reached in September 1982 would have restored cost-of-living adjustment payments and provided quarterly wage bonuses if the company were profitable enough, the proposed contract was overwhelmingly rejected by the rank and file. Repercussions were felt in Canada, where contract talks stalled and the union voted to go out on strike. A subsequent proposal by Chrysler, substituting up-front pay increases for profit sharing and containing other provisions leading to a 15 percent wage increase over the life of the eighteen-month contract, was accepted by a two-to-one margin. The Chrysler workers were clearly not betting on the future profitability of their employer.

When an extension of the Chrysler labor agreement was negotiated in September 1983, up-front cash rather than a profit-sharing plan was again the autoworkers' objective. To avoid a work stoppage when two new models were scheduled to go into production, Chrysler was forced to agree to a contract that would raise labor costs 29 percent by 1985. That agreement had the effect of narrowing the company's labor cost advantage to $1.12 by September 1984 when its rivals' labor contracts were to expire. In the 1985 negotiations, the UAW was finally successful in gaining, among other things, wage parity with GM employees by the end of the contract period.

Such an agreement could not have come at a worse time. With the industry having passed through its cyclical peak and the company committed to a large capital investment program, the company's relative labor cost advantage was completely eroded. This will have the effect of pushing Chrysler further and faster into the arms of its Asian partners. In turn, Chrysler's production employees will feel increasingly left out of the company's future. It is not surprising that Chrysler's labor relations staff noted that grievances and absentees were back up to "unacceptable levels" by 1985.

Throughout the early 1980s, Chrysler recognized that its competitive position and financial prospects could be substantially aided by the tax, trade, and antitrust policies of the U.S. government. After several years of keeping a low profile in Washington, Chrysler went on record in 1982 in support of a program to strengthen the auto industry. First, Chrysler argued that the U.S. government should collect a tax on Japanese cars sold in this country to compensate for the estimated $1,750 in tax revenues that an American-made car would have contributed in manufacturers' and employees' taxes to local, state, and federal governments. In addition, the company called for consumer tax credits to encourage consumers to purchase fuel-efficient, American-built cars. Chrysler also helped found in 1983 the Basic Industries Coalition, a group seeking tax breaks for "smoke-stack" America. Finally, Chrysler began touting a new protectionist machine. Called the U.S. Trade Policy Council, it is intended to be a coalition of businesses and unions for "mobilizing the American people to fight back against unfair foreign competition." In marked contrast to Ford and GM, Chrysler advocated reducing Japanese imports to 15 percent on the U.S. market (their share in mid-1984 was just under 20 percent).

Chrysler also vehemently opposed the GM-Toyota joint venture on antitrust grounds. In its lawsuit the company argued, among other things, that GM's cost savings from using an existing design and buying major components in Japan would force any new, domestically built small car into an untenable position. Chrysler stated publicly that if the courts allowed the GM-Toyota deal to proceed, the company would be forced to substitute a Mitsubishi model for its current line of American-made subcompacts (Omni/Horizon).

By 1985, Chrysler's tax, trade, and antitrust initiatives waned as the company redoubled its own efforts to force coalitions with Asian car makers. It was a simple case of joining the parade rather than trying to redirect it.

TRENDS AND PROSPECTS

There are common themes in the emerging strategies of the Big Three. None of the Big Three can afford to live with its current cost structure. Thus, each is restructuring the way it does business in the United States. Each has retired inefficient production capacity and is now automating its remaining facilities. All are lowering their fixed costs by reducing the number of personnel and the level of vertical integration. As a result, volume required for profitable operation has been cut. Since 1979, the number of new car sales required for the industry as a whole to break even has declined by one-third.

Each of the Big Three has also launched an unprecedented number of new car models. In doing so, they appear to have recognized the inadequacy of past quality control practices and the need for new approaches to remedy the situation. Robert Decker, GM's vice-president for quality and reliability, whose position was created in 1982, has argued that management must accept a large share of the blame. "For years management said to the workers, 'We design the product, we design the tools and we bring 'em out here and you just push the button and we'll make whatever comes out,' " he said. "Quality wasn't at the top of the list. We were doing better than anyone else. Selling more than anyone else. Selling all we could build. We were making lots of money. So why do anything different? Now, however, all that has changed. The quality push won't ever stop.

We've really learned our lesson. The competition won't ever let it slacken."[35]

In addition, GM and Ford have managed to improve their labor relations and have made radical, procompetitive changes in the way that their business policies are formulated and implemented. The information and policy sharing that followed the innovative 1982 and 1984 labor contracts at Ford and GM demonstrates that many auto executives have developed a realistic view of their enterprise as an assemblage of overlapping and competing interests. The creation of QWL and EI programs, mutual growth forums, and a wide variety of joint labor-management committees demonstrate that corporate management is increasingly willing to accommodate the interests of employees and their union in the conduct of ongoing operations. So, too, does the current presence of the UAW's president on Chrysler's board of directors indicate management's willingness to listen. Problem solving and negotiation also seem to be slowly but steadily entering the relationships between management and labor, thereby pushing the less effective "command and control" approach to administrative leadership into the shadows of history. Importantly, each of these changes in industrial governance can facilitate the exchange of the kind of quid pro quos between labor and management necessary to regain global competitiveness.

Despite these advances, the Big Three remain uncompetitive in cost and quality in the small-car business. Each of the Big Three understands this and is relying more and more on coproduction and importing arrangements with Japanese automakers. All totaled, by 1990 the Big Three will import about 820,000 cars for their dealers and coproduce another 630,000 cars with Japanese and Korean partners, a combined amount greater than 10 percent of the estimated sales of passenger cars. With the possible exception of GM's Saturn program, most of the new product investment of the Big Three is committed to midsize, large, luxury, and sports cars. Meanwhile, the Japanese are blanketing the small and midsize car markets with an increasing number of models. From 1980 to 1985, Japanese and Korean automakers introduced five times as many small cars and three times as many midsize cars as U.S. producers. New product announcements for the 1986–1990 period show Japan with twice as many new cars planned.

The implications of this trend are spelled out in detail in Appendix A, which analyzes competitive product programs and anticipated domestic production for 1990. The resultant scenario shows that if the current pattern of new product introduction continues, U.S. automakers will either abandon or be forced to abandon most of the nation's small-car manufacturing capacity by 1990 in a free trade environment. Utilization of anticipated small-car capacity will be a meager 14 percent. Only federal CAFE regulations, which forbid U.S. automakers from counting new vehicles with less than 75 percent local manufacturing content in their corporate fuel-economy averages, will keep U.S. automakers from totally abandoning the domestic production of small cars. Again according to this scenario, U.S. automakers will only utilize 43 percent of their anticipated midsize-car manufacturing capacity in 1990, if current trends continue (see Appendix A, Exhibit 7). Based upon these production estimates, the employment of hourly and salaried workers involved in the production and assembly of automobiles at plants operated by GM, Ford, Chrysler, and AMC, which declined from 700,000 in 1978 to 480,000 in 1983, will decline an additional 140,000, to 340,000 jobs in 1990 (see Appendix A, Exhibit 9).

This scenario, based on conservative assumptions, poses great risk for the Big Three and the nation as a whole. If U.S. automakers cannot manufacture small cars profitably at home, they will eventually lose the capacity to compete profitably in the midsize market, which is already under attack by the Japanese. Many manufacturing processes are common to both market segments. In addition, components subject to economies of scale, such as air compressors, fuel injection systems, and transmissions, are also used across several car platforms. Finally, if the Big Three end up importing significant portions of their product lines and major components from abroad, the zone of overlapping interests between management and labor, as well as many state and local governments in the industrial Midwest, will shrink rather than expand. Efforts to reduce domestic manufacturing costs and increase craftsmanship across all car lines through innovative industrial governance processes will then be jeopardized. This problem is recognized by U.S. auto executives. Lloyd Reuss, the first head of GM's new Chevrolet-Pontiac-Canada Group, has said, "We cannot get out of the domestic, small-car-manufacturing business because credibility with our work force is key to our future success as an automaker."[36] But the scenario for 1990 suggests that this will be an extremely difficult philosophy to live by.

The prospects for the Big Three are complicated by a highly uncertain economic and political environment. As the auto industry enters its next round of global competition, producing new car models—whether produced at home or abroad—will become even riskier than in the past. For one thing, energy prices and availability, which influence consumer demand in powerful ways, are especially unpredictable. Without exception, U.S. automakers recall the period between December 1978 and June 1979. At the end of 1978, U.S. producers were rationing their popular gas-guzzling V8 engines to meet federal fuel-economy standards The U.S. consumer had swung back to big cars after the supply interruption of 1974; Japanese imports were languishing on West Coast docks with a 148-day inventory of unsold cars. Six months later, V8 engines were obsolete and the Japanese inventory was sold out. Today, American automakers are concerned about another such swing—this time downward. "We are humble about our forecasting ability after going through the 1970s," said Ford's David McCammon. "The difficult variable to get a hold of is energy prices—and to a lesser extent U.S. energy policy."[37]

At General Motors, John F. Smith, Jr., formerly director of worldwide product planning and currently president of GM of Canada, shares McCammon's view. "Clearly energy has caused a significant change in the industry in terms of its planning process," says Smith. According to Smith—whose office wall sports a slogan reading, "No amount of planning will ever replace dumb luck"—about six years ago General Motors adopted a system of forecasting that utilized three scenarios, looking at high, medium, and low ranges for the economy and energy. Even this system, however, was not able to anticipate the changes in energy price and availability that actually occurred. "Today what we are dealing with is below our low, and it's very troublesome to deal with," says Smith. "How long does this last? Is it going to last five years, two years, ten years? That is the difficult part of this thing. I find energy to be difficult. Other people say it does not matter that much. I think it matters a hell of a lot."[38]

In fact, energy not only matters a lot, but in a lot of different ways. From the time when a new car is conceived until it finally appears in the market, a change in energy prices can make it miss the market— or make the market miss it. Again, swings in energy price and availability can create unexpected markets for entire new lines of cars and make obsolete current production capacity for existing lines. Uncertainty over energy swings also burdens U.S. automakers with the tangible cost of maintaining a large and more flexible, but more costly production capability to cover the full range of possible energy futures. GM's Smith explained, "We are carrying more product lines today than we were before the energy situation descended on us. We are carrying all kinds of product lines. There is a cost to that. The result is that we carry a higher fixed cost base in order to have that flexibility."[39]

The sensitivity and the volatility of the energy issue illustrate only one element of a larger problem: the difficulty U.S. automakers face in assessing future demand in the world auto market. The range of published forecasts of worldwide demand for autos illustrates the enormous uncertainty that afflicts the industry in this basic building block of operations. For 1985, reliable and credible published reports of worldwide demand for autos and trucks began at a low of 35.8 million units and climbed to a high of 57.9 million units. For 1990, the range of forecasts is even greater: from a low of 31.2 million to a high of 92.7 million units. In the North American market alone, the spread presented by forecasts is just as large: for 1985, demand forecasts ranged from 11.9 million units to 15 million units; for 1990, they range from 9.4 million units to 24.1 million units.

The gap in these forecasts and the uncertainty they reflect pose major problems for U.S. automakers. Although automakers still derive much of their competitive advantage from the sheer scale of their operations, the cost of a mistake in actually deploying and operating the facilities is steadily increasing—a 30 percent increase in the penalty for error in the past five years according to GM.

The involvement of governments is another uncertainty influencing the future of auto competition. Around the world, the auto industry is a major source of employment. In 1981, for example, the world auto industry and its direct suppliers employed roughly 6.5 million people building and assembling vehicles. These jobs are not taken lightly by their governments. In a future of intensifying global competition among automakers, government intervention in a variety of ways is increasingly likely. The competition of the late 1970s and early 1980s has already heightened trade tensions as governments seek to protect their domestic producers from import penetration. Virtually all the developing markets of any size—Brazil, Mexico, Argentina, Korea, Taiwan, Venezuela—have adopted high tariffs, quotas, or local content legislation designed to capture jobs for their country in auto production. In addition, traditional free traders,

such as the United States, West Germany, Canada, and the Nether-
lands, have recently resorted to a variety of protectionist measures to
restrain Japanese imports. Other Western European countries, such
as France, Italy, and the United Kingdom, have longstanding agreements with the Japanese to limit imports. As the trade issue has
flared, governments have sought to use other instruments to support
their industries: direct grants, tax incentives, and bail-outs have
become increasingly common. Governments around the world appear
intent on capturing a piece of the auto industry or keeping what they
already have.

The uncertain economics and politics of the auto industry make
forward planning for the small, midsize, and large car business a
highly tentative game. Some cards, however, have already been
played. As a result, it now appears that a large portion of U.S. small-
car production will move offshore. A significant portion of domestic
production capacity for midsize cars is also at risk. The anticipated
two million cars produced by foreign automakers in North America
by 1990 (see Appendix A, Exhibit 6) will not replace the anticipated
losses of U.S. automotive production. Most of the high-value-added
components in foreign models produced in North America will still
be imported from abroad. Whether or not the Big Three, together
with the UAW and public policymakers, can successfully defend the
rest of its domestic manufacturing base is therefore the critical question for the remainder of the 1980s.

CHAPTER 7

Choices and Dilemmas of the United Auto Workers

While the financial crisis of the early 1980s has subsided, the United Auto Workers (UAW) has not matched the Big Three's return to prosperity. Record profits have not restored employment, and the automakers' drive to improve competitiveness is likely to come at the expense of still more jobs. Most analysts agree that technological change and competitive onslaught from East Asia will cause further employment losses in the auto industry, perhaps as many as 200,000 additional jobs by 1990.[1]

At the same time as its absolute numbers (and financial resources) are dwindling, the union's relative strength in the industry is eroding. Although at least five Japanese automakers will operate assembly plants in the United States by the early 1990s, to date none has agreed to recognize the UAW in plants that will not be jointly operated with American partners. Unless the union is successful in organizing these new plants, its ability to influence the U.S. automakers' decisions and policies may be in jeopardy.

In these circumstances, the UAW is facing some hard choices. Since employment levels seem destined to fall, should the union try to delay the process by negotiating job guarantees, or should it expedite the inevitable while maintaining high levels of compensation for current membership? How far should the union go in cooperating with management to improve productivity and competitive performance? Should the union give up or modify its traditional demands for guaranteed wage hikes in return for profit sharing or other forms of contingent compensation? Can the UAW continue to maintain its tradition of industrywide pattern bargaining as more nonunionized foreign automakers locate their operations here?

The UAW is grappling with these problems and dilemmas at a time of great vulnerability. Declining membership and income in the 1980s will make it more difficult for the union to achieve the solutions to the auto crisis that it would most like to see. Although it has tried valiantly to stem the pressures on job levels and on its control of labor in the industry, the UAW has limited ability to shape the course of events through conventional techniques of collective bargaining, political lobbying, and organizing drives. And as yet, the union has not found a strategy that will allow it to control its own destiny.

THE UAW AT FIFTY

The UAW marked its fiftieth birthday in 1986. The world in which it now lives is radically different from the one in which it grew up. Public support of the labor movement is ebbing, and trade union membership in the United States has been in continuous decline for the past quarter century. In 1955, the year of the consummation of the AFL-CIO merger, 25.3 percent of American workers belonged to unions. Thirty years later, only 18 percent of the nonagricultural labor force was unionized.[2]

The UAW itself seemed immune to these trends until recently. Peak membership stood at 1,530,870 in 1969, and as recently as 1979, it was at virtually the same level, 1,527,858. But the auto crisis of the early 1980s hit the UAW with devastating force. In 1978, the five unionized U.S. automakers employed 723,402 workers; in 1982, only 438,217. Even with the recovery, 1985 employment at the same five companies stood at only 542,910. Employment impacts in other industries have been even worse. The UAW's membership in the agricultural equipment and construction equipment industries is less than half its 1978 level. Although UAW membership has climbed back to about 1.15 million, that total is still nearly a third below the level before the crisis. During the worst years, 1982 and 1983, more than 200,000 UAW members were on indefinite layoff. By 1985, the union had ceased reporting this statistic because so many people had been laid off for so long that the number no longer had meaning.[3]

The auto crisis coincided with a turning point in the UAW's own history. In 1983, when Douglas Fraser, vice-president Martin Gerber, and five regional directors retired, the last of the men closely associated with Walter Reuther left power in the union. The current officers, including the four most influential—the president Owen Bieber, the secretary-treasurer Ray Majerus, and vice-presidents Don Ephlin and Steve Yokich—assumed high positions in 1980.[4] Some observers have wondered whether these leaders will command the same loyalty as their predecessors. The new officers seem popular with the rank and file, although they are not as well known as Reuther, Leonard Woodcock, or Fraser. At the 1983 convention, for instance, Owen Bieber had to take a moment after his election to introduce himself. Since Reuther's time, UAW presidents have been addressed by their first names: Walter, Leonard, and Doug. Bieber is continuing the tradition—"Call me Owen"—but it is significant that he had to announce it to the convention.

The rank and file has also been changing in a number of ways over the years. In the first place, the auto and supplier industries account for fewer members. In 1983, slightly less than half (545,000, or 49.5 percent) of the active members worked for manufacturers of cars and trucks, down from more than 60 percent a decade ago. An additional 250,000 (22.7 percent) members were employed by suppliers to the auto industry, also down from recent years.[5] Second, the UAW is graying. The auto crisis, the adoption of labor-saving technologies, and the UAW's seniority-based contracts can lead to no other outcome. At Chrysler, before the most recent call-backs, workers had to have at least fifteen years of seniority to survive the drastic cutbacks of 1979 and 1980. The average age of the UAW membership is in the midthirties and climbing.

Finally, one thing has not changed. Autoworkers may be fewer and older, but they remain well paid. At the end of 1985, an assembly-line worker earned an hourly wage (not including profit sharing) of $13.36 at GM; $13.365 at Ford; and $13.35 at Chrysler. These wages are about 35 percent higher than general manufacturing wages in the United States. The costs of benefits, including pensions, unemployment insurance, and health care, pushed the total compensation package at the Big Three to about $25 per hour, according to company estimates.

Declining membership has had significant financial implications for the UAW. In 1984, the union reported an income of $380.3 million.

Between two-thirds and three-quarters of this total came from dues, with the rest accounted for by investments and interest on existing funds.[6] UAW dues are currently assessed at two hours of income per month. At this rate, the 400,000 members lost since 1979 represent nearly $100 million per year in lost income. During the crisis years, most of the UAW's funds and expenses were cut, including programs for education, organizing, citizenship, fair practices, and recreation.

It is against this background that the UAW confronts its future. How it is currently behaving follows directly from its analysis of its problems.

STRATEGIES FOR SURVIVAL

To cope with its darkening environment, the UAW is pursuing a variety of strategies, but it has not as yet settled on a definite course. The union's various approaches reflect partly a defensive reaction to being blamed for the auto crisis by early analysts, and partly its own difficulties in coming to terms with the forces driving change in the industry.

When the auto crisis first hit in 1979, many commentators, including some top auto company executives, fixed the blame for the Japanese cost advantage on greedy overpaid workers. For example, Roger Smith's initial speeches as chairman of GM dwelled on an eight-dollar per hour wage differential between American and Japanese workers as a principal source of the U.S. companies' problems. Some of the more zealous supporters of President Reagan echoed the same view. Having been blamed by management and the government for the auto industry's woes, the union responded, naturally enough, in kind. In 1982, for example, Doug Fraser argued that the companies handled the two oil shocks of the 1970s poorly, adding, "The auto crisis is also a result of poor product engineering. The industry designed the wretched Vega and Pinto models, and we had nothing competitive in the small-car segments. I remember Walter Reuther telling GM thirty-five years ago that the American public wanted a small car, but nobody in the industry would listen."[7]

Irving Bluestone, a retired vice-president who was a close associate of Reuther's, echoed the sweeping indictments of management, but included more specific causes of the crisis: the companies exercised bad judgment in not building small cars; management was slow to perceive the Japanese advantage in quality; "stockholder tyranny" and a short-term view among management got in the way of essential investments; management focused on high-margin but otherwise useless products like vinyl roofs at the expense of substantive innovation; the industry's annual model change discouraged innovation; and finally, the absence of meaningful competition in the industry after its earliest years contributed to the companies' sluggish response to Japanese import penetration.[8]

UAW leaders also criticized the federal government for failing to come to the industry's aid. Fraser and Owen Bieber have been openly and frequently contemptuous of the "Reagan economic fiasco" and its "Bonzo economics." Fraser reprimanded the administration and its "right-wing ideologues" for "using their screwball economic theories which threaten to destroy everything that is decent and fair and equitable in American society." Top union officials blast the administration for maintaining high interest rates, accepting unconscionable levels of unemployment, and its dogmatic adherence to supply-side economics.[9]

The UAW has also been advocating a more active federal role for several years. "Government involvement is essential to help the industry become competitive," says Fraser. "Contrast our auto industry with those of Germany and Japan. Governments there plan what will happen to their industries. We don't and we are hurt by it." Rather, "we have had inadequate fiscal actions and disastrous monetary policies, the wrong energy program, and an international trade posture which increasingly leaves our industries at the mercy of other governmental designs."[10] Adds Bieber:

> Most other countries which have an existing auto industry or which are looking at building an auto industry treat it as one of the basic parts of their economy. We haven't done that. We have been so-called free traders, free marketers. There's not much free about it anymore other than a free ticket to foreign producers to come in and take this market away from us. . . . I think the number one step is for this country, this government to recognize what other governments have, that there must be some type of orderly rules and regulations to protect the market.[11]

UAW spokesmen have reacted sharply to claims that the union bears responsibility for the auto crisis, although they do allow that workers might have paid more attention to product quality over the years. The frequent charge that U.S. autoworkers are overpaid raises union hackles. "The auto worker's job oftentimes is monotonous, it's repetitive," counters Fraser.

If you go in our assembly line people work very, very hard. . . . I am not going to apologize for the high wages that the auto workers receive. . . . We received the high wages and frankly the rich fringe benefits because we were negotiating with an auto industry that was very, very rich and very profitable and you're dealing with an industry where the workers' productivity increased at an annual rate of 3.4 percent over the last twenty years. I mean, that is an outstanding rate of productivity and when you go to the bargaining table you negotiate based upon economic realities of that bargaining table. So here we have a profitable industry, workers with high productivity and that combination provided for our rich agreements.[12]

Bieber admits that workers here do make more money than Japanese autoworkers. But he points out that Japanese employers do not bear the costs of health care, pensions, and workers' compensation, and he hastens to add:

Looking beyond Japan, it is clearly in neither the workers' interest nor the nation's interest for U.S. auto labor to "compete" with Mexican auto labor, paid $3 to $5 a day, or with Korean auto labor, currently available at $2 to $2.50 an hour. The goal is not to make our people poor, after all. Subsistence wage rates defeat the goal of balanced growth and fulfill Walter Reuther's prophecy that nations paying bicycle wages will have bicycle economies.

Indeed, Bieber claims, "the problem is not that American or European auto workers make too much. The problem is that Japanese auto workers do not receive enough for their labor."[13]

The union has also directly challenged the research studies detailing the Japanese cost advantage. Emphasizing "the amount of guesswork involved" in analyzing cost data supplied by the companies, vice-president Don Ephlin argued that "it is irresponsible to state as a 'finding' something necessarily subject to a wide margin of error when the effect is to reinforce the damaging notion that Japanese vehicles represent a vastly superior value and thereby to paint our beleaguered industry further—and undeservedly so—into a corner."[14] Ephlin also points to the changing conclusions of consultant James Harbour, the source of the original cost comparisons, who now argues that inadequate management systems in American companies account for more of the Japanese cost advantage than comparative labor rates.[15]

Moving from defense to offense, the UAW offered its own distinctive analysis of the Japanese competitive advantage in 1983. Like the Big Three, the union believed that the undervaluation of the yen was a critical problem. Testifying before a House subcommittee, Fraser argued that the yen was undervalued "by 20 percent or more." "An appropriately valued yen," he asserted, "would raise the 'landed cost' of a $5,000 Japanese vehicle to $6,000, wiping out two-thirds of the often claimed $1500 Japanese advantage."[16]

The UAW also isolated two other sources of Japanese competitive advantage. First, argued Fraser,

> the remarkable success of Japanese exports . . . depends heavily on the dualism of the Japanese economy. On the one hand, the export sector has technological parity with its competitors in other advanced countries. On the other hand, most other sectors of the Japanese economy (e.g., services, agriculture, and other primary goods) have a very low productivity which brings down the pay scale of the entire country.

In other words, Japanese autoworkers' wages seem disproportionately low only in comparison with what American autoworkers make, but Japanese autoworkers earn extremely high wages for Japan, just as they do in the United States. Second the UAW contended that Japanese industrial policies positively aid Japanese automotive competitiveness. At one time or another, says Fraser, "the Japanese government has used credit allocation, import restrictions, subsidies, corporate restructuring, etc.," to support the auto industry's growth.[17]

Given this diagnosis of the problem, the UAW's strategies for coping with the industry's future follow in straightforward fashion. From management, the union is seeking a greater role in business decisions and greater security for its members. From the government, the union looks for positive action to protect the American automakers from the effects of Japanese competition. And for itself, the union is exploring ways to decrease its dependence on the auto industry through organizing drives and mergers with other labor organizations.

The Bargaining Agenda

Asked how they think strategically about the future of the UAW, most union officers talk in terms of familiar means—collective bargaining with the companies—to meet workers' long-term needs. After all, it was through collective bargaining that the UAW achieved high wages, seniority protections, a pension plan, unemployment benefits, generous vacations, an impressive array of medical and hospitalization benefits, dental care, and even a prepaid legal plan. But a bargaining system that worked so well for so long to divide greater and greater wealth has worked far less well to apportion diminishing rewards.

In the years since the auto crisis, the UAW has pursued bargaining strategies based on different, and to some extent, conflicting goals: security, involvement, and recovery. From 1980 to 1982, the union made substantial economic concessions to the Big Three in return for a limited form of employment security, a greater voice in management decisions, and compensation contingent on company performance. Since that time, the UAW has emphasized different goals at different companies. The 1984 master agreements with GM and Ford represent a continuation of wage restraining and exploratory, problem-solving bargaining characteristic of the previous contracts. At Chrysler, on the other hand, the union has seemed less concerned about long-term issues, pushing hard instead to recover benefits sacrificed in the company's darkest hours. The 1985 Chrysler contract not only brings wages and benefits at that company into line with those at GM and Ford but also provides automatic wage increases and includes a profit-sharing agreement.

The UAW's shifting bargaining strategies are in part a response to the industry's recovery, but they also reflect tensions within the union's leadership over how best to represent the members' interests, and tensions between the UAW leaders and members over how far the union can stray from its traditional role.

Bargaining for Security

Employment security has been a UAW concern for a long time. The union's earliest contracts featured provisions to protect workers with a certain level of seniority from layoffs and dismissals. In the 1950s, the union addressed the problem by negotiating agreements for supplemental unemployment benefits to protect workers during the periodic layoffs experienced in a cyclical industry. In the 1970s, aware that new technologies would increasingly displace workers, the UAW sought to preserve jobs by negotiating more time off for its members—up to fourteen "paid personal holidays" in addition to regular vacations (2.5 weeks) and statutory holidays. In all, if the 1979 master agreements had run their course, workers would have been paid for more than forty days not worked each year.

The crisis of the early 1980s forced the union to consider wholly different approaches to preserving jobs. Although the government mandated many concessions that the UAW made to save Chrysler from bankruptcy in 1980, the 1982 master agreements at Ford and

GM—negotiated months ahead of schedule at the union's behest—featured innovative approaches to protecting jobs. The UAW traded wage restraint and some time off with pay for limited income guarantees, profit sharing, and what amounts to consultative rights in major managerial decisions.

The Ford contract, settled first, broke the three-year pattern, running for thirty months, until September 1984.[18] The most significant changes were the suspension of the annual improvement factor (AIF) and the automatic wage increase first negotiated in 1948, and the abandonment of nine personal paid holidays. The UAW also agreed to defer three quarterly cost-of-living adjustments (COLA) and to phase in full pay for newly hired and certain rehired employees over a period of eighteen months. Finally, the union pledged to approach subsequent local contract bargaining with an open mind about modifying work practices.

For its part, Ford met a longstanding union demand by negotiating a profit-sharing agreement that would make payments to workers whenever the company's pretax earnings exceeded 2.3 percent of sales. Ford also agreed to consult with the union on basic managerial decisions, from manning levels to plant closings and investments, and to accept some conditions on plant closing decisions. The company promised to give employees six months' notice of intended closings and would not, for two years, shut a plant because of increased outsourcing. To help displaced workers find new jobs, the company agreed to contribute five cents for every man-hour worked to a jointly administered UAW-Ford National Development and Training Center to provide training, retraining, and job counseling services.

Ford also satisfied some of the union's concerns about employment security. The company established a guaranteed income stream (GIS) for most employees; workers with at least fifteen years of service were guaranteed at least 50 percent of their last hourly wage and insurance coverage in the event of layoffs. Certain seniority employees were given preferential placement opportunities during the life of the contract. In addition, the company increased its contributions to the union's supplemental unemployment benefits (SUB) fund. Finally, Ford agreed to establish experimental "lifetime employment" programs at three pilot plants. About 80 percent of the workers at these plants were to be guaranteed jobs; in the event of a downturn, manning levels would be reduced by attrition, work time would be reduced, "and/or alternative work assignments either within or external to the Company" would be provided.[19]

The 1984 contracts at GM and Ford continued in this vein. Before the negotiations opened, Don Ephlin pointed out that "in the past the UAW has done very well by the membership in wages and benefits. And we have done very well in providing for our senior and retired workers. Now is the time to turn our attention to the needs of the next generation of autoworkers."[20] An improved economic climate allowed the union to recapture some wage concessions and periodic adjustments, although the COLA and the AIF were not restored to their precrisis forms. The companies agreed to continue the 1982 provisions such as the SUB and GIS benefits to protect workers from cyclical layoffs, and agreed also to continue consultations about outsourcing and plant closings.

But the most novel features of the 1984 agreements centered around provisions to deal with the forces permanently eroding employment levels: new technologies and competitive pressure on costs. Besides beefing up the training and retraining programs, the companies and the union agreed to establish a jointly administered venture capital account. This account (up to $100 million at GM and $30 million at Ford) would be used to help establish new lines of business within the automaker and perhaps entirely new companies to employ displaced autoworkers. At the same time, GM issued a statement of intent to build its new entry in the small-car market, the Saturn, in the United States with UAW involvement in the planning from the outset.

GM and Ford also agreed to work with the UAW toward the creation of a wholly new program to preserve employment. To support a cascading set of joint committees on employment security at the national, regional, and local levels, GM agreed to allocate up to $1 billion ($280 million at Ford) payable between 1984 and 1990 into an account for workers with at least one year of seniority whose jobs are threatened by new technologies, outsourcing, or negotiated productivity increases. This money would be used to retrain and relocate eligible employees for other jobs within the company. According to GM industrial relations planners, during the life of the program, the company would in effect treat employees as a fixed cost. Because the fund is administered at the local level, plant managers would have to consider bearing the costs of relocating workers when evaluating new investments.

The UAW leaders are proud of these bargaining innovations. Owen Bieber and Don Ephlin point to the success of the retraining programs under way at GM and Ford. The companies and the union have already begun using the nation's community college network as places to retrain autoworkers for employment in other industries and in the service sector. At Henry Ford Community College in Dearborn, for example, displaced workers have been trained for jobs in welding, aerospace, and cable TV operations. By the end of 1984, some 11,000 workers across the nation had taken advantage of these programs. The 1984 master agreements extended the program to provide training for active employees as well.[21]

Other programs, however, have proved hard to implement. For example, by the end of the 1982 contract, neither GM nor Ford had settled on a workable formula for the experimental "lifetime employment" plants. At Ford's Chicago assembly plant, for instance, Byron Cooper, president of Local 551, negotiated for the job guarantees by agreeing to relax some work rules and to abolish some relief time. But the proposed contract was rejected, and Cooper lost his bid for reelection shortly thereafter. He had served as president for seven years and had been a local union officer for nineteen years. "I think we moved too fast on this contract," reflects Cooper. "We simply pushed the workers too much at one time. There's a lot of reluctance to change."[22]

And the new job bank programs at GM and Ford have proved unwieldy. As of the end of 1985, the program had not been fully tested at either company.[23]

BARGAINING FOR INVOLVEMENT

The auto crisis also triggered the realization among top officials of the UAW that collective bargaining cannot, by itself, reconcile the employment concerns of workers with the competitive interests of employers. Although gaining a greater voice for the union in managerial decisions affecting long-term investments and employment levels was a bargaining agenda of a distinctly second order in the last four decades, the auto crisis brought this concern to the fore.

In the 1982 bargaining round, the UAW agreed with Ford and GM to establish joint committees to meet at least four times a year at both the national and local levels to discuss general business conditions. The agenda of these meetings, called mutual growth forums at Ford and joint committees for enhancing job security and the competitive edge at GM, was deliberately left vague, although spokesmen for both sides expected the forums to supplement collective bargaining. The joint committees have met with varying degrees of success. At Ford, they have been more important than at GM, largely because of evangelistic leadership on both sides. Don Ephlin, who was director of the Ford Department from 1980 to 1983, and Peter Pestillo, Ford's vice-president of labor relations, have been vocal and highly visible champions of better communication between labor and management. Before Ephlin moved on to the union's GM Department, he met frequently with Pestillo to discuss substantive business developments at Ford and implications for employment. For example, when asked about the agenda of these meetings in the summer of 1982, Ephlin reached into his pocket and pulled out a three-by-five-inch card with four items on it: a new absenteeism plan, negotiations on the sale of Ford's steel plant at River Rouge, progress on contract talks in Canada, and the temporary institution of a ten-hour workday at one of Ford's California plants.[24]

At the local level, results are mixed, since the programs depend on sympathetic and able plant managers and local union officers to make them work. At Ford's Wayne assembly plant, both managers and workers credit the mutual growth forum for making dramatic improvements in the industrial relations climate. "It's not the company that's giving us a hard time anymore," says a skilled tradesman in the plant. "It's the outside world. We now have access to much better information from the company. I now know the cost of contracting work on the outside and can use that information in talking with management about saving money. The more informed we are, the better the decisions we can make."[25]

The last two bargaining agreements at Ford and GM have also emphasized improving relations between the companies and the workers on the shop floor through quality of work life (QWL) and employee involvement (EI) programs. Recognizing that efficiency and quality are bound up with the employees' general well-being, GM and the UAW introduced a formal QWL program in 1973; Ford's similar EI program dates from 1979.[26] Both programs are founded on the belief that the traditional, authoritarian pattern of labor relations that developed in the auto industry is no longer acceptable from the standpoint of human relations or competitive reality. QWL and EI programs represent the simultaneous attempts of labor and management to come to grips with worker "alienation," on the one hand, and with inadequate productivity and product quality on the other.[27]

The most extensive QWL program at GM is in operation at the company's Cadillac plant in Livonia, Michigan.[28] Hourly workers at Livonia are organized in business teams that make decisions and share responsibilities for production, quality, materials, daily job placement and rotation, housekeeping, and safety. First-level supervisors are called team coordinators and are expected to act as "facilitators" of effective team performance. Traditional job classifications and pay scales have been abolished in favor of a pay-for-knowledge system that rewards competence and skills acquisition as well as seniority. The management level of general foreman has been eliminated along with special privileges and dress codes for other managers.

The UAW's agreements with New United Motors Manufacturing, the GM-Toyota joint venture in Fremont, California, and the new Saturn Corporation represent extreme forms of cooperation and involvement. The two contracts are similar, though the Saturn agreement is potentially the more far-reaching. The UAW has worked with GM managers from December 1983, the outset of planning for Saturn. At the very start, the two sides agreed that a radically new approach to making cars would require radically different industrial relations. As two members of the joint labor-management planning committee put it, "union and management are partners and share in the responsibility for assuring success of the enterprise," and "Saturn cannot be successful if it's just business as usual." In the "Saturn People Philosophy Statement," management and labor jointly profess, "We believe that all people want to be involved in the decisions that affect them, care about their jobs and each other, take pride in themselves and in their contributions and want to share in the success of their efforts."[29]

The Saturn complex will be highly automated—in fact, an automatic guided vehicle system will control the manufacturing process instead of the traditional assembly line—but its most innovative feature will be its labor contract. The final assembly process will employ half the workers of a conventional assembly plant. These workers, or work unit members, will be organized in teams and share responsibility for a variety of tasks. Indeed, the factory will have few job classifications, one for all nonskilled workers and three to five additional classifications for the skilled trades, in sharp contrast to conventional plants, which have dozens. Workers at Saturn will be paid a guaranteed salary that totals only 80 percent of standard industry wages. Performance incentives and a profit-sharing plan are expected to help workers make up and perhaps exceed the balance. Finally, four-fifths of the employees will receive a permanent job security guarantee based on a seniority formula.

At this writing, the Saturn contract is under fire from several different directions. The National Right to Work Legal Defense Foundation challenged the contract on the grounds that the UAW will represent all Saturn workers even though few have been hired and a representation election has yet to take place. The UAW dissidents declaim against the agreement for abandoning the union's traditional adversarial role as a representative of the worker. The contract has even drawn fire from one of the union's founders: after hearing about it, Victor Reuther worried about "what's happened to our trade union movement." He denounced the contract because the UAW executive board hurriedly endorsed it without seeking a vote of the GM bargaining council or the bargaining committee, and because the compensation incentives seem a throwback to the piecework systems the UAW struggled long to overcome.[30]

Such criticisms of the Saturn agreement are symptomatic of genuine controversy inside the UAW over the value of workers' obtaining a greater voice in management. Although workers say that they want better relations with management and an end to capricious supervision, some of them, at least, do not see these as worthwhile trade-offs for economic benefits. "Better treatment in the plants is something that should happen anyway," says Al Gardner, a UAW dissident at Ford Local 600.[31]

BARGAINING FOR RECOVERY

For all their advances in terms of employment security, information sharing, and profit sharing, the concessionary contracts of 1980–1982 were controversial in the union. During the crisis, the union was forced to trade off two of its most cherished principles: pattern bargaining—the practice of negotiating the same economic package at every automaker on the same date—in return for contracts at Chrysler different from Ford or GM; and automatic wage hikes in return for contingent forms of compensation. With the recovery, the UAW has been pushing to restore both principles.

Concessions, obviously, were never popular among the leaders or the rank and file. Workers at GM ratified the 1982 master agreement by a razor thin margin of 52 percent to 48 percent. The margin at Ford was much wider (73 percent to 27 percent), though opponents of the contract claimed that about 100,000 eligible voters registered their unhappiness by not voting at all. The unhappiness of Chrysler workers was even more pronounced. In 1982, once Chrysler began to show profits again, workers insisted on immediate restitution. In September, the union's international bargaining council negotiated a contract that contained a profit-sharing mechanism instead of an immediate pay hike. Chrysler workers rejected this contract by more than two to one—one of the rare occasions in UAW history that the rank and file overturned a national agreement recommended by the international leadership. Chrysler's Canadian employees, moreover, followed the contract rejection with a five-week strike that ended only when the company restored the automatic wage escalators— the COLA and the AIF—and granted immediate wage increases ($0.75 per hour in the United States; $1.15 per hour in Canada).

Although top officials of the UAW leadership threw their weight behind the 1982 agreements, they regarded the concessions as temporary. At the union's 1983 convention, President Bieber received his loudest ovation when he thundered, "No one can predict exactly where we'll be when we sit down with the auto companies in the '84 talks. But I want to say one thing to management," emphasizing the verb tenses, "we've made our sacrifices . . . we've made our concessions . . . we've given all we're going to give . . . I'm deadly serious when I say it's [management's] turn to do some giving."[32]

Bieber's first negotiations, at Chrysler in 1983, made still more progress toward the goal of restoring wage parity among the Big Three. The union settled for an immediate $1 per hour wage hike and a promise to move wages to the levels at GM and Ford by the end of 1985. At GM in 1984 and at Chrysler in 1985, Bieber resorted to strikes to achieve better economic packages than the companies had been willing to offer. These recovery contracts proved much more popular with the membership: the 1984 agreements at GM and Ford received more than 57 percent and 65 percent favorable votes, respectively, and the 1985 agreement at Chrysler, which fully restored wage parity, the AIF, and COLA, and includes a profit-sharing agreement to boot, was approved by 87 percent of the voting members.

Although pattern bargaining has been restored, some UAW leaders argue that profit sharing may be a way to mitigate its anticompetitive effects. As Don Ephlin points out, "You can have a pattern agreement on minimum wages and benefits and then use profit sharing as a supplement." This would mean, for example, that AMC would not have to pay the same labor costs as GM. Under recent contracts, GM workers received, on average, profit-sharing pay-outs of $606 in 1983 and $515 in 1984; Ford workers received $440 and $2,000 in those years. Despite these rewards, however, profit sharing remains controversial in the union. "They're meaningless in bad times," grumbles one international representative, who points out, "That's why the first Chrysler contract failed in 1982." Opponents also cite difficulties in finding an agreeable profit-sharing formula. AMC has had profit sharing since 1961 but has earned enough to begin pay-outs to workers in only two years since then. As a result, few people in the union consider profit sharing an acceptable trade-off for a COLA and the AIF.[33]

By the end of 1985, the UAW clearly retained enough clout to restore pattern bargaining and regain most of the economic ground lost earlier in the decade. The membership just as clearly regards recovery bargaining as a success. Less clear, though, is whether collective bargaining is a process that can serve the union's long-term interest in preserving jobs. The trade-off between negotiating a better economic package for workers now or exercising restraint to maintain or increase employment levels is posed most vividly in national bargaining at Chrysler. The 1985 contract is the most rewarding in the industry for workers; on the other hand, Chrysler continues to deverticalize and outsource at the expense of UAW jobs. Local bargaining at Chrysler in 1986 has mitigated the effects of the national agreement by reducing wage classifications and broadening job responsibilities. Nonetheless, some observers believe that the new Chrysler contract illustrates a classic tension between workers choosing to satisfy short-term financial needs at the expense of their long-term employment interests.

The difficulties the union experienced in balancing its short-term and long-term interests through collective bargaining are understandable. Collective bargaining is a slow and unsteady process, complicated by traditional expectations and the inherent turbulence of union democratic politics. The UAW leaders understand this, and they have pursued political and legislative answers to their dilemmas as well.

Lobbying for Government Intervention

The union's political activities are unfolding along several lines. In general, the UAW is an ardent supporter of the Democratic party and its agenda of full employment policies including public works programs, retraining assistance, and funding for regional and community adjustment.[34] Along with the AFL-CIO, the UAW endorsed Walter Mondale before the 1984 presidential primaries and worked actively on behalf of Democrats during the national elections. As for the specific problems of the auto industry, the UAW has strategies for the short and long terms. First, the union is lobbying for protection from Japanese imports. Second, the union is pushing for the creation of a national industrial policy to promote the welfare of American industries, including autos, in global competition.

The UAW has been lobbying the government for a variety of protectionist measures since the late 1970s. In 1980, the union filed a petition in support of Ford's unsuccessful petition to the International Trade Commission (ITC) for relief from injury caused by Japanese imports. In 1980 and 1981, the union pressured Congress for a resolution supporting an orderly marketing agreement with Japanese automakers. And from 1981 through 1985, the UAW supported the voluntary restraint agreement and protested the relaxation of restraints in 1984 and 1985.

In addition, the UAW mounted an intense effort in the early 1980s to persuade Congress to enact domestic content legislation to require automakers that sell a certain number of vehicles in the American market to build a corresponding percentage of their value in the United States. For example, the union's proposed Fair Practices in Automotive Products Act (1983) would have imposed its requirements on a sliding scale over several years. Manufacturers selling more than 100,000 units in the United States would have been required to buy or build at least 10 percent of the car's wholesale value in the United States; they would have had to add another 10 percent of domestic content for each additional 100,000 units sold, up to 90 percent for sellers of 900,000 units or more. In practice, the legislation was primarily aimed at Toyota and Nissan, which each sold more than half a million vehicles in the United States annually.

In testimony before the House in 1983, Doug Fraser asserted that local content legislation would create nearly one million jobs in autos and related industries in the United States and produce a number of other salutary effects on the economy. Fraser also argued that the law would stimulate foreign investment in the United States, curb outsourcing by the domestic manufacturers, improve the balance of payments, respond fairly to Japanese trade practices, and help end the recession. The UAW claimed that local content would not violate international trade agreements, and union leaders pointed out that many other countries have similar policies.[35]

The UAW mounted a major lobbying effort for the bill, demanding a statement of support for the principle of local content in its master agreements with all five American automakers in 1982. The UAW's political arm, its Community Action Program (CAP), sent out lobbying kits to local unions, other labor organizations, and its general sympathizers to drum up support for the legislation. CAP pulled out the stops: editorials were placed in newspapers and magazines, letters to the editor composed, speeches delivered, telegrams, mailgrams, and postcards sent, interviews granted, TV spots filmed. *Solidarity*, the UAW's monthly magazine, sponsored a major write-in campaign to Congress, and President Fraser warned "that the union and its allies would be closely scrutinizing the support behind the legislation" as national elections approached.[36]

These efforts were rewarded in 1982 and 1983 when the House approved versions of local content. Neither bill went much further, however, because many Democrats as well as most Republicans opposed it. Critics claimed that the law would raise prices, imperil the companies' efforts to improve productivity and quality, continue an unwarranted disparity between wages in the auto industry and general manufacturing, restrict competition, and undermine if not violate the General Agreement on Tariffs and Trade (GATT) and other trade policies. Some opponents even disputed the claim that local content legislation would produce more jobs. In 1982, for example, the Congressional Budget Office calculated that "the increase in jobs created by increased domestic content could be negligible."[37] And it was (and is) an open question whether the jobs created, if any, would be jobs for the UAW. Of the foreign automakers that have opened or announced assembly operations in the United States, only Volkswagen has recognized the UAW as a bargaining agent in plants that are not jointly administered with American partners.

Although the union continued to advocate domestic content legislation into 1984, the debate has become moot with the voluntary arrival of the Japanese and Asian producers. Nevertheless, union leaders regard their lobbying efforts as worthwhile for encouraging the Japanese automakers to build plants in the United States and for increasing public awareness of the effects of the auto crisis and the role the government might play in its solution.

Beyond local content, the UAW has been pushing for increased government involvement in the economy. Believing that a critical part of Japanese automotive competitiveness lies in Japanese industrial policy, the UAW is urging the United States to respond in kind. At the constitutional convention of May 1983, the union released *The UAW Blueprint for a Working America* as its contribution to the growing debate on industrial policy. From now on, said Owen Bieber, "workers and their unions must play a major role in shaping new policies geared to achieving sustained growth and a better quality of life for our people."[38] The *Blueprint* spells out general guidelines for an American industrial policy: "industrial policy must be coordinated" in recognition of the linkages between sectors of the economy; "industrial policy should be bargained" among representatives of business, government, labor, and the public; "there is a legitimate role for the government" to intervene in the economy and coordinate sectoral policies; and "finally, industrial policy must be based on a system of social accounting" that would balance public costs and benefits with private gains and losses in making policies affecting industries, companies, and regions.[39]

To formulate and carry out this industrial policy, the UAW proposed creating new federal agencies and structures. These include a tripartite National Strategic Planning Board, separate Industry Strategy Committees, a National Strategic Development Bank to provide capital, a National Civilian Technology Administration, and a Bureau of Conversion Assistance "for the purpose of effecting orderly conversion through advance notice of plant closings and concerted efforts to prevent closings."[40] The reconfigured government would set about reexamining tax policies, trade relationships, labor-market conditions, and various federal, regional, state, and community programs that affect industrial competitiveness. In the case of the auto industry, an industrial policy might include domestic content legislation, reduced consumer interest rates, targeted tax policies, measures to discourage plant closings, and regional adjustment assistance.[41]

Like the UAW's proposed local content legislation, its recommended industrial policy has few allies outside the labor movement. The companies stand firmly against most of the union's proposals. Despite language in the 1982 contracts, the automakers do not really support local content, since they are themselves multinational enterprises worried about retaliation abroad and restrictions on foreign investments. Nor are they enthusiastic about an American industrial policy, since they are suspicious of government intervention in almost any form. Finally, there is considerable bipartisan skepticism about content legislation and industrial policy in the federal government as well.

In proposing these political solutions to its long-term predicament, the union appears caught between the unlikely and the undoable. As a result, the UAW is exploring still other avenues to reduce its dependence on the automakers. Like the auto companies themselves, the UAW is looking for ways to avoid the industry's cyclical crises by diversifying into other sectors of the economy.

Diversifying from the Auto Industry

The UAW has worried for decades about its dependence on the auto industry. Over the years it has diversified its membership by expanding into other industries and sectors of the economy in a somewhat desultory fashion. The auto crisis has brought a new urgency to the problem, however, and the UAW has stepped up its organizing efforts and opened talks with other industrial unions as a means of stabilizing its membership and its political clout. Its diversification strategy, however, is fraught with problems.

The relationship between the UAW and the auto industry, of course, has been close since the beginning of the union. Before World War II, in fact, the UAW organized only car and truck manufacturing and supplier companies. The union was pulled into other industries by its primary employers. Ford was a major tractor and farm implement producer. Both Ford and GM had interests in aircraft. The war obviously stimulated other defense contractors, including North American Aviation, Douglas Aircraft, and other aircraft companies and suppliers, which the UAW subsequently organized. In the late 1940s, the UAW moved more vigorously into agricultural and construction equipment at International Harvester, John Deere and Company, and Caterpillar as part of its rivalry with the communist-led Farm Equipment Workers Union.

Although the UAW now represents workers in many industries, the leadership and membership are dominated by the auto and supplier industries. All of the international officers and the vast majority of regional directors started out working in auto or supplier plants. Together, employees of auto and supplier companies account for more than 70 percent of the total membership. In contrast, less than 10 percent work in the agricultural implements industry, with another 7 percent employed in aerospace. The remaining members work in industrial settings as diverse as aluminum and universities. According to the "best guesstimate" of the UAW Research Department in late 1982, the union's white-collar membership stood at about 40,000 (3.6 percent).[42]

The UAW has attempted to organize beyond its blue-collar manufacturing origins for many years. In the late 1950s, an Organizing Department memorandum sounded a cautionary note.

> It is obvious that unless greater effort is exerted in the task of organizing the white-collar employees, the UAW in the years immediately ahead will tend to become a second rate union unable to match its progress of the past in meeting the future needs of its membership. It will become more and more difficult to influence the social, economic, and political life in the community as it has in the past.[43]

Organizing drives in aerospace and the consumer electronics and appliance industries, however, have made little headway since the 1950s.[44] Attempts to organize white-collar workers at the automakers succeeded only at some Chrysler locations.[45] In 1982, a major drive to represent clerical, secretarial, and supervisory employees at GM produced dismal results. Indeed, the UAW has had little luck in attracting technical, office, and professional employees over the years.

The UAW failed to grow much outside the auto and closely related industries for a variety of reasons. Until very recently, there was little incentive to look outside, since the auto industry was the largest and most lucrative industry in the economy. Second, the UAW is constrained by jurisdictional agreements with various labor federations. When it has been affiliated with the CIO and AFL-CIO (1937–1968 and 1982 to the present), UAW organizing drives were subject to federation guidelines. The UAW could not, for example, organize plants in the steel industry (unless operated by an auto company like Ford's steel mill at the Rouge complex) without trespassing on the territory of the United Steel Workers, an AFL-CIO affiliate. In aerospace and some machine tool and supplier companies, UAW growth is constrained by the presence of the International Association of Machinists (IAM).

Third, it is one thing to talk about organizing outside autos and closely related industries, but another thing altogether to do it. Management has grown much more determined to resist unionization in recent years, according to Martin Gerber, retired head of the UAW Organizing Department. "In no other country that I know of," he says, "is management's adversarial attitude toward unions more explicit than here in the U.S. Management bitterly opposes unions. They try to intimidate workers and our organizers with union-busting techniques." Organizing is made still more difficult by economic conditions in the Midwest, the UAW's home territory. As Gerber says, "Employers have a lot of power now, which comes from the changing nature of our economy. The number of blue-collar workers is down. There are a lot of facilities with fewer than fifty people working at them. Employers threaten loss of jobs or other reprisals for union activity—even though this is against the law."[46]

On occasion UAW officers have expressed doubts about their ability to work with people with substantially different backgrounds, education, and training. The union has consistently had trouble finding qualified organizers to break into new territory. The unorganized, moreover, have their own doubts about the UAW. Even though the UAW has a lot to offer in terms of experience, financial support, research abilities, political clout, and a good reputation, the vast majority of its members—and all of its top officers—have blue-collar backgrounds. If it is difficult for UAW members to identify with white-collar, technical, or service sector workers, it is equally difficult for these "outsiders" to identify with the concerns of autoworkers.

Finally, in addition to its other difficulties, organizing is an agonizingly slow and expensive process. Between 1980 and 1982, when the UAW lost hundreds of thousands of members, organizers brought in just over 30,000 new members. This total amounts to just over half the number organized in the preceding three years. Moreover, the union's financial plight has affected the organizing budget: the UAW spent $1 million less on organizing in 1982 than in 1980.[47]

All of this has led the UAW to explore other ways of dealing with the problem of its dependence on the auto industry. In 1979, District 65 of the Distributive Workers of America affiliated with the UAW, adding several thousand white-collar workers to the membership. The UAW-District 65 partnership has since led several successful organizing drives among white-collar workers in the Northeast. It has been more difficult to arrange more formal mergers with other industrial unions. In the early 1980s, for example, the UAW discussed merger with both the United Rubber Workers and the Machinists. But these unions could not agree on a common agenda, and the talks have since broken off.

Despite difficulties in diversifying, Martin Gerber likens the UAW's organizing drives to "getting a transfusion of new blood. The new members have a lot of ideas and enthusiasm. They can help rejuvenate the union."[48] The point is well taken. But organizing is a cumbersome process, complicated and slow. For the foreseeable future, organizing offers an unlikely solution to the UAW's dilemmas.

CRACKS IN SOLIDARITY

The UAW's ability to realize its plans for the future depends partly on the officers' ability to lead their own members. And there is some cause for worry. The auto crisis brought to the surface a number of tensions and conflicts in the UAW that had lain dormant during the years of prosperity and the Reuther consensus. Moreover, the factionalism of the 1930s and 1940s never fully disappeared and is emerging once more. Radicals and dissident groups continue to thrive in some local unions and in the UAW's Skilled Trades Department. More ominous is the growth of an increasingly vocal opposition movement and mounting rivalry between local unions inside the UAW. A well-organized opposition group nearly defeated the 1982 GM contract and mounted spirited campaigns against the 1984 master agreements and the Saturn contract. In 1985, the Canadian branch of the UAW seceded from the international union over disagreements on collective bargaining strategy.

The UAW represents a broad spectrum of beliefs. The leadership of the UAW has been associated with the center and left wing of the Democratic party since the late 1940s. The rank and file, however, have not followed the official line with much consistency. In recent years, the gap appears to be widening. In the 1972 presidential primaries, for example, significant numbers of UAW members voted for George Wallace. In 1980, according to some estimates, about 40 percent of the UAW members who voted in the U.S. presidential election chose Ronald Reagan over the union's candidate, Jimmy Carter. And in 1984, despite the union's endorsement of Walter Mondale, President Reagan carried every auto-producing state handily.

The recent growth of an outspoken opposition movement within the UAW is a more serious problem for the union's leadership. Dissent has a long history in the UAW and the current opposition inherits much from the past. In the early 1960s, a group calling itself the National Committee for Democratic Action in the UAW (NCFDA) organized around a platform calling for referendums on dues increases, direct election of officers, and "rank-and-file control of the UAW."[49] The NCFDA was a loose coalition of locals whose program has reappeared in various guises in the past two decades. In the late 1960s, for example, the United Caucus—the name perhaps a play on the old Reuther-led Unity Caucus of the 1930s—opposed the international leadership on many of the same issues as the NCFDA.

In recent years, the dissenters have been disproportionately strong among skilled tradesmen, who account for about 15 percent of the union's membership. Relations between skilled and nonskilled workers in the UAW have frequently been touchy, reflecting historic divisions in American labor between proponents of craft unionism and advocates of industrial unionism. On the shop floor and at the bargaining table, the interests of the two groups periodically clash. Skilled workers aim to maintain control over job classifications, training, and wage premiums, and nonskilled workers find each point a source of resentment.

Recent concession contracts, which have restricted work organization in many plants, have reopened old disputes. Indeed, skilled workers have opposed the policies of the leadership frequently in UAW history. In 1955, in fact, a majority of skilled workers in the union attempted to defect to an independent labor organization, the Society of Skilled Trades, but were prevented from doing so by the National Labor Relations Board.[50] Walter Reuther, himself a skilled tradesman, was able to head off that crisis and the union subsequently moderated some tensions by guaranteeing skilled workers a separate right of ratification for UAW contracts. Nevertheless, some dissatisfaction still remains. In 1973, an Independent Skilled Trades Council (ISTC) was formed in the UAW out of the ashes of the United Caucus with an agenda that transcends the interests of skilled workers. According to Al Gardner, a dissident shop chairman at Ford Local 600, "The production workers are hard to organize into any kind of national organization, since there are so many of them and they are so diverse. It's hard to build up the necessary communication links. . . . The ISTC [formed] when we realized that the best chance of organizing a real opposition was in the skilled trades."[51] The ISTC continues to serve as an outpost of opposition in the 1980s.

In 1982, a group overlapping with the ISTC gathered under the name Locals Opposed to Concessions (LOC) and campaigned actively against the national auto contracts. Funded by donations from twenty-three locals in Michigan and Ohio and from individual members, LOC claimed credit for the close vote at GM and the defeat of the initial votes at AMC and Chrysler.[52]

Of course, LOC drew strength from the inherent unpopularity of concessions. The group published analyses of the Ford and GM contracts that concluded that if ratified, workers would get "an unbelievably bad deal." "We find no redeeming provisions [in the contracts]. The giveaways are more far-reaching than is widely recognized. Jobs are not protected. Job security is not increased in any way. The gains that have been represented to our members as great beginnings of new programs are all so seriously flawed that they are close to useless." As Pete Kelly, an LOC leader based at Local 160 at the GM Technical Center, pointed out:

> The concessions were absolutely meaningless. Look at the outsourcing clause. Management has to close the plant before the language takes effect. It's not tied to effects on employment! I'm not opposed to concessions if the company has a problem. But we should get our benefits back when things come back to normal. We lost $200 million in SUB benefits. The guaranteed income stream is a joke. People get less money than they would from SUB.

Leaders of the LOC also see larger issues at stake in the auto crisis. QWL and mutual growth forums are meaningless, claims Kelly.

> The corporations still make the final decisions. Even in the joint committees, the executives have the tie-breaking vote. I don't like this kind of collaboration. I have more respect for a tough, principled opponent than a wishy-washy friend. If labor becomes partners with management, that's an abuse of the system set up in the 1930s. We have a system of checks and balances. If labor gets too cozy with management, we give up the union's role of protecting the workers.[53]

An aspect of the crisis that particularly disturbs UAW dissidents is the emergence of rivalry between local unions to outdo one another in making concessions to save jobs. Indeed, many union officials are alarmed by the companies' practice of "whipsawing," using work rule changes or other contract modifications made in one location to gain concessions in another. As Gardner points out, "The new contracts breed a kind of selfishness. If one local bends to management, it can take work away from another local. The Employee Involvement program and the Mutual Growth Forums pit workers against other workers."[54]

In 1983, UAW dissidents regrouped themselves once more, abolishing LOC in favor of a new, permanent organization to rally around the bargaining cry, "Restore and More in '84" (RAM). The 1984 contracts proved less controversial, and although RAM opposed particular provisions of the settlement, ratification votes were much less ambiguous: at GM the margin was 57 percent to 43 percent.

Although RAM has succeeded in winning publicity, a more serious problem for the UAW was the secession of 123,000 Canadian autoworkers early in 1985 under the leadership of Robert White, formerly vice-president and head of the UAW's Canadian Department. White had long been a maverick in the union. He opposed profit sharing because "it makes people much too concerned about the enterprise they are working in, not the union and broader concerns of the day." White also challenged the union's moderate bargaining strategy of the early 1980s. In 1980, he bridled at accepting U.S. government-mandated concessions at Chrysler; in 1981, he was the only member of the UAW executive board to vote against contract reopeners at GM and Ford; in 1982, over the objections of the executive board, he led a five-week strike at Chrysler Canada that resulted in a richer settlement than Chrysler workers in the United States received. When the UAW executive board refused White's request for more autonomy in December 1984—in the wake of another unpopular thirteen-day strike at GM of Canada—the Canadians pulled out. They took with them not only members and roughly $30 million in settlements but also the potential to disrupt auto production and bargaining strategy south of the border.[55]

AN UNCERTAIN FUTURE

The UAW is currently in the midst of a painful transition from long years of stability and prosperity toward a future of declining membership, diminishing financial resources, and dwindling political clout. In such circumstances, the union is wrestling with choices and dilemmas. How can short-term and long-term interests be balanced? Is pattern bargaining realistic in a globally competitive industry? Can decentralized, company-specific contracts be tolerated? Can the union simultaneously manage in factory environments as different as those in Saturn and in traditional plants? If the UAW fails to organize the Japanese auto plants in the United States, will it lose leverage in negotiations with the Big Three?

The questions are easy to multiply, the answers hard to find. In part, the leadership is itself uncertain about the future. "We don't have anyone now like Walter Reuther who understands the big picture," says one union official. And, in part, the UAW recognizes that it does not control its own destiny. Decisions being made (or avoided) by corporate executives and public officials will largely determine the future shape of the American auto industry. The UAW is inevitably consigned to a secondary role in this pageant, but it is a role that can be played with distinction. As Doug Fraser observes,

Like the mine workers a generation ago, we are facing an era of declining employment. The UMW [United Mine Workers] and the coal industry were facing new technology, and the union decided not to fight trends but to keep up the wages and benefits. The UAW is in a similar position now. We can't stop the tide. We'll be a smaller UAW, but society can live with a smaller UAW. The power of an institution is not based upon size alone. It's based upon its program, its philosophy, and how it allocates its resources.[56]

CHAPTER 8

The Government-
Management
Relationship:
Trapped in the Past

To many observers, the ups and downs of the U.S. automakers' roller-coaster ride since 1979 have been most clearly marked by headline events and decisions that occurred, not in Detroit or even Toyota City, but in Washington, D.C. In 1980, then-Congressman David Stockman told a Harvard conference on the auto industry that federal interventions "have caused the design, engineering, and cost accounting departments of the automobile industry to be shifted from Detroit to the banks of the Potomac."[1] For example, the industry's low point came with the day-by-day agony of Chrysler as it slowly slid toward bankruptcy while the Carter White House and the Congress debated whether the free enterprise system would permit a federally guaranteed bail-out. The seriousness of the Japanese competitive threat in autos first became a matter of public record in the UAW-Ford proceeding before the International Trade Commission in 1980, with the auto company and auto union appealing to the government for protection. The issue surfaced again in 1981, with the negotiation of a voluntary restraint agreement limiting Japanese auto exports to the United States.

On the regulatory front, the Reagan administration popularized the notion of "deregulating" the auto industry, identifying thirty-four separate federal regulations that it proposed to relax or revoke, modifying fuel-economy standards when General Motors and Ford were facing noncompliance with the law, issuing only one new safety regulation in five years, and permitting GM and Toyota to go forward with their joint venture. Finally, in the area of macroeconomic policy, the government's ballooning budget deficit fueled the auto industry's cries that it was being forced to compete against the Japanese on uneven terms: the overvalued dollar was helping the Japanese auto industry expand its already significant landed cost advantage, boosting imports in the American market and forcing more U.S. auto production and sourcing to move offshore in order to be competitive.

These headline-grabbing events have contributed to a perception that much of what has happened and will happen with the U.S. auto industry is decided in Washington, in negotiations between government and management—in the overlap of public policy and business policy. There is, however, an irony to this perception. It is antithetical to the philosophies of both the government, particularly the highly ideological Reagan administration, and the automakers, particularly the industry leader, General Motors. As a result, notwithstanding newspaper reports that make Washington center stage in the auto industry's ongoing drama, both sides have done their utmost to maintain a relationship that thinks about and acts upon global competition as if there were no need to adapt the old American system to the new reality.

In fact, since 1979 when the auto industry clearly was overtaken by the Japanese, the government-management relationship has exhibited none of the six characteristics of a competitive enterprise system—and has done so as a matter of choice. Instead, both government and management have continued to espouse the philosophy of the past, of separate responsibilities, separate authority, and separate interests, while settling into the practice of business as usual in handling day-to-day regulatory matters and ignoring long-term questions of strategic thinking.

Significantly, this business-as-usual relationship is not a function of partisan politics. It is not a matter of one political party having right answers and the other wrong ones; nor is one political party holding the auto industry hostage while the other side seeks to win its favor.

Nor can the nature of the government-management relationship be traced to one or another wrongheaded administration, a weak Congress, or a rogue bureaucracy. For the most part, the relationship transcends party differences and reflects both longstanding beliefs and practices that define the interaction of the two sides and, just as important, the absence of an alternative that has conceptual clarity and practical applicability.

It is a relationship with two dominant themes: first, that macroeconomics is the only appropriate role for the federal government in the economy and in the competitive performance of the industry; and second, consistent with the first theme, that government should only respond to the demands placed on it and should not attempt to formulate or execute a specific competitive strategy. Together, these two principles frame a classical definition of American economic-political theory: laissez-faire economics, responding to the dictates of the marketplace, and demand-responsive government, balancing competing claims.

These two themes have direct implications for the shape and conduct of the government-management relationship, implications best measured against the template of the Japanese enterprise system. In the current American system, the concepts of shared authority, shared responsibility, and shared interests are effectively ruled out as a matter of philosophy. Instead, the free market and competing interests are presumed to determine the competitive performance of the industry. Howard Paster, a former UAW lobbyist and officer of Timmons and Company, which lobbies for Chrysler among other clients, says, "The administration is willing to let the marketplace determine whether there is an auto industry and if so at what size and level."[2] Second, the government neither practices strategic thinking with regard to the auto industry nor attempts to make distinctions between the individual companies competing in the globalized environment. Unlike the Japanese enterprise system, which develops strategy after considering the impacts on individual companies within the context of global competition, the American approach tends to operate at the level of the U.S. industry in the national context. This approach applies across the spectrum of policy areas, including taxes and trade and union regulations where company differences give a different result to the application of public policy. Says Bob Bedell, deputy administrator of the OMB Office of Information and Regulatory Affairs, "In the case of a regulation, I almost never know how it will affect the different companies. All I want to know is the science and the data."[3]

Third, because of its laissez-faire, demand-responsive orientation, government as an institution operates in a cumbersome, slow-moving manner; it is generally inflexible and slow to adapt. Says an auto specialist in the Department of Commerce, "Right now trade is hot, so the White House is looking at trade as an issue. But we're also facing an unemployment problem in the near-term future, and I'm not sure I see the administration handling it. You don't see in the White House staff real concern over unemployment."[4] And fourth, as a local consequence of all these elements, decision making both within the government and between government and management lags behind events, and is not efficient, effective, or economic in application.

The relationship between government and management is the same system based on the same thinking and the same practices that obtained prior to the globalization of competition. It is a relationship that still has not adapted to the new reality where national enterprise systems, not individual companies, must compete. Says Michael Finkelstein, a ten-year veteran administrator in the National Highway Traffic Safety Administration (NHTSA), "Nobody in Washington has yet understood the fundamental change going on as a result of Japan's entry into the market."[5] Rather, the government-management relationship continues to reflect preglobal competitive thinking: a preference for an arm's-length government-management approach and for less government, in general. But at the same time that the government-management relationship in Washington appears to be locked into the philosophy and practices of the past, a large number of state governments have been experimenting with the elements of another model, one that incorporates the six key features of competitive enterprise systems.

THE MACRO-MICRO ENTANGLEMENT

Although the Reagan administration has been more fervent in its expressions of faith in the marketplace and bolder in its assertions that macroeconomics is the only level at which government should intervene, this mainstream view has, in fact, consistently run through contemporary American government. In parts of the federal government, the opposition to anything other than laissez-faire economics may be as old as the government itself. Says one official of the

Department of the Treasury, "Our resistance to industry-specific tax breaks dates back to 1791."[6]

This macroeconomic orientation was, for example, deeply ingrained as a principle in the Carter administration's handling of the auto industry's competitive crisis. Even in 1979–1980, when the auto industry foundered and Carter faced tough election-year politics, including a challenge from within his own party, the administration strayed very little and only reluctantly from this dominant economic philosophy. For instance, the Carter administration approached the Chrysler bail-out with deep misgivings, agonized over the philosophical legitimacy of the company's plea for help, and finally agreed to the package only after seeing evidence of the devastating social and economic impacts of a Chrysler bankruptcy on predominantly black Detroit. Even in approving the concept of the bail-out, however, the administration felt a moral responsibility to use its leverage in the negotiations to insist that management and labor make sacrifices to earn the government's support.

Similarly, Carter opposed special tax treatment for the beleaguered automakers and rejected the repeated requests of Ford, Chrysler, and the UAW to use protectionist measures against the Japanese to hold down import market share. Even in the area of regulations, where the combative Joan Claybrook headed the National Highway Traffic Safety Administration, much of the clamor was over rhetoric rather than substance: during her tenure as NHTSA administrator, Claybrook proved remarkably ineffectual in intervening in the industry's affairs. Says Finkelstein, who worked under Claybrook at NHTSA, "If you look at what she did, there was not some enormous body of new regulations. But her views, her rhetoric that Detroit was immoral, poisoned the relationship. It was hard to deal with the companies where there was an absence of trust."[7]

In part, the macroeconomic orientation of government reflects the origins of economic policy making in any administration, regardless of the political stripe of the party in power. Without exception, the macroeconomists of the Council of Economic Advisers (CEA), the Department of the Treasury, and the Office of Management and Budget (OMB) have held the high ground. Advocates of more interventionist government policies—often employing the perspective of business policy or competitive strategy, and usually led by the Department of Commerce—have had to argue their cases on an ad hoc basis from positions outside the official economic policy-making apparatus.

Says Stuart Eizenstat, domestic policy adviser to Carter, "Both Charlie Schultze [CEA head] and Mike Blumenthal [Treasury secretary] opposed any microeconomic policies. For example, they felt that tripartism was too interventionist and that government involvement in a tripartite effort meant that government would get its pocket picked by industry and labor."[8]

For the most part, members of Congress embrace this economic philosophy, as well. Ari Weiss, former aide to then-House Speaker Thomas O'Neill, says, "There are almost no microeconomic thinkers in Congress. Most take the view that macrolevel economic policies play out differently in different districts. They think economically at the macrolevel and politically at the microlevel."[9]

Not only is this the dominant economic theme within the government, it is also the strong philosophical preference of the automakers. Rather than accepting the legitimacy of the government's participation in shaping the competitive performance of the auto industry, management continues to recite the old orthodoxy. "We want to make decisions based on economics," says James Johnston, GM's vice-president for industry-government relations. "GM is strongly in favor of the market. We believe we're better off if the government doesn't direct or impede where we're going but sets a climate where the market can decide. The most important thing for the government is the macropicture. Our job is to worry our way through the micros."[10]

This view of government's limited role in the competitive environment is not limited to GM, although its position as market leader may engender a heartier endorsement of the philosophy. Both Ford and Chrysler, while looking to the government for specific targeted help, have remained wary of becoming too deeply enmeshed in the government. Even Chrysler, with its record as a ward of the state, turned to the government only as a last resort and got out from underneath the government and the Loan Guarantee Board as quickly as possible. If anything unites the three usually divided automakers, it is the conviction that government continues to represent a burden.

What the Reagan administration has done since 1981 is simply to express this philosophy in starker terms, carrying it to its logical extension and consolidating the power to effectuate it in the Office of Management and Budget and in a more ideologically driven White House. In 1981, for example, while the auto industry was suffering through its most difficult period, the Reagan administration took the position that its supply-side macroeconomic policy—and not a sector-specific auto policy—would provide the environment for the industry's recovery. Testifying before a Senate Finance subcommittee, the then-assistant secretary of commerce, Robert Dederick, first reviewed a program of regulatory reform designed to save the automakers an estimated $500 million to $600 million and "get the government off the industry's back," and then cautioned the senators not to draw the wrong conclusion about the administration's relationship with the industry: government was only attempting to reduce its authority over the industry and was accepting no responsibility for its competitive performance. Said Dederick, "It is important to recognize that the president's program never intended that government should 'solve' the problems of the auto industry. While the government is firmly committed to building a strong economy and dismantling unjustified interference in industry affairs, it is just as fairly committed to insisting that business should solve the problems of business."[11] Five years later, OMB's Bedell echoed Dederick's philosophy, with even more conviction. "We see no more reason for the government to be involved with the auto industry," Bedell said, "than for it to be involved with the grocery industry."[12]

Nonetheless, in spite of these deep philosophical convictions, even under the Reagan administration the government has remained deeply involved with the microlevel operations of the automakers. In fact, the United States, like every other major auto-producing nation in the world, has a set of microlevel auto sector policies involving trade, investment, competition, financial assistance, and regulation.[13] (See Appendix B for a summary of the auto sector policies in France, West Germany, Japan, the United Kingdom, and the United States.) What distinguishes these interactions is not that they have been eliminated or even significantly reduced; certainly it is not that they have been limited to macroeconomics. Rather, it is that they have been conducted without a sense of shared authority, shared responsibility, or shared interests to shape and direct them, precisely because of the dominant laissez-faire philosophy. Says auto industry lobbyist Howard Paster, "We have no ongoing auto policy in this country. There is no institutional continuity or capability in the government, no industry-driven consensus, no long-term thinking, and no congressional authority or capacity to look long range at autos. As a result, we seize simplistic solutions and fight over the wrong issues."[14] Two categories of government and auto industry policy making illustrate the disjunction between philosophy and practice: regulatory policy in the areas of the environment, safety, and energy and the GM-Toyota joint venture.

Early on, the Reagan administration announced its intention to "deregulate" the auto industry. Wrote the *New York Times* in November 1981, "The automobile industry was virtually free of regulation at the federal level until the mid-1960s, when it was required to march to rules set by dozens of agencies. Today, regulators in Washington set standards for emissions, safety, and mileage that affect the size, shape, and performance of new automobiles as much as designers at G.M.'s Technical Center in Warren, MI. Occupational safety inspectors prowl through factories while equal opportunity officials have a say in who gets hired and promoted. Until earlier this year, lawyers at the Federal Trade Commission were contemplating a suit aimed at splitting the company (General Motors) into pieces. But last April, the Reagan administration said it would assist the ailing auto industry by reducing the burden of regulation. . . . Vice President Bush, who heads the administration's deregulatory effort, predicted that the proposed changes would save the industry $1.3 billion in capital costs, and consumers more than $9 billion over five years."[15] The package, announced in 1981, identified thirty-four federal regulations that were to be revoked or relaxed. And, in fact, after five years in office, the Reagan administration had promulgated only one new safety regulation, the requirement for high mounted stoplights in the back of all autos sold in the United States.

Nevertheless, the Reagan administration never really sought or achieved the deregulation of the auto industry. Howard Paster says, "The Reagan administration has actually done less in regulations than is perceived. They said they wanted to 'get government off the backs of the industry.' But government will continue to be on the industry's back. The only question is how heavy it will be."[16]

In a number of instances, the administration either never tried to lighten a major regulatory burden, tried and failed, or, at the auto industry's own urging, made only minor revisions. For example, wholesale revisions in the Clean Air Act once appeared to occupy an important position on the administration's agenda—important enough to warrant inclusion in the text of a presidential State of the Union message. But after five years of the Reagan administration, the Clean Air Act has remained unchanged. Says Chris DeMuth, former administrator of the OMB Office of Information and Regulatory Affairs, "An administration effort never came together on the Clean Air Act. No one was really able to take it on."[17] Just as important a factor in preempting any move to change the law was the extreme rhetoric of deregulation: the threat of an attempt to gut the Clean Air Act in the name of the free market only served to galvanize consumer groups and congressional opposition to making any changes at all in the law.

The administration's handling of the passive restraint regulation is another example of the extensive authority the government has continued to exert over the auto industry, and its inability to exercise that authority in a way that also acknowledges responsibility for it. The debate over the government's requirement of air bags or some other form of passive restraint in all passenger cars is probably the most time-consuming, least productive regulatory debate in modern American political history. Regardless of the merits of the issue, the record on air bags shows that as of 1985 more than fourteen years of government rule making had produced fewer than 11,000 vehicles with air bags sold in the United States.

In 1981, the Reagan administration sought to end the issue with one bold stroke: it simply rescinded the passive restraint requirement. A court challenge, however, overturned the government's action and, as a result, the secretary of transportation, Elizabeth Dole, issued a new passive restraint requirement: passive restraints would be phased into passenger cars in a growing proportion between 1987 and 1990, the new regulation said, unless two-thirds of the population of the United States was covered by mandatory seat belt laws adopted by state legislators. Moreover, according to the secretary's regulation, the seat belt laws passed by the states would have to meet certain criteria, including, for example, the amount of the fine to be paid as a penalty for failing to wear a seat belt.

This escape clause in the regulations has, predictably, triggered a nationwide legislature-to-legislature footrace between the automakers, who continue to chafe at the notion of government-mandated restraints, and the insurance companies, who favor the imposition of the passive restraint requirement by the federal government. The resulting spectacle featured the automakers preaching safety in the halls of state capitols and lobbying for mandatory state-level seat belt measures, and the insurance companies opposing state-level action as a way to get federally mandated passive restraints. As of 1985, sixteen states accounting for roughly 50 percent of the American public had passed some form of mandatory seat belt law. But even these results have proved expensive and ambiguous. According to GM's Johnston, the state house lobbying has thus far cost the company between $5 and $6 million. Moreover, in a number of states, where the insurance companies have not succeeded in preventing a seat belt requirement from becoming law, they have gotten states to incorporate provisions that do not match the secretary's criteria, raising the as-yet-unanswered question of whether these states will, in fact, count toward the required two-thirds.

A third example of the disparity between philosophy and practice is the area of energy policy. Since its adoption in 1975, the Energy Policy and Conservation Act has represented one of the most intrusive government requirements. In essence, because of the central role of energy in the economy, and because of the major link between the automobile and energy use, in the name of national security the government has dictated an annual miles per gallon standard for fuel efficiency that the overall fleet of each automaker must average, the corporate average fuel economy (CAFE) standard. Failure to meet the standard represents "unlawful conduct" on the part of the auto company and carries a substantial fine. More important than the potential penalty, this one regulation has reached deep into company planning: it has affected the allocation of research and development funds, guided the efforts of engineers, touched company product planning, sourcing, and marketing—none of which conform to a laissez-faire economic philosophy.

And yet, in 1985, when it became clear that both Ford and GM would fail to meet the 27.5 miles per gallon standard for 1986, there was no suggestion that the law be fundamentally rethought and rewritten in light of global competition. Instead, the two automakers sought and received a minimal adjustment in the standard for one year. In fact, according to former OMB administrator DeMuth, as far back as 1980 when he was in OMB, he could never rally the support for a wholesale deregulation of energy policy and the auto industry. "In 1980, I wanted to trash CAFE," says DeMuth. "I thought it was politically doable. We were trashing energy conservation regulations and there was not one peep out of Congress. I needed support from the auto companies and it wasn't there. Chrysler opposed changing CAFE, on the grounds that it would be a government bail-out for Ford and GM. And GM's arguments were so tepid, so weak."[18] In the perception of government officials, the automakers never marshaled the evidence to attack the fuel-economy regulations head on, or perhaps it was never a high priority for the industry.

Perhaps the most interesting example of the macrolevel and microlevel entanglement in the government-management relationship is the 1984 decision by the Federal Trade Commission to permit General Motors and Toyota to enter into a joint venture agreement. The proposal from the two companies—the two largest automakers in the world—was to form a jointly owned company, New United Motors Manufacturing, Inc. (NUMMI), which would use an idle GM plant in Fremont, California, to produce a small car. Toyota would provide the design, much of the high-value-added componentry, the design and layout of the plant, the machine tools, and the management and management systems. GM would supply the facility and a set of managers to work with the Japanese, and would purchase the output of the plant and market the cars as Chevrolets. The workers would be UAW members, drawn largely from the laid-off Fremont pool.

Although enormously complex and difficult to assess in terms of its long-term implications for U.S. competitiveness, the proposal was approved by the FTC on two rather simple and straightforward grounds: first, that the joint venture would serve as a learning laboratory for GM, giving the company a chance to get firsthand experience in the Toyota production and human relations system; and second, that since no clear harm from the joint venture could be demonstrated, laissez-faire economic philosophy would dictate that the two partners to the agreement should be allowed to proceed without government hindrance.

The FTC approval of the joint venture was conditioned on explicit stipulations as to how the joint venture should operate. Significantly, the macrolevel philosophy gave way to strict microlevel intervention, covering production volume, product pricing, the project's lifetime, and rules for communication between the two sides. In sum, the government, and not the two companies, decided how many cars the joint venture would produce (a maximum of 240,000 per year, with no option for a second assembly line, regardless of demand for the product); how the price for the product should be set (based on a government-specified formula applied to a weighted average of a number of comparable small cars); how long the joint venture could last (twelve years and no longer); and how the two sides of the joint venture could communicate (a "Chinese Wall" was to be built between

GM and Toyota and a complete file on all communications kept for annual government review).[19]

These examples are only among the most visible illustrations of the continued persuasive influence of the government in affecting the performance of U.S. automakers. At a more mundane, less visible level, the business-as-usual relationship grinds along, doing what needs to be done, processing routine requests from the automakers for a large number of technical amendments to federal regulations, consistently defining how fuel tanks should be filled for testing, changing the basis for crash testing when seats stay in the car during the test, altering the glazing standard for windshields, and more.[20]

According to former OMB administrator DeMuth, the lesson of the current relationship is that the government and automakers are now more in equilibrium. Rather than mounting head-on attacks against government regulations, for example, the auto companies go after modest changes around the edges. Says DeMuth, "The auto industry has been domesticated."[21] Gone is the adversarial rhetoric and public posturing that characterized much of the 1960s and 1970s. In its place is a surface-level agreement that government should limit and reduce its intervention in the industry's affairs: a status quo holding action between the two sides. But the relationship is as much out of step as ever, in terms of both the conflict between philosophy and practice and the conflict between the relationship and the new competitive environment. The simple reality is that the government continues to play a major role in shaping the policies and performance of the automakers while both sides vigorously deny it. The philosophy of the relationship faces in one direction, the practices in another. The government continues to exercise authority over the automakers; neither side, however, holds the government responsible for its significant impact on the industry's performance. As a consequence, the two sides continue to operate as if the government could or should be a neutral agent in the global competition. The auto industry is left with the worst of both worlds: all the costs and none of the benefits of government's participation in industry affairs.

DEMAND-RESPONSIVE GOVERNMENT

The second major theme that defines the government-management relationship is of a piece with the first: government should have no coherent strategy of its own; instead it should be responsive to the often conflicting demands placed upon it by various constituencies or factions. Like the Treasury's dislike for sector-specific tax breaks, this view of government's operating principles has a long and distinguished history: as far back as 1788 in *The Federalist*, American political thinkers advanced the argument that separating and balancing the powers within the federal government was the best way to control the effects of "faction"—the inevitable play of special interests before and within the government.

Almost two hundred years ago, James Madison observed, "Shall domestic manufacturers be encouraged, and in what degree, by restrictions on foreign manufacturers? [These] are questions which would be differently decided by the landed and manufacturing classes; and probably by neither with a sole regard to justice and the public good. . . . The regulation of these various and interfering interests forms the principal task of modern legislation, and involves the spirit of party and faction in the necessary and ordinary operations of the government."[22] Today former OMB administrator DeMuth says simply, "The content of policy is completely determined by forces brought to bear on the government."[23]

This view of government gives the American government-business relationship a particular flavor: to get the government involved, management has to have both a solution and a story that is simple. When management looks to the government, it needs to ask for a simple and specific solution, usually some form of relief, if management is to succeed in its special pleading. Says Susan Schwab, an aide to Senator John Danforth who specializes in trade policy, "When someone walks into your office, it means they're in trouble."[24]

Moreover, in the Washington policy tangle, management tries to find government actions that will apply to a limited area, for a limited time. In the case of the auto industry, for example, which has felt the tight squeeze of government's visible hand for too long, there is no enthusiasm for an ongoing, structured, consultative relationship. Observes Don Campbell, an assistant to Senator Donald Riegle from Michigan, "The auto companies are more likely to ask for relief from the government, not help by the government. In their eyes, government is neither capable nor desirable as a partner for business." Another element of responsive policy making is the need for a simple story. In the demand-responsive environment of Washington, complex and messy issues get short shrift, because they are both hard to deal with inside the political process and hard to explain to voters back home. Says Campbell, "If you're smart, you only come to Congress if you've got a simple story to tell."[25]

The example of the auto industry and trade policy both illustrates how demand-responsive government works and suggests its drawbacks in the new global competition. In 1981, with a recession choking off demand and Japanese imports claiming U.S. market share, Ford and Chrysler, the hardest hit automakers, and the UAW had a simple solution and a simple story. The story was verified by closed auto plants and laid-off autoworkers, and carried one message: it was now a case of "them versus us"—and "they" were winning and inflicting heavy costs. The solution was equally simple: impose protectionist legislation on the Japanese, reserving market share for the U.S. producers and providing breathing room for necessary capital investments, retooling, and new products. The auto industry brought its simple story and simple solution to the Congress, which responded by threatening to pass protectionist legislation, the Danforth-Bentsen bill. To head that measure off, in April 1981 the Reagan administration negotiated a two-year voluntary restraint agreement with the Japanese; in the year before Reagan's reelection campaign the limit was quietly extended for another year, after which the Japanese announced yet another year of self-imposed restraints at substantially higher levels.

Even though the negotiation of the voluntary restraint agreement showed demand-responsive government working as intended, in fact it also demonstrated its flaws and limits. First, because government was not viewed as a legitimate partner and had no competitive strategy of its own for the industry, it accepted trade policy as a simple solution, but not necessarily the right one or even the last one. The restraint agreement developed as an isolated policy instrument, rather than as a component of a larger, more comprehensive package designed to attack the causes of the automakers' competitive failure, of which trade was really only a symptom. Moreover, even within the area of trade policy the argument was not rooted in a larger vision of a national trade strategy. Says Robert Lighthizer, a former deputy in the Reagan administration's Office of the U.S. Special Trade Representative, "There really is no United States trade strategy. We simply lurch from crisis to crisis."[26]

Most important, demand-responsive government precluded the administration from negotiating quid pro quos with the automakers and the UAW in exchange for the restraint agreement. Instead of acting as a legitimate player in the national enterprise system and negotiating a mutually acceptable strategy, the government simply acceded to the industry's pressure for relief, with no agreement on collateral issues: from management, an understanding on investments, prices, profits, bonuses, plans; from labor, on wages, work rules, training. As a result, when the market returned and U.S. automakers garnered record profits—and awarded themselves big bonuses—the government felt betrayed. Stuart Keitz, director of the Office of Automotive Affairs in the Department of Commerce, offers the government's view of what went wrong: "The industry never came in and talked about price or profits. They never offered to strike a deal. But Bill Brock (then the special trade representative) thought he had an agreement that they wouldn't kill the golden goose during the restraints. After the big bonuses, the trust was busted. It left a very bad taste in the administration's mouth for a long time."[27] As a consequence of the way the restraints were handled, the government-industry relationship ended with less cooperation, a diminished sense of shared interests, and a poorer level of understanding. Says OMB's Bedell, "The auto industry doesn't have many friends to begin with. Then they pass out $2 million bonuses and that makes it even tougher."[28]

Second, the Reagan administration negotiated the trade agreement, not because it was committed to a strategy designed to promote the competitiveness of the American auto industry, but because it wanted to head off a threatened worse violation of administration orthodoxy, the even more protectionist Danforth-Bentsen trade bill. As a general operating principle, the government in the absence of a positive strategy continually finds itself fighting a holding action across a variety of policy fronts, giving ground grudgingly once it becomes clear that some movement is necessary in order to prevent the entire position from being overrun. Riegle aide Don Campbell says, "The theme is that there is no theme. The administration is only taking a series of steps that defuse the really hard choices. They're accepting a lesser evil to hold off the worse threat of 'big government' or 'protectionism.' The only theme is that government shouldn't frame a longer-term strategy."[29] This approach is not limited to the Reagan administration, or to the executive branch. Rather, it reflects a general government principle. Says Congressman Richard Gephardt, "In more ways than not, the government operates like a bystander, hoping that the industry will change its ways."[30]

The third problem with demand-responsive government is that it is, by definition, completely ad hoc and situational. As a result, government policy on any problem must be created and recreated from scratch as the situation changes in focus, disappears, and then reappears with different characteristics. There is no strategic process that allows the government to monitor the competitive situation as it changes and think ahead about the initiative that would fit into broader goals.

This last problem is of critical importance to the future of the auto industry. Four years after the government negotiated a voluntary restraint agreement with the Japanese, the U.S. auto industry has disappeared from the government's screen as a matter worthy of national attention or concern. The Office of Automotive Affairs, established in 1981 in the Commerce Department as a visible, high-level policy coordinating center, has been downgraded to a small subbranch of the International Trade Administration (ITA).

This demotion only reflects the larger ambivalence of demand-responsive government to the auto industry in 1985. There is no simple story and no simple solution, and as a result the government has no interest in the industry. Is it sick? Or is it healthy again? Even more complex, in the face of industrywide joint ventures, U.S. sourcing of finished autos from Japan, and Japanese direct investment in America-based production facilities, who is "us" and who is "them"? And if the intermingling of U.S. and Japanese automakers has taken away trade policy as the simple solution to the American industry's future competitive problems, then what kind of substitute simple solution could government turn to?

It is not even clear at what point in the future the government would once again perceive a problem. Notes Stuart Keitz of the Commerce Department, "With the end of the VRA, Japanese market share will go up. Is 30 percent acceptable? Is 40 percent? No one has ever said."[31] At Chrysler's Washington office, the forecasts are even worse. Says Robert Perkins, vice-president of Chrysler's Washington office, "By 1990, we expect the Japanese to have 50 to 54 percent of the U.S. market, including imports, transplants, and total outsourcing. Three to four years out, we will face another crisis, not just of manufacturers but also suppliers. Somebody should be thinking about this now."[32]

These questions only serve to illustrate why demand-responsive government ultimately puts the American auto industry at a disadvantage. Because the government does not think strategically about its participation in the enterprise system, its inevitable interventions lack a longer-term sense of direction. Moreover, there is no coherent policy context that provides continuity to decisions as they need to be made. As a consequence, decision making is rarely efficient, economic, or effective. In fact, because government decision making depends so heavily on the play of pressures being brought to bear, it lags behind events and is subject to constant reconsideration: the debates over passive restraints and clean air, for example, seem never to be resolved. Instead, these issues, which are marginal matters in comparison to the larger question of the industry's ability to compete, occupy a disproportionate share of the political system's time and energy. Finally, the government does not anticipate change, but tends only to respond to it, rendering its policies and practices inflexible and slow to adapt.

STATE-LEVEL STRATEGIES

Even though the relationship between the federal government and the auto industry appears to be mired in preglobal orthodoxies, at the level of state government across the country a new model is emerging, one that emphasizes the value of government as a competent partner, a catalyst for competitiveness. It is, interestingly, a model that closely parallels the Japanese enterprise system.

One example is auto-dependent Michigan. There, Governor James Blanchard, who as a member of Congress played a pivotal role in engineering the Chrysler bail-out, seized the initiative to redefine the government-management relationship at the state level. His administration's efforts began with the philosophical view that government, even at the state level, had a role in determining the competitive performance of the auto industry, that government's programs and policies exerted authority over the companies, which implied, in turn, the need to assume responsibility.

The result of this view of the government-management relationship was a broad-gauge strategy to help the industry—and the state—compete by reducing costs and improving quality. The government fulfilled its responsibilities by cutting the costs of regulations, including workmen's compensation and unemployment insurance, investing in education and training for new and displaced workers, creating the Michigan Strategic Fund to provide venture capital to innovative start-up companies, investing in infrastructure improvements, and, perhaps most impressive of all, paying off an inherited $1.7 billion state deficit in three years. Not only did the state adopt a competitive strategy, it also created a forum—the Governor's Commission on Jobs and Economic Development, cochaired by Doug Fraser and Lee Iacocca—where the strategy could be negotiated.

At the state level, the goal of a competitive strategy is to develop programs and policies that will both help the existing companies in the state compete and attract new investment. Clearly, some elements of policy are beyond the reach of state government: the macroeconomic policy of the federal government, for example, federal trade policy, or procurement policy. But state governments are discovering that they still do have a significant number of policy instruments that can not only affect the competitive performance of business within their borders but also enhance the attractiveness of the state as a location of economic enterprise. Some of these instruments are fairly traditional factors that generally cover the cost of doing business: the tax and regulatory burden, for example. In most instances, state governments are looking for ways to reduce these costs or disguise them so that they no longer are an easily identified target.

Some state governments are pushing in even more far-reaching ways to use their resources and powers to promote competitiveness as a public and private goal. Most of this activity falls into three categories. First, state governments are investing in human resources. They are putting more money and more attention into education, at all levels. Because of the perceived link between quality institutions of higher education and high-tech industries, that level has received a great deal of publicity. Just as significant, however, are new initiatives aimed at elementary and high school education and new efforts to use community colleges as training and retraining centers. The second area for state intervention is in promoting and advancing technological innovation. By investing directly in research and development, coventuring with private industry in technology centers, and promoting technology transfer from new to mature industries, states are investing in technological change. Third, states are using some of their broader powers to create an entrepreneurial environment within their borders. Instruments as diverse as state-controlled venture capital funds for investments in roads, sewers, bridges, and water facilities give state governments tools with which to leverage private investment decisions. The overall aim is to help the state compete not only against other states, as in the past, but against other countries by helping the state's companies and workers compete.

According to Raymond Scheppach, executive director of the National Governors Association, Michigan's orientation is typical of the new effort at the state level to promote competitiveness. "The federal programs for economic development are, for all practical purposes, gone," Scheppach says. "The governors have gotten a lot more sophisticated than they were. They're not just smokestack chasing. They are the ones in a position to take the lead because they are a lot closer to the real economic issues—infrastructure, education, job training, venture capital, one-stop economic development offices. States are sorting out their economic strategies and figuring out what is their comparative advantage."[33]

It is conceivable that in the future the federal government may turn to the example of the states to rethink the federal government-management relationship. At least some people on both sides of the relationship are looking for a new model, one that avoids both the "less government" laissez-faire philosophy and the "more government" industrial policy approach. On the industry side, Chrysler's Perkins says, "Three to four years from now, we will face another crisis in the auto industry. It's essential that we come up with a strategy if we are to compete with other countries that have a strategy."[34] On the government side, Congressman Richard Gephardt says, "Our major competitors are highly organized and we need a measure of parallel organization. We need the capacity to gather and analyze competitive information."[35] At the staff level, Riegle aide Campbell asks, "What should the government's attitude be? A healthy nationalism, a concern for the long-term consequences of policies, the ability to analyze specific industries, and the capacity to define and pursue our long-term national interests."[36] And William Krist, former deputy in the Office of the U.S. Special Trade Representative, says, "Our government doesn't look at issues in an industry-by-industry way. There's no unit that really understands marketing and production; there is no industry analysis and industry capability. The debate in the United States is between chaos and industrial policy and those aren't the only options."[37]

PART IV
Trends and Prospects

CHAPTER **9**

Signs of Change

In 1963, after twenty-three years as GM's chief executive officer, Alfred P. Sloan wrote in his memoirs, "Every enterprise needs a concept of its industry. There is a logical way of doing business in accordance with the facts and circumstances of an industry, if you can figure it out." Today these are the facts and circumstances of the American auto industry.

• Globalization has permanently altered the circumstances of competition.

• The new competition pits companies from vastly differing enterprise systems, rather than from within a single system. In the new competition the rivalry is between national systems. The national enterprise system of foreign automakers is the source of their competitive advantage.

• If American companies in a broad cross-section of industries are to compete in the future, the American system must change.

• The failure of the U.S. auto industry to change has caused deep and irreparable damage. The Japanese automakers already dominate the low end of the market; to compete against them, U.S. companies are both moving offshore and purchasing foreign-made products to import and sell under domestic nameplates. Moreover, Japanese automakers are building strength in the midsize and sporty segments of the market. The implications for American companies, workers, and the larger national interests are serious, particularly if the auto industry is regarded as representative of a larger competitive challenge.

• The primary responsibility for leading change in the American enterprise system belongs to American management. Although both labor and government share in the responsibility, neither can initiate or lead the process. Management can lead the way, both because the company—rather than the labor union or the government—is the actual instrument of competition and because management has the firmest grasp of corporate information and resources. Consequently, American managers must bear a disproportionately heavy burden not only for the direction of the corporation but also for the future economic, social, and political well-being of the country.

These are sobering, if not somber, conclusions. They suggest that for many industries change is already too late; that for much of the American auto industry—and perhaps all of it—time is quickly running out; and that unless managers across the economy alert themselves to the facts and circumstances of the new global competition and respond in alliance with union leaders and government officials, a significant part of the American economic base faces an uncertain future. Fortunately, there is some encouraging evidence that suggests that change is possible and that some change has been taking place in the auto industry.

Since the onset of the auto crisis in 1979, each of the Big Three has made noticeable strides in adapting to the new competitive environment. In a number of respects, Ford has made the greatest improvement. For example, Ford most quickly realized the important role of the UAW workers in contributing to the company's competitiveness. The 1982 Ford-UAW contract was a tribute to management's new understanding and commitment to act. Similarly, Ford consistently sought to draw the federal government into a dialogue that would redefine the management-government relationship. Moreover, Ford adopted a comprehensive "defect prevention" approach to quality that has yielded dramatic improvements and boosted Ford's standing in consumer quality ratings.

Perhaps the most significant testimony to Ford's competitive strides has been the successful introduction of the Taurus and Sable lines. In a number of important ways, this $4 billion project, which was launched in 1980 when the company was reeling from losses for the first time since 1956, illustrates how systemic change in the way American automakers approach the design and production process can yield a competitive product. In virtually every important respect,

Ford committed itself to pursuing product quality and to using a team approach to achieve it. The impressive result was a car that not only won the Car of the Year Award but also gained immediate acceptance in the marketplace: the 1986 supply was sold out in the first months of production. The Taurus program demonstrates the competitive capability of American automakers and suggests what it will take to launch a comeback.

To break through the old bureaucracy within Ford, tap creativity across the company, improve efficiency, and reduce costs, Ford created Team Taurus, a one-hundred-member team that approached the design and production of the car in a concurrent, rather than sequential fashion. This program management approach brought together planning, design, engineering, and manufacturing partici-pants to work as a group. The integrated team approach reduced the time from planning to production, improved the quality of the prod-uct, and, with other front-end improvements, saved Ford approxi-mately $400 million.

Ford accurately assessed the real scope of today's competition— the world, not just the Big Three—and then set out to take on the best. To do this, Ford used the concept of Best in Class, analyzing four hundred separate features from fifty midsize cars from around the world. After establishing which car had, for example, the most accurate fuel gauge, most comfortable seats, best windshield wipers, easiest-opening trunk, and more, Ford set out to do better.

Ford went to the workers to get their suggestions and to engage their enthusiasm for the Taurus project. At the Atlanta assembly plant, for instance, the plans for the car were literally put on the wall for workers to comment on. The approach yielded real results: one worker suggested an idea for smoother operation of the windows; another suggestion convinced Ford to adopt a single standard size for all screw heads, reducing the number of tool changes. Overall, more than five hundred employee suggestions were incorporated into the Taurus program.

The project involved mutually advantageous bargaining between Ford and UAW locals. For example, to win the job of making the transmissions, Ford workers at the Livonia plant agreed to flexible job classifications, a move toward greater production efficiency and reduced costs. In return, they won the work and a total of 75,000 hours of training for the nine hundred workers.

Ford recognized that suppliers were a key factor in cost and quality. As a result, the company invited four hundred suppliers to become early members of the Taurus program.

Ford even delayed the introduction of the car several times—in the past, a cardinal sin—to make sure that the product's quality would not be jeopardized.

The Taurus experience illustrates how widespread change must be for the American automakers to meet the new global standards. Taken together, the steps in the Taurus program represent Ford's effort to create a new system for the design and production of cars. But the Taurus experience also illustrates that this kind of widespread change both can be done and will work.

At Chrysler, changes have been less far-reaching. Nevertheless, the brush with bankruptcy and the government bail-out have made the company particularly sensitive to the management-government relationship and the impact of public policy on company performance.

Largely because of its size and market dominance, GM's reponse is pivotal. Three specific examples—the 1984 GM-UAW contract, the Saturn project study process, and the GM-Toyota joint venture—illustrate that progress can be made, particularly in the relationship between management and labor. Each of these examples, described in previous chapters, demonstrates the following key principles.

First, the old relationship is obsolete. The traditional model, dating back to the early 1950s, called for management to insist on control of the work place and the union to wrest economic rewards from management on behalf of the workers. Now the two sides are seeking to junk that approach as out of touch with the new competitive reality.

Second, both sides are responsible for the company's competitiveness. Management and labor together accept the fundamental proposition that the two sides are mutually dependent and mutually responsible for the company's performance.

Third, both sides work toward more effective and efficient communication and decision making. The nature of the communication and decision-making process between management and labor must change in order to institutionalize change in the overall relationship.

The 1984 GM-UAW contract embodies each of these principles. In many of its key elements the 1984 contract refined or reestablished the experiments attempted in the 1982 agreement. Most significantly, the contract represented a test of the lessons learned by the two sides during their years of crisis. Negotiated at a time of huge industry profits, and with new and untested leadership at the bargaining table for the UAW, the contract that finally emerged is a historic document with the potential to point the way toward a new understanding of the labor-management relationship in global competition. There are four breakthrough agreements in the contract.

The first accomplishment reflects what the 1984 contract is fundamentally about: a shift from bargaining over pure economics to bargaining over global competitiveness. At the beginning of the negotiations, many observers felt that, given the less-than-innovative record of GM in contract talks and the political needs of the new UAW leadership, as well as the industry's enormous profits, the most likely outcome would be an expensive, inherently noncompetitive agreement—that GM would once again attempt to "buy off" the union and that the union would opt for a future of high wages and few members.

The outcome was the opposite of this gloomy prediction. GM took the position that it had a genuine need for the union. Its negotiating stance indicated that, more than ever before, the company saw its future linked with that of its workers. And the UAW's position represented a historic shift from wages and benefits to employment security. For the first time, GM said that its future competitiveness depended on the quality of its workers and the UAW responded that the place to begin was not with money but with work. Both sides acknowledged that the bargaining terms of the old relationship were obsolete.

The second breakthrough came in the innovative approaches devised to create employment security. Again, management and labor dodged a dangerous historical trap: seeing job security for workers as something that could be won only at management's expense. Rather than constraining management's competitive flexibility by limiting outsourcing, plant closures, or new technology in exchange for job security, the two sides agreed that job security for the workers was dependent on competitiveness for the company, that is, that the two sides had shared interests.

They then defined mutually advantageous ways in which they could realize their shared interests. GM committed itself to go forward with the Saturn project, potentially a $5 billion investment in building a competitive small car in the United States. In addition, GM set up a $100 million new venture fund to be managed jointly by the company and the union. The fund's mission was to develop opportunities for new GM enterprises and new UAW jobs, focusing in particular on communities with longstanding ties to the company. Finally, the contract called for a $1 billion Job Opportunity Bank Security (JOBS) program, a jointly administered system of worker retraining, relocation, and assistance designed to guarantee that all GM employees with at least one year of seniority would not lose their jobs because of outsourcing, technological improvements, or productivity gains.

Each of these innovations represented an expression of shared interests. Overall, GM retained its flexibility to allocate its production resources in the most economic way and at the same time committed itself to an investment program to train and retrain its workers—also a sound economic decision. The commitment to continued small-car production in the United States clearly is in the interests of both GM and the UAW; a successful Saturn project would serve the interests of both sides. The new venture fund is not only an opportunity to create new businesses and new jobs in old communities but also a vehicle for members of the UAW to learn more about running the business, a business for which they now have a share of the responsibility. Finally, the JOBS program meets both the UAW need for a major commitment to the future of the workers and management's need for more highly skilled, better trained workers.

The third breakthrough in the contract came in the area of compensation: the economic bargain shifted from one of entitlement—the annual improvement factor (AIF), which had been part of the basic package since 1948, guaranteeing a wage boost regardless of the actual performance of the company—to one of contingent performance, specifically, profit sharing and performance bonuses. This new arrangement reinforces the link between management and labor—the better the company does, the better the worker does; the better the worker does, the better the company does—and moves toward greater flexibility and adaptability in the company's wage costs.

The final innovation developed in the contract was the establishment of a variety of joint GM-UAW committees to carry out the different elements of the agreement: new forums for sharing information, discussing common problems, developing a common perspective. Virtually every feature of the contract was assigned a new joint committee for its implementation: the JOBS program was placed under the joint control of UAW-GM JOBS committees at the local, area, and national levels; the $100 million new venture fund was handed to a new Growth and Opportunity Committee, with an equal number of GM and UAW representatives; a Joint Skill Development and Training Program called for the creation of a joint committee at the level of each local union, with the participation of the UAW local president and the chairman of the shop committee along with the GM plant manager and personnel director; a National Joint Health and Safety Committee was created and given a $4 million fund to use in investigating occupational health hazards; and a Hazardous Material Control Committee was established at each GM plant.

The expanded use of joint committees significantly changes both the nature and quality of the management-labor dialogue. It is a structural expression of the fact that in many areas the two sides actually comanage the company. That requires joint decision making up and down the two structures, places where discussions are more frequent and different from those of the past. The committees serve as an invaluable mechanism for the two sides to reintroduce themselves to each other, this time in a nonadversarial, problem-solving relationship.

Moreover, the committee structure begins to answer a key question raised by a new management-labor relationship: What do the midlevel representatives on each side do to justify their positions? In the traditional relationship, the functions and modes of conduct of the plant manager or personnel director and the local union president or shop steward were clear. The plant manager and his representatives cracked the whip; they made sure that discipline and control were maintained on the factory floor. And the local union president and his agents responded in kind. They won elections by showing that they could and would stand up to the boss by filing grievances or refusing to go along with changes that threatened to boost productivity.

But functions and conduct are far from clear in a cooperative relationship, one where worker job security and company competitiveness go hand in hand. If heavy-handed discipline is out and quality of work life is in, what is the new function of the midlevel manager? And if grievances are a hindrance to productivity and productivity is now as good for the worker as it is for the company, then how does a new-style union official get elected?

The new committee structure represents a partial answer to these questions. Rather than making the plant manager and local president less important, the committees make them vital elements in the establishment of the new management-labor relationship. Their joint decisions become the building blocks of competitiveness. Each side is able to point to real improvements, delivering on a mutually benefi-cial agenda instead of concentrating on wasteful sparring with each other.

Overall, the 1984 contract demonstrated that both sides had clearly grasped the underlying messages of the previous years of crisis. Neither side was fooled by the huge profits; both sides resisted the temptation to revert to a business-as-usual attitude. The contract that was negotiated spoke directly and creatively to the need for a new relationship between management and labor. The key provisions afforded both GM and the UAW an opportunity to move the Ameri-can enterprise system in a more competitive direction.

The second illustration of the capacity of the existing system to change is the Saturn project study center. When GM chairman Roger Smith presided over a Detroit press conference in early January 1985, most of the media attention was directed to the flashy parts of his announcement: that GM had decided to go forward with its "clean sheet" approach to building a competitive small car in the United States; and that Saturn would not only be a separate nameplate—the first new one added by GM since 1918—but also a separate corpora-tion with assets of $5 billion. When Smith called Saturn "the key to GM's long-term competitiveness, survival, and success as a domestic producer," most observers assumed that the proper focus of this moonshot effort was technological—an attempt to come up with modular assembly techniques, paperless information systems, and advanced manufacturing systems that could catapult GM past the Japanese.

In fact, however, the potential for a successful American entry in the small-car market—indeed, the potential for GM's future—may rest more with the solid year of thinking and self-examination that went into the Saturn announcement than with any technology that would go into the factory or the car. The real news at Smith's press conference was that GM was endorsing the findings of the GM-UAW Saturn study center, the most dramatic of which concluded: "GM cannot become internationally competitive under the current UAW-GM relationship." Instead, the study said, there had to be a whole new relationship constructed between the two sides, one based on "mutual trust and respect." GM and the UAW had to become "one team with common goals," a new philosophy that then had to drive the entire system.

Interestingly, these sweeping conclusions emerged as the result of a failure. In 1981, at the peak of the Japanese small-car onslaught, GM was forced to scrap its plans for an S-car—an American-made small car to take on the imports. After years of publicly denying the existence of a Japanese competitive advantage, GM through its own internal analyses of the cost to produce the proposed S-car had confirmed that such a car simply could not compete: manufacturing in the United States under traditional assumptions, GM could not produce a competitively priced small car. The project was scrubbed.

At the end of 1983, the GM-UAW Joint Study Center was announced, not to build a small car, but to rethink how to build one. In January 1984, the ninety-nine members went to work on a statement of mission, philosophy, and objectives. A short three weeks into the project, the word *joint* was dropped from the center's name because, as team members explained, "We felt the word *joint* implied two parts coming together and we no longer thought of ourselves as two parts but one team with common goals."[1]

To emphasize the importance of philosophy, the study members produced a half-humorous but pointed hypothetical statement.

> We believe that close controlling supervision that embodies the characteristics of coercion, blandishment, manipulation, and exploitation is the best approach to motivating people.
>
> Moreover, by pitting people against people, by selectively lying to them, by showing favoritism, and by threatening them, we believe they will, in turn, care about their job and support us as dedicated, cooperative, motivated, and confident employees.[2]

Such an operating philosophy, said the study team members, would have a profound effect on both the work force and corporate performance. To make the lesson even sharper, the Saturn study participants honed in on the issue of job security and company values: "At GM, as well as many other companies, one of the first things that happens during slack periods is that workers are cut back. This would lead one to believe the company's philosophy is more that employees are expendable than one that our human resources are our most important asset."[3]

Consequently, the Saturn team members developed a statement of philosophy that reflected the kind of management-labor relationship they believed was necessary for GM to compete.

We believe that all people want to be involved in decisions that affect them, care about their jobs, take pride in themselves and in their contributions, and want to share in the success of their efforts.

By creating an atmosphere of mutual trust and respect, recognizing and utilizing individual expertise and knowledge in innovative ways, providing the technologies and education for each individual, we will enjoy a successful relationship and a sense of belonging to an integrated business system capable of achieving our common goals which insures security for our people and success for our business and communities.[4]

The study participants noted how this philosophy could contribute to GM meeting its goal of reducing cost and improving quality. For example, trust between management and labor would reduce the need for management layers, supervision, and security: increased trust means reduced overhead. As the Saturn team went about its mission of figuring out how to integrate people and technology into a competitive U.S. small-car project, the philosophy served as a template for testing the design of each subsystem: plant layout and design, technology, work units, and job design. In each case, the most cost effective and quality conscious solution matched the statement of philosophy behind the entire mission. In the end, the study team arrived at a clear understanding of the systems nature of global competition and the need to adapt accordingly: "Only by achieving our common goals can we achieve our individual goals of job security, profits, and our collective goal of preserving our smokestack industry, which is in our national interest."[5]

Not surprisingly, the philosophy so carefully and painstakingly nurtured at Saturn is in practice at New United Motors Manufacturing, Inc. (NUMMI), the Toyota-GM joint venture. Operating in a former GM assembly plant that was closed because of the success of Japanese imports and a history of nasty management-labor relations at the facility, NUMMI represents a twin stroke for the U.S. auto industry: it is a source of small cars and jobs for GM and the UAW and it is a laboratory for experimenting with a new enterprise system, combining the Toyota philosophy and production system with UAW representation.

According to Jim Peters, senior adviser to the joint venture and on loan from GM, "The philosophy comes first. If you get that right, then everything else follows."[6] At NUMMI, the company philosophy comes directly from Toyota; the design of the enterprise system is as much a Japanese product as the design of the Corolla spinoff produced at the plant. "What makes any company unique is its management policy," says Tatsuro Toyoda, NUMMI president. "Toyota believes that the company's greatest asset is its people. This belief generates the spirit, mutual trust, and respect between labor and management. Open communications and the realization that the welfare of labor and management are interdependent are the keys to mutual trust."[7]

Just as the Saturn study group found, what follows from mutual trust and respect is a new architecture for the management-labor relationship: shared authority and responsibility, shared interests, greater adaptability and flexibility, and, finally, better quality and lower costs. Says Peters, "The UAW has always said, 'If you only give us a say, we could help you out.' So now we're saying, 'OK. But with a say comes responsibility not just to bitch but to offer businesslike ideas.' "[8]

The sharing of authority and responsibility at NUMMI is extensive: small groups of workers are given wide latitude to participate in developing company policy, even to the point of reviewing the company's annual plan; teams of workers created the job descriptions of group and team leaders, instead of the other way around; hourly workers participated in the development of their own work standards. To Peters, the point is a simple one: "The idea is to show the link between the worker's future and the company's future."[9]

The link is secured by the same set of quid pro quos negotiated between management and labor in Japan. Workers are accorded job security, authority, and responsibility for their own operations, and equal respect and status with management; there are no divisions between the two sides in the parking lot or the cafeteria, important symbols of NUMMI's intent to live by its philosophy. In return, management has eliminated most job classifications and work rules, implemented a system of job rotation for maximum flexibility, and motivated the workers to concentrate on quality and productivity.

One dimension at NUMMI that goes beyond the Saturn findings is the approach to the public sector, the management-government link in the enterprise system. According to Thomas Klipstine, NUMMI community relations manager, "The philosophy of trust and cooperation should extend to the government and the community."[10] To put this philosophy into practice, NUMMI managers visited every level of state and local government to introduce themselves well before the facility even began turning out its first preproduction models. In response to an expression of concern by the local sanitation district, the company spent $3 million to upgrade the waste treatment system. "Why spend $3 million?" asks Klipstine. "Because if you don't, you may end up spending $6 million later. And because it creates trust and credibility. From the long-term point of view, it's very important to foster good relations with the community."[11]

Moreover, NUMMI managers see a connection between their relations with labor and with government. To help introduce top managers to state government officials, NUMMI hired a consultant, a man who had formerly represented the UAW in state matters. "We wanted to send a signal to the UAW," says Klipstine, "that we are all in this together."[12]

The 1984 contract, Saturn, and NUMMI, as well as a vast number of plant-level initiatives across the auto industry, illustrate two important points. First, it is clear that a number of top officials of both the automakers and the autoworkers have given deep and careful thought to the competitive dilemma facing their industry and have concluded that fundamental systemic change is necessary. Second, on a variety of fronts they have moved to implement change—and they have succeeded. In a relatively short time, they have demonstrated the ability to adapt a system that took almost half a century to mature.

Furthermore, their efforts have been rewarded by external objective measurements, which demonstrate that both their conclusion of the need for change and their choice of the direction for change were well considered. Over the past several years, the American automakers have recorded significant improvements in critical areas such as product quality and productivity, as well as in plant-level factors such as absenteeism, grievances, and unauthorized work stoppages. In fact, evidence from the Big Three shows that those plants that have moved the farthest in practicing the new philosophy of management-labor relations have made the greatest progress in improving their performance, providing their workers with the strongest possible form of job security.

But the evidence also shows that the changes so far, although substantial, are insufficient. The competition is a moving target; foreign automakers continue to shave costs and improve quality to maintain their competitive edge. The Japanese automakers retain their advantages in cost and quality and, with the expiration of informal trade restraint, have demonstrated their ability to win additional sales and market share in the United States. Moreover, the highest quality cars being made in the United States today are coming out of Japanese-operated plants. And the changes attempted in the

American system are still fragile experiments. Much of the change is largely rhetorical, waiting for the test of implementation. Where change is in progress, other questions remain.

CHAPTER 10

Rethinking the Principles

The best of the foreign competitors and the examples of changes begun in the American auto industry make the same point: the principles that underlie the enterprise system are as critical as the practices. The traditional American enterprise system has been driven by a particular way of thinking about management, labor, and government, their roles, responsibilities, and relationships. If American managers are now to lead a revision of the system in response to global competition, these underlying principles bear a hard and careful look: the idea of a "clean sheet" approach is as necessary in the design of the American enterprise system as it is in the design of the auto production system.

Testing the principles underlying the American enterprise system afresh against the new competitive reality means that managers who expect to lead their companies into the future will have to stop living in the all-too-comfortable past. The old managerial habits may offer the warmth of familiarity and the comfort of peer group approval. But in the new competitive environment, managers' old ways of thinking about their enterprises, themselves, their employees, and the government can mean the failure of the business. And where labor and government officials are unprepared or unwilling to address the new global competition, company managers may have to drag them into the present as well. In spite of the progress that has been made, it is clear that the UAW still has yet to achieve a realistic understanding of the full meaning of globalization and its impact on the union. Similarly, the government still lacks a coherent concept of its role and responsibilities in global competition. Until and unless they both achieve an integrated understanding of the way in which systems compete in a global market, American companies will be working at a substantial disadvantage. For that reason, managers may have to assume the additional burden of describing for labor and government the new principles to guide the American enterprise system, including making it clear to both sides how their real interests can best be achieved.

To adapt to the new environment, managers, labor leaders, and government officials will have to come to terms with three conceptual changes: the need to think competitively, to think globally, and to think systematically. In each case, the principles that used to describe the basis for competition need a fresh consideration; simply, they need to be tested against the changed circumstances and, where they no longer fit, adapted to match the environment.

In the case of the U.S. auto industry, thinking competitively means shaking free of the assumptions and attitudes of nearly three-quarters of a century of economic success. For almost that long, the Big Three, the UAW, and the government enjoyed the benefits of a stable, predictable, comfortable oligopoly. The circumstance was not without competition—both among the automakers and between the sides of the enterprise system. But it was controlled competition. As a result of that element of control, as well as the prolonged stability and predictability of the environment, the auto industry grew complacent. Its success yielded smugness, a sense that there were no new questions to be asked, no outside opinions to be investigated. As Peter Drucker wrote in the 1972 update to the *Concept of the Corporation:*

> GM has been all along a "managerial" company rather than an "innovative" one . . . . But we will need to understand increasingly how to organize and to manage innovative organizations. And for this the GM model is not adequate and may not even be appropriate. . . . Not to have changed anything has been the foundation of GM's success in terms of sales and profits. But it is also clearly the source of GM's failure as an institution . . . . The failure of GM as an institution—for failure it is—is to a large extent the result of . . . an attitude which says: "We are the experts and within our area of competence, we make the decisions. Other areas are not our business. They are the business of other people."[1]

Drucker's description of the attitude problem at GM was true not only of that organization—and true all the way up through the crisis years of the early 1980s, until a fundamental reorganization of the company sought to begin to address the problem—but also of the other two members of the Big Three and for labor and government.

The attitudes of each of the American players, imprinted by years of success, are the most serious obstacles to the American auto industry's return to competitive health.

As the Japanese auto industry clearly portrays, competitiveness is achievable only as a result of a constant, relentless search by all sides for improvements in cost and quality. One Toyota worker conjured up an instructive image of the company's operation: the metaphor of management and workers drying a wet towel. "We are constantly wringing out the towel," said the Toyota worker. "But it is never completely dry."

In the new environment, competitiveness, to be won, must be sustained. It is never the result of a single managerial masterstroke; nor is it enough to have one, or even several, highly profitable years. Indeed, profitability alone is no longer a satisfactory indicator of competitiveness, which was demonstrated by the American auto industry's superficial recovery in 1984. Like the relationships between management, labor, and government that drive competitive performance, competitiveness itself is the result of ongoing efforts, continued negotiations, persistent change.

The second broad conceptual change is for all three sides to think globally. The shift from national to global competition is an accomplished fact in the auto industry. In the very simplest of terms, there no longer is an American auto industry—there is only a world auto industry. Management's definition, therefore, of its competitive situation needs a thorough reassessment. Moreover, the old assumptions about the economic roles of the union and the government are subject to reexamination. All sides need to expand the relevant frame of reference from the North American continent to the world. The competition stretches from Japan and South Korea to Europe and South America. No longer can the UAW act as if the union had no competition. In fact, the long-term survival of the UAW may depend on how well and how carefully it studies and understands the principles and practices of unions, workers, and companies in competitor nations. Perhaps most significant, the government has a profound obligation to suspend its own ideological preconceptions long enough to take a practical, common-sense look at the principles behind the role played by government in other countries.

The change to a global competition means that the categories of principles and practices now embrace the world. To improve the competitive performance of American industry requires learning from the foreign competition, particularly where they have surpassed American standards.

A global perspective also means looking at markets around the world—selling to them and learning from them. Prior to globalization, the American producers could be content with the American market. But now the U.S. market enjoys the distinction of being the most open auto market in the world. Producers around the world are able to mass-market or find a profitable niche in the United States—the Big Three have lost their exclusive franchise. To compete, American producers need to embrace the same conviction that Japanese automakers espoused immediately after World War II: the whole world is the market.

Finally, for the U.S. auto industry to become competitive again means thinking systematically. Acting on its own, no side in the U.S. enterprise system can reverse the current Japanese competitive advantage. It is that understanding, along with an intrinsically global perspective, which defines the center of the Japanese enterprise system. The enterprise system is, most fundamentally, a system. When it is in the proper equilibrium, all of the elements are in harmony; each component supports and reinforces the others. The consistency of the system becomes its greatest strength: like the product that the system is turning out, the system itself exhibits integrity.

The developmental history of the American enterprise system has served to mask this underlying principle. Rather than seeing the system as a system, each side has regarded its role in isolation. Changing the enterprise system necessarily means changing the way each side looks at itself, its role, and its responsibilities in relation to the other sides in the system.

The driving force for change is as fundamental as a new concept of the corporation. In many ways the old concept of the corporation has been the bedrock of the traditional American enterprise system. It is a concept that finds expression in the notion of "management's rights"—those prerogatives that managers historically fought to preserve and protect against the incursions of organized labor and government. These prerogatives have defined the way in which American managers have traditionally viewed their jobs: to design and implement corporate strategy, to decide on the allocation of resources, to hire and fire, to determine products, standards, and specifications, to define, measure, and evaluate overall corporate performance.

In each of these instances, the key has been the presumed unilateral authority vested in the manager. The concept has carried into the definition of corporate purpose, which in the case of GM was expressed in this phrase: "We make money, not cars." This traditional concept of the corporation pervaded not only management's view of itself but also its view of labor and government: management and management alone would retain the authority and responsibility for the competitive performance of the company. Labor and government were adversaries and externalities. Labor policy and public policy issues were unwelcome interventions that inevitably resulted in higher costs or escalating demands. Consequently, the union and the government were to be kept as far from the substance of the business as possible; the less they knew and the less they were involved, the better. Their participation in the affairs of the company was, in the eyes of most American managers, both unwelcome and illegitimate.

A new concept of the corporation begins by revisiting that basic principle. As the examples of Germany and Japan show, and as the growing evidence of experimentation in this country confirms, the new concept requires that the old battle cry of management's rights give way to legitimacy and trust in management's dealings with labor and government.

To some, this may sound like a hopelessly naive and idealistic notion. Nevertheless, the real value and strength of this idea derive from its practical and pragmatic appraisal of America's competitive dilemma: it is the only viable course left open to American management, the only course that will work.

In practical terms, most of the prerogatives that managers think they need to defend were long ago bargained or legislated away; today managers are staunchly defending a fallen citadel. In reality, most of the presumed unilateral decision making of managers is the result of a bilateral agreement arrived at jointly with either labor or government. A short list makes the point: within the plant, labor now has a voice in deciding who works, when they work, how fast they work, how much it costs for them to work, how the job is designed, and how it is carried out. In the larger affairs of the company, the government now has a voice in who gets hired, fired, and promoted, how the product is designed, where the product is made, how safe the product is, how safe the plant is, and, in the case of the auto industry, even how much energy the product consumes. Managers who attempt to run their companies adhering to the old-time religion of management's rights inevitably will inflict substantial costs on themselves—the costs of trying to make an old myth fit a new reality.

But managers who abandon the myth of management's rights are doing more than giving up an obsolete way of thinking about themselves and the enterprise system. They are moving to a new positive approach for the enterprise system based on legitimacy and trust, a pragmatic attitude that not only implicitly accepts reality for what it is but also seeks to exploit the new opportunity. As the experiences in the Japanese and German auto industries indicate, those companies that treat labor as a key ally and an important fixed cost can realize substantial advantages in product cost and quality. Just as important is the change in management's thinking about government, a shift from an unwelcome economic externality to a legitimate catalyst for competitiveness.

The painful irony of the recent past is that American management, by its show of strength in protecting management's rights against labor and government, has actually increased its vulnerability to foreign competition. Rather than recognizing the system as a system and using the overlapping interests as a source of strength, American managers have preferred to view each side as a rigidly self-contained entity with strictly patrolled borders. Neither labor nor government has been encouraged to invest in the competitive performance of the company. Consequently, though both labor and government have systematically eroded management's authority, neither side has accepted a share of management's responsibility for performance.

In the past, when the company performed poorly, which it did in the crisis years of 1979 to 1982, it was regarded as an example of management's failure to plan ahead. Labor leaders and government officials took square aim at "shortsighted auto executives." And when the company performed well and profits soared, which happened in the rebound years of 1984 and 1985, it was regarded as an example of management gouging the public. Labor leaders and government officials took aim at "profit-hungry auto executives." Bestowing legitimacy on labor and government, recognizing their right to participate in company decision making, represents an important step toward forcing them to accept responsibility. It is a step toward adapting the

American system both to the reality of global competition and to the reality of current practice.

This is not to suggest that managers should expect labor leaders or government officials suddenly to start acting like corporate officers; that is neither possible nor desirable. Conflict between the sides is inevitable; there are real and valid differences that should be recognized and must be respected. The question for American managers is how best to manage these differences while building on shared interests, how to manage both conflict and cooperation so that the results are competitively advantageous.

Again, the experiences of both the German and Japanese enterprise systems serve as instructive lessons. Both of them consistently confront difficult issues involving substantive disagreements between management and labor and between management and government. Their success is not that they have eliminated conflict. It is that they have learned how to negotiate their differences toward mutually satisfying outcomes. The implication of their examples and of the lessons of change already under way in this country is that the most practical, common-sense basis for the operation of an enterprise system is for managers to seek to negotiate with labor and government beginning with the principle of shared authority and shared responsibility.

Another implication suggested by this change is that the traditional definition of leadership will change as part of the new set of relationships. Under the old guiding principles of the American enterprise system, leadership of any of the three sides conformed to a narrow definition consistent with adversarial relations and perceived self-interest. Leadership under this traditional paradigm consisted of accomplishing the short-term self-interested goals of the organization—whether making a larger profit, demanding a fatter contract, or getting reelected—and doing so at the expense of the other side. But under a new concept of the corporation, this definition changes: Leadership consists of the capacity to negotiate and create joint gains with the other parties in the enterprise system.

At the core of this new concept of the corporation is the idea of negotiated strategy. The real task of the manager in a salient, global industry is to negotiate a mutually rewarding strategy with labor and government to produce and sustain global competitiveness. To achieve this, the manager must both develop business policies that are in the interest of the company and bring to bear labor policies and public policies that reflect and respect the legitimate interests of the workers and the public at large.

One small piece cut from the larger fabric of issues involving the auto industry serves to illustrate the point. In order to meet the Japanese challenge, the U.S. auto industry will have to have both higher productivity and better quality. This twin requirement represents an enormous challenge for the automakers, not so much in developing the strategy to meet both goals but in negotiating that strategy with those most directly affected: the workers. The problem is that the need for both productivity and quality presents an internal tension in management's relationship with its workers, particularly under the traditional paradigm. Achieving higher productivity means fewer workers. Achieving higher quality means more motivated, involved workers. How does a company dramatically cut its work force and at the same time win the commitment, confidence, and support of those who remain but who may be the next to go?

William B. Chew, who is charged with strategic planning for GM's Industrial Relations Department, explains the problem this way. "Our major problem is to define an economically viable configuration and then figure out what this means for the size and nature of the work force of the future. Either we become more productive and need fewer people or we stay as is and lose market share," says Chew. "Either way it's fewer people. Once that is known, then the question of a declining work force becomes one which has implications for and consequences on employees, on union leadership, on the community, on local tax structure, on government policy and so on." The solution, suggests Chew, cannot come at the expense of the workers or the community. Ultimately, a competitive strategy can emerge only through negotiation with those who have legitimate interests in the company's performance: all sides in the enterprise system. It is a process designed to establish what Chew calls "the price of change."[2]

The measure of a successful strategy is no longer whether it meets the narrowly defined self-interests of the company. In salient, global industries, a successful strategy must accommodate an assemblage of overlapping, competing, and sometimes conflicting interests. This recognition is a key principle in Japan. Honda's Hideo Sugiura says, "We have learned from experience that any project we have undertaken simply for ourselves has never turned out well." It is also explicitly stated as part of the Saturn philosophy: "If it feels good to only one [side], chances are it's wrong."[3]

The basis for implementing negotiated strategy is the exchange of quid pro quos; the thrust becomes the creation of joint gains and shared interests. In the example of the auto industry's need for productivity and quality, the solution begun in the 1984 contract was just such an exchange. According to Al Warren, GM's vice-president of industrial relations, the negotiation of that contract was a marked departure from past practices. "We shared information with the UAW that we've never shared before," says Warren. "We didn't take positions. Instead we looked at problem solving. I think we have put into place a structure that will materially change both institutions."[4] Significantly, as Warren suggests, these principles—shared authority and shared responsibility, shared interests and negotiated strategy— suggest the need for new practices and structures to carry out the new concept of the corporation. Those practices and structures are the subject of the next chapter.

CHAPTER **11**

Reworking the Practices

The new principles of a changed enterprise system are dependent on the day-to-day practices of management, labor, and government. Although the principles may provide a fresh conceptual frame for thinking about the relationships of the three sides, ultimately the operation of the system depends on the practices. Indeed, one of the greatest problems within the American system has been the lack of a consistent connection—an internal equilibrium—between principles and practices.

It is axiomatic that just as structure relates to strategy in the design of the company, so must practice support principle in the design of the enterprise system. This consistency is one of the important sources of power in the Japanese system. On a day-to-day basis, the practices and structures within the Japanese system deliver on the promises made in the principles.

If, for example, an underlying concept of the enterprise system in Japan is that management recognizes and accepts the legitimate participation of the workers in sharing authority and responsibility in the company strategy, daily practice reinforces that principle. In ways large and small, workers experience the philosophy in the work place. It is embodied in visible symbols that Western observers have often remarked on: the presence of a yellow cord for workers to pull to stop the assembly line if they spot a defect or the absence of separate dining facilities and parking areas for managers and workers. Taken individually and out of context, these practices may seem little more than symbols, and can easily be dismissed as such. Indeed, it would be laughable to suggest that the world dominance of the Japanese auto industry is attributable to a parking policy.

But seen as a part of a larger system, these small symbolic gestures do, in fact, matter. Regardless of whether or not a Japanese autoworker ever pulls the yellow cord to stop the line, the cord is there, every day, as a physical statement from management to workers that their participation in decisions on quality and productivity is fundamental to the company's competitive performance. And this is only one small example. The strength of the Japanese system is that one practice after another has evolved to support the guiding principles: the employment practices, reward system, communication system, negotiating practices, and more, all send consistent messages between management and labor.

In much the same way, management and government have cemented their understandings with ongoing practices that enact the philosophy of shared responsibility and shared authority. In addition to the practices that embody the sense of mutual trust and respect within the system, the Japanese have developed a structure that gives shape to the system: they have created a series of places where the relationship can occur. The sum of these parts—the practices and the structures—is an internally consistent system, an approach to dealing with each other and with the outside world that promotes competitiveness. There is an equilibrium within the system not only between principles and practices but also between management, labor, and government.

The implication of this for the U.S. auto industry is simple: to regain its competitive footing, the automakers must support the new principles discussed in chapter 10 with new practices. Particularly in light of the long history of distrust and adversarialism between both management and labor and management and government, reforming the American system requires careful attention to the day-to-day dealings that will test all sides' adherence to the principles. This point is aptly dramatized by the Saturn study project's mock philosophy, designed to illustrate how a company's guiding principles can be decoded from the way in which the system actually performs on a day-to-day basis; and it is a point demonstrated by the trenchant observation that a company that truly regards its workers as its most valuable asset would surely not lay them off as the first response to an economic downturn.

Nor are these inconsistencies between principle and practice purely hypothetical. One major reason for the lack of real progress in the GM-UAW relationship after the 1982 contract—which called for many of the advances reintroduced in 1984, such as new joint committees, profit sharing, and closer cooperation between the two sides, in addition to wage concessions by the UAW—was that on the same day that the give-back contract was ratified, GM chairman Roger Smith announced a new executive bonus program. The message the workers got was that GM was preaching equality of sacrifice and practicing something far different. Over the life of the contract, a substantial portion of the UAW membership steadfastly believed not that the two sides had aptly perceived the nature of the foreign challenge and responded intelligently, even heroically, but that the sharp-penciled bosses on the fourteenth floor of the GM building had once again outmaneuvered the union and the workers.

The result was more than a breach of faith and bitter feelings. Because of the perceived gap between philosophy and practice, UAW leaders who had hoped to be able to use the contract to educate their members to the new realities of global competition instead faced a difficult credibility problem with their own rank and file. To government officials monitoring the crisis in the auto industry, it looked like another example of the ineptitude of management and the hopeless tangle between management and labor—yet another reason for government not to get involved with this self-destructive industry.

The point, though simple, is fundamental. As former Japanese auto union president Ichiro Shioji says, "The key to the stability of the labor-management relationship is trust. It can't be achieved just by talking. It has to be built up by practice and experience."[1] A company has to practice what it preaches.

NEW PRACTICES

Changing the American enterprise system means adopting innovations that lead to new, procompetitive consultative practices among the three sides. The emphasis needs to be on information and information sharing, on communications and negotiations conducted at all levels of management, labor, and government. In addition to focusing on process, the three sides need a practice of consultation with new structures, a path of communication on which the sides can begin to meet and share information on a fresh footing. A final area for experimentation in new consultative practices is the exchange of trade-offs between the sides, the continued brokering of quid pro quos that can break down the old rigidities and preconceived notions that calcify these important relationships. Overall, these innovations can contribute to changing the operation of the enterprise system. They are closely related to four of the six attributes, discussed in chapter 1, that enhance the competitive performance of the enterprise systems: more efficient, effective, and economic decision making; greater flexibility and adaptability; strategic thinking; and company-specific relationships set in a global context.

New Information

In more practical terms, what do these points mean? Procompetitive consultations translate into several requirements. Each side, for instance, needs better information about the other. Managers, as the most influential group in the enterprise system, need a clearer understanding of how both labor unions and public officials operate. In particular, they need a more political—and less cynical—frame of reference for viewing their transactions with labor and government. One UAW leader complains, "Business schools don't really teach managers how unions work. We're always sticking our neck out to come to an understanding with management and then they chop it off. Most of the time, they don't even realize how what they do affects union politics."[2]

Within the ranks of management, this new requirement has organizational implications. Specifically, companies need to elevate to a greater prominence the roles played by their human relations and government relations executives. Traditionally, these posts have been akin to second-class corporate offices. After a decision had already been made from financial and production data, for example, the labor and government relations vice-presidents would be called in, told of the decision, and instructed to "sell" it to the union and the government. But in a system where business policies affecting labor's interests are negotiated, these two vice-presidents will need to be involved from the beginning in structuring the key trade-offs. Moreover, any sense that these jobs have been dead-end positions will have to change. The skills of negotiating with labor and government are exactly the skills needed at the top of the company to create a sustainable competitive future. In the past, chief executive officers and company presidents have come from finance and engineering departments. In the future, more will need to come with human relations and government relations backgrounds.

The demand for better understanding extends to labor and government, too. In order to represent their own interests, as well as participate with management in the ongoing process of strategy negotiation, both labor and government need a more complete and sophisticated understanding of the world auto competition and its strategic dynamics, as well as the business situation of each of the U.S. automakers.

For the government, the problems have been chronic and crippling: an absence of trained analysts in key staff positions with real comprehension of business and competition; endless turnover, which virtually guarantees the need for constant on-the-job training; sunshine provisions and open meeting laws that effectively prohibit serious, ongoing negotiations between industry and government representatives; leaks and narrow personal electoral agendas that threaten to turn every document and piece of economic analysis into a political weapon.

It is purely a matter of academic debate whether these obstacles can ever be completely surmounted. In real terms, the government's influence in setting the overall economic environment, in acting as a catalyst through capital and human investments, and in intervening at the microlevel of industries and companies through a wide assortment of policy instruments is too significant and far-reaching to be written off. On a day-to-day basis, the government is incapable of "making" any industry or any company competitive. But as the example of the U.S. auto industry shows, the government can certainly contribute to the decline of an industry's competitiveness over time—or, as the example of Japan demonstrates, contribute to its rise.

The evidence also indicates that the real issue regarding the participation of the government in the enterprise system is not one of more or less government but better government. In particular, better government calls for two things. First, it demands political representatives who can translate public policy requirements into economic considerations. This is a far cry from reflexively abandoning public interests at the behest of company lobbyists who may plead that safety, clean air, worker health, or other concerns are too costly and therefore the source of failing U.S. competitiveness. The interaction of economics and public policy is just not that simplistic. After all, the Japanese auto industry has consistently been confronted by environmental regulations that are every bit as stringent as those in the United States, regulations that became a source of competitive advantage in the Japanese industry's drive to export. Moreover, the example of the Reagan administration's wholesale abandonment of the passive restraint regulation, which led to a lengthy and costly court case and more delay and indecision for the automakers, illustrates how overzealous friends can do just as much damage as underinformed enemies. In the words of one auto executive with the responsibility for working with the government safety agency, "Most regulators don't want to do dumb things. If they do, it's our fault. We should be down at the grass-roots level, working hard to help them do the right thing—what's right for the government, right for the consumer, and right for the free enterprise system."[3] The real point is that productive negotiations between management and government can take place only when each side is capable of speaking the other's language.

For government, that means a greater capacity to translate legitimate public issues into workable approaches that make economic sense. It is noteworthy, for example, that after the worldwide energy crisis in the early 1970s, both the Germans and Japanese increased their gasoline taxes as a way of using the marketplace to stimulate energy conservation and signal their automakers to stress fuel efficiency. Only in the United States was the economically perverse course taken of passing a law that simultaneously depressed the price of gasoline to the consumer and required automakers to meet higher government-mandated fuel-economy standards. In part, better government simply means smarter government, government with a more economically realistic understanding of how its public policy interventions consistently affect the competitive position of American industries and companies.

Producing smarter government, in turn, suggests the second requirement: better information. Government data and statistics are not only critical to negotiations between the public and private sectors and to the process of making public policy in agencies and the Congress. In large measure, government data and statistics are also responsible for determining how the country thinks about the performance of the economy. National unemployment figures, the federal deficit, the rate of inflation, the balance of trade: these aggregate figures have come to be a shorthand description of the economic well-being of the nation in the eyes of the public.

But current government information is inadequate for and obsolete in forming public policy and informing public opinion. For the most part, government data today track and report on an American economy that no longer exists: the SIC (standard industrial classification) codes, for example, date back to the days of Herbert Hoover—before he was president, when he was secretary of commerce. The industry groupings in the SIC codes are totally irrelevant to the current shape of the economy. Moreover, the predominant way in which the government collects and reports its economic information corresponds to the old competitive environment, to national competition at the industry level, rather than the new one, to global competition at the company level. As a consequence, the government is not only hindered in playing a more constructive role within the enterprise system but also hinders the nation as a whole in developing a better understanding of the new global reality, because of the way it describes the national economy.

For all of these reasons, perhaps the most practical and useful place to initiate change within the government is in the collection and analysis of information. Better government can begin by using the enormous capacity of the public sector to assemble and analyze information as a source of competitive advantage for American companies: looking at the auto competition, for example, not from a national perspective but from a global one, and not from the industry level but from the company level. Realistically, that is how competition today is being conducted; it is the basis on which successful competitor nations assess the environment and negotiate strategy. By operating on the basis of information that reflects a competitive environment that no longer exists, the government ultimately produces decisions that serve neither the competitive interests of American companies nor the larger public interests. In effect, the U.S. government has been building the Maginot line of global economic competition.

For organized labor, the task is more direct—largely a matter of advancing economic education free of the traditional ideological limits of the labor movement. In the case of the auto industry, the UAW has one of the most talented research departments in organized labor. But even there the problem of doctrinaire interpretation persists. One UAW official who understands the problem says, "We have a hard time recruiting people with a background in economics or business. And all too often, when they do come to work for us, they feel like they have to overcompensate and become even more committed than the guys in the factories. I'm not sure that really serves our interests."[4]

Even more fundamental is the lack of appreciation for the facts of business life embedded in the union rank and file. Labor's detachment from business matters is a logical but unfortunate consequence of management's own policy, a legacy of the myth of management's rights, which absolved labor of any responsibility for learning about business, and, in fact, insisted that labor had no real need or legitimate interest in company affairs. Says one UAW official, "We always worried about people. We didn't give a damn about the business. We used the business as a tool to get what we needed for the people. Now it's reached the point where we've got to learn about the business and go back to the people and explain about the business."

The need to explain "the business" to the rank and file applies to management and government as well. The experience of the auto industry demonstrates that in each of the three sides of the enterprise system there are at least some top-level leaders who have a clear-eyed understanding of the need for change and the direction change must take. But in addition to solidifying the new concepts and practices at the top, each side faces a similar critical task: educating the middle ranks and bringing them along in the process of change.

For the automakers, it may be middle managers who feel threatened by a change in operating principles and practices that appears to take away their authority and give it to the workers. For the union, it may be the old-guard rank and file who were weaned on the stories of the Battle of the Overpass and who would regard any move by labor toward accepting more responsibility for the performance of the company as a sign of co-optation by management. In government, it may be the bureaucrats within the special interest agencies, the staff of congressional committees, or even cabinet members who regard themselves as ideologically pure standard-bearers. These midlevel participants are essential to any change in the enterprise system: on a day-to-day basis they run the system. Without their willful participation, comprehensive change will never take place. For that reason, leadership on each side will be tested to develop information, education, discipline, and reward systems that galvanize midlevel participants into supportive, contributing members of a reformed enterprise system.

New Structures

In addition to more accurate information and more sophisticated understanding within the three sides, procompetitive consultation suggests new structural elements to provide a location for ongoing communication and negotiation between the three sides. There are a variety of names for previous and existing structures: Ford and the UAW created mutual growth forums; GM and the UAW are experimenting with joint committees; for a brief period in 1980 the government attempted to convene an Auto Industry Committee composed of representatives of the U.S. automakers, the autoworkers, suppliers, dealers, and the government.

Regardless of the name, the functional purpose of these forums is essentially the same: to create a new structure within which management, labor, and government can conduct a new kind of relationship, outside traditional collective bargaining or legislative lobbying. The object is to change the nature of the dialogue: from periodic to ongoing; from adversarial to respectful and trusting; from competing interests to joint problem solving; from exclusively top-level contact to structured contact from bottom to top. It is a lesson borrowed from both the Germans and the Japanese: The best way to achieve efficient, effective, and economic decision making and to build flexibility and adaptability into the system is through lines of communication that solve problems before they can become crises and eliminate unwelcome surprises that may freeze one side into a defensive reaction.

Both the German and Japanese enterprise systems have evolved with highly symmetrical communication structures; in both cases, it is almost as if management, labor, and government could be represented by three ladders, with their parallel rungs lined up as channels of communication and negotiation. Until recently, this parallelism has been entirely missing from the U.S. system. The 1982 and 1984 auto contracts, however, represent conscious efforts to design a new structure between management and labor, one that will regularize contacts up and down the two organizations and promote information sharing and joint decision making.

There appears to have been no such progress, however, in restructuring the relationship between management and government at the federal level. At the state level, where the direct impacts of faltering competitiveness are felt more quickly and government is expected to respond, more attempts have been made to create new communication channels. As described in chapter 8, Michigan Governor James Blanchard in 1982 appointed the Governor's Commission on Jobs and Economic Development, a committee of statewide leaders, cochaired by Lee Iacocca and Douglas Fraser, to review public and private initiatives designed to help revive the state's economy. Moreover, the subcommittee structure of the governor's commission matches the internal structure of government agencies established to coordinate the efforts of state government, the Cabinet Council on Jobs and Economic Development.

At a more targeted level, the cabinet council has authorized a special auto-specific information and analysis effort: the AIM (Autos in Michigan) project. The AIM project, which includes an advisory committee of auto executives, suppliers, consultants, and state government staff, entails a careful analysis of the trends affecting the competitive position of auto manufacturing in Michigan. As such, it represents a formal vehicle for management and government to develop and share information on joint concerns and to arrive at a situation report on the industry to which both sides can subscribe. As important as the written product, however, has been the ongoing process: the AIM project has served to open new and important lines of communication between the two sides. Says Peter Plastrik, former director of the governor's cabinet council, "Over the past two years the number of people we talk with in the auto industry has grown by factors of tens. It used to be that the only people we'd ever talk with were from the political group and maybe a vice-president. Now we have contacts up and down the organization."[5]

Moreover, although unsuccessful, the Michigan bid to land GM's Saturn plant displayed path-breaking creativity and originality. Michigan officials downplayed traditional economic incentives, such as reduced land costs or tax breaks. Instead, the state proposed the creation of a new forum, the Saturn Institute where managers, workers, and government officials could train and learn together, and offered to "Saturnize" the state government. The formal Michigan proposal to GM said, "We will Saturnize our relationship with Saturn. We will create an integrated Michigan government unit to engage Saturn as a partner. Its mandate from leadership: innovate for competitiveness. We will begin with a clean sheet of paper."[6] Michigan's offer was, in essence, to recreate the management-government relationship by creating a new governmental structure to negotiate with Saturn on a long list of items: training and education, site development, permits and regulations, relations with suppliers, even some items of social service, such as unemployment insurance and workmen's compensation.

But at the federal level, no such restructuring has been offered or attempted. Along with a change in federal information collection and analysis, the single step that would go the farthest toward the goal of reshaping the management-government relationship would be the establishment of an institutional focal point for government participation in the national dialogue on global economic competitiveness: an Office of National Economic Competitiveness in the White House.

It would be an overstatement to suggest that an office with a presidential adviser and a small staff could turn around the nation's competitiveness problem. But such an office could make a number of concrete contributions while symbolizing government recognition that current structures are simply inadequate to attend to the major change that has taken place in the economy. An Office of National Economic Competitiveness could address two broad needs. It could provide a visible, top-level point of entry for management and labor leaders seeking to establish a dialogue on the competitiveness issue. Currently there is no such focal point in the U.S. government. The approaches used by Germany and Japan—reliance on a highly skilled bureaucratic corps or a far-reaching, powerful ministry—are clearly not applicable to the American system. But structure is important for change; new structure must promote a different kind of information exchange between management and government from what has taken place in the past.

Second, the office could serve as a watchful eye to make sure that broad national economic policies are developed with an eye to their impact on company performance in the global marketplace. Much as the creation of the Council of Economic Advisers institutionalized the perspective of the macroeconomist in shaping economic policy, so would the establishment of this office institutionalize the skills of the business strategist and competitive analyst in the government.

The creation of the Council of Economic Advisers represented a slow and measured response to the changing economics of another generation. The idea for an advisory committee to monitor and analyze national economic change first surfaced in 1931. At that time, it was seen as a response to the crash of 1929 and the Depression. By the time the idea became law in 1946, as part of the Employment Act, the council had become an economic weather bureau, monitoring the national economic climate and issuing periodic reports. The immediate concern was that the end of World War II would mean a new depression, with unemployment spiraling as high as 20,000,000.

But that the council became law and has served a valuable purpose in the government and in the economy demonstrates the capacity of national institutions to change in response to new conditions. Perhaps the strongest argument for a new Office of National Economic Competitiveness is the existence of the Council of Economic Advisers: just as it was an appropriate institutional response to the economic changes of the Depression and the end of World War II, so an Office of National Economic Competitiveness is an appropriate institutional response to globalization.

The purpose of these new structures between management and labor and between management and government is to promote ongoing discussions, communication, and information sharing. But implicitly, the structural arrangements serve a broader goal: to break down the traditional rigidities of principle and practice that have been built up over time and to supplant them with more flexible, adaptable, mutually advantageous arrangements. The structure represents the channel; just as important are the messages, the negotiations that determine the working agreements in the enterprise system.

New Quid pro Quos with Labor

The lesson of the auto industry in one area is unambiguous: the traditional bargaining that has governed the relationships between management and labor is not consistent with a competitive enterprise system. Different agreements, consistent in style and substance with the principle of shared authority and shared responsibility, will have to be struck. The new deals will need to emphasize quid pro quos that serve the interests of both sides.

From the German and Japanese experience, the kinds and categories of exchange are evident. In exchange for the elimination of restrictive work practices and job classifications and the negotiation of wage and benefit packages that are company specific and performance weighted, management promises the workers employment security, more responsibility and power in the work place, ongoing training, and respect. The principle that the workers are the company's most valuable asset is put into practice in the way workers are hired, trained, rewarded, addressed, promoted, and disciplined. In return, management expects a commitment from the workers that is company specific—a shared sense of responsibility for, and pride in, the performance of that company.

Since 1982, both GM and Ford have been moving with the UAW in the direction of a similarly structured set of trade-offs. But some elements of the package have been easier to achieve than others. The companies have formally expressed their commitment to employment security, less so their willingness to empower workers on the plant floor; the UAW has accepted a moderated wage and benefit agreement, but backed away from company-specific economic bargaining. Moreover, at the level of the individual plant, the progress toward practicing the new philosophy embodied in the 1982 and 1984 contracts has been notoriously spotty, depending almost entirely on the character of the plant manager and the president of the UAW local.

Simply continuing this pattern will not secure a competitive future: the rate of change is too slow and the scope of change too narrow. The experiments now being attempted are responses to changes in the competitive environment that began almost twenty years ago. But catching up to yesterday is cold comfort when the competition has moved on to tomorrow. American management and labor will need to extend their reach if they hope to grasp the future. "Business as usual," even if modified by the incremental changes introduced in the 1982 and 1984 auto contracts, inevitably will only mean going out of business.

The place to begin again is the formal agreement between management and labor. Initially, the contract between the two sides was a small and straightforward document, a short statement of the terms and conditions of employment and of the wages and benefits earned in exchange. By way of illustration, the first contract between the UAW and Ford in 1941 was no more than five pages long, small enough to slip into every worker's back pocket. But over the years, this basic agreement took on more and more. Like the federal tax code, it became an instrument of policy. New issues found their way into the contract. It became the place where the differing interests of management and labor confronted each other; in the absence of any other forum, collective bargaining became the arena for management and labor to argue over power sharing and policy sharing—the elements of negotiated strategy—as well as the traditional aspects of their relationship involving work, wages, and benefits.

Untangling these issues into two discrete agreements with two discrete sets of communication would provide the management-labor relationship with a new competitive impetus. One package would treat the traditional issues in collective bargaining. A second package would be devoted solely to the issues related to long-run competitive strategy: questions of company and union philosophy, and questions of business policy that affect the common interests of management and employees. This second package would constitute a new compact between the company and its workers. It could address such issues as investment decisions related to capacity expansion and reduction, and vertical integration and disintegration; supply choices with respect to the sourcing of components and finished product; and technology choices regarding the development of new products and the installation of new manufacturing processes leading to increased competitiveness in world markets.

Ideally, both the collective bargaining agreement and the negotiated competitive strategy agreement would be renewed annually rather than every three years, which is now the case with collective bargaining in the auto industry, and would be bargained on a company-specific rather than industrywide basis, which is the case with pattern bargaining.

There are a number of reasons why this approach not only makes sense but also would advance the cause of American competitiveness: the explicit legitimacy it confers on labor, the clear sharing of responsibility and authority, the structure it creates for negotiating management-labor cooperation, the link between principles and practices, the mechanisms it would create for communication, and the flexibility it would permit. The annual update, in particular, recognizes that periodic consultation is the key to ensuring that the evolving relationships between management and labor remain on a procompetitive track. In a host of ways it is a logical outgrowth of an analysis of the changing paradigm of the enterprise system. But perhaps the best reason to move to this approach as quickly as possible is, very simply, that it represents the future direction of management-labor relations in the auto industry—and quite likely all industry.

Three developments, in particular, indicate the direction of the auto industry. First, the growing presence of Japanese auto producers in the United States is changing the definition of accepted practice in management-labor relations. Within several years, more than one million autos will be manufactured in the United States by Japanese-managed companies employing Japanese-style management-labor relations: Nissan, Honda, Toyota, Mazda, Mitsubishi, Subaru. Whether workers are unionized or not, management typically begins its relationship with its workers by explicitly stating its philosophy, in effect, by negotiating with the workers an understanding of the principles that will guide the overall operation of the company.

At Toyota, for example, the basic principles were even embodied in a written document, a letter of intent between management and labor, stipulating the philosophical basis for proceeding with the relationship. Progress toward the full-scale operation of the plant and the development of the product continued at Fremont, California, for almost a full year with no formal contract between management and labor. The sole basis for the relationship was the philosophy expressed in the letter of intent and the mutual trust and respect it engendered. When a contract finally was negotiated, the practices in the agreement governing wages and benefits, job security, and job classifications represented a logical outgrowth of the letter of intent. The contract was ratified by a 92 percent vote of the workers.

Where these new Japanese-managed projects are unionized—thus far, Toyota and Mazda—the UAW has realistically accepted the need for a negotiation over philosophy and a negotiation over wages and benefits. Where the facility is not unionized, the company has followed such an approach on its own initiative. In both cases, the result is the same: two separate agreements, company specific, with a close connection between principles and practices and a close identification between management and labor.

The second development is suggested by GM's Saturn project. The decision to make Saturn a separate, wholly owned corporation clearly meant that Saturn would have a separate labor agreement with the UAW: in effect, GM succeeded in establishing a situation comparable to that of the Japanese producers located in the United States. And while the new workers employed at the Saturn plant are almost entirely UAW members, they are working under a different system and in a different relationship with GM from that of their fellow UAW members. First, they have an extensive body of writing and thinking produced by the Saturn study team, designed to define the philosophy of the relationship. Second, they have a separate contract with terms and conditions, wages, and benefits different from the GM-UAW master agreement. Third, the new labor agreement established a joint Strategy Advisory Committee, whose agenda will be the "long-range goals and health of Saturn." The real significance of this development, however, is not the Saturn experiment itself and the thousands of workers. Rather, it is GM's conviction that the future health of the company depends upon its ability to Saturnize its relationships across the board, not only in the context of a limited experiment but throughout the system. To make that happen requires duplicating the Saturn format in the other GM divisions, working in partnership with the UAW—and doing it as soon and as quickly as possible.

The third development in the management-labor relationship is the implicit end of pattern bargaining. In reality, the old paradigm has already died; all that is wanting now is for both sides to recognize the fact, accept it, and move on in a conscious way to a system of contingent compensation based on company-specific deals. The original purpose of pattern bargaining, whether in autos or any other industry, has been to remove direct labor costs as a competitive factor among rival companies. In the case of the American auto industry, as long as the competition was strictly limited to the Big Three, pattern bargaining could be justified. But globalization knocked the conceptual underpinnings from underneath the pattern; in relatively short order, the reality of the pattern changed, if not the rhetoric.

Chrysler was the first of the Big Three to break the pattern with the blessing of the UAW in 1979 as a result of its brush with bankruptcy. Then in 1984, although the pattern was never explicitly renounced, it became clear that the resources, structure, and strategies of GM and Ford were so different as to require bargains tailored to the capabilities of the company. The new reality is that under the pressure of globalization, Ford and GM each defined a philosophical approach to its relationship with the UAW and shaped its bargaining to that philosophy. Over time, the different approaches, played out against the backdrop of the competitive stage, are producing widely diverging results. What has yet to change, however, are the policies of the UAW in response to this development.

The UAW's bargaining goal with Chrysler in 1985 was restoration of wage parity with Ford and GM (rather than more innovative profit sharing), thereby forcing the automaker into more coproduction with Mitsubishi, its Japanese partner. The structure of the UAW also needs to change. Just as Sloan brought a balance between centralization and decentralization to GM in the 1920s, so today the UAW needs a rebalancing in its organization between company-specific relations and industrywide concerns.

Like the myth of management's rights, the concept of an industrywide pattern is becoming a less and less credible fiction. Once again, the handwriting is on the wall; the sooner management and labor heed the message, the greater the opportunity to shape a sustainable competitive direction for the future.

Moving Management and Government

The relationship between management and labor clearly has a direct and immediate effect on the competitive performance of the company. In recent years, both principles and practices have begun to change—sadly, only gradually—to reflect the new global reality. At a minimum, both sides have recognized the need to change and even grasped a number of the fundamentals that must be adjusted in order to realign their relationship. Between management and labor, the issue that remains is the rate and range of change: whether the two sides can push ahead in their own internal adaptations and their bilateral arrangements to catch up with the international competitors. There is a general philosophical understanding between the leaders of management and labor in the auto industry that correctly corresponds to their joint competitive challenge. The questions for the future are whether, how fast, and to what extent that understanding can be converted into purposeful practice.

In the relationship between management and government, however, no such philosophical agreement exists; as a consequence, the practices between the two sides remain chaotic and anticompetitive. Since 1979, when the auto crisis really began, the two sides have been locked in ideological trench warfare over the proper role of government in the economy: the fundamental question of the legitimacy of government's participation in the enterprise system. Not only has the debate proved fruitless, it has also yielded some incongruous results. For example, when the Japanese tidal wave hit the U.S. automakers in 1979, the Carter administration steadfastly refused to give in to calls from Ford, Chrysler, and the UAW asking for trade protection, citing its philosophical commitment not to intervene in world trade. On the other hand, the Carter administration saw no philosophical problem in creating a special Auto Industry Committee, with representation from all U.S. auto producers, the UAW, suppliers, auto dealers, and the government—an experimental forum where information could be shared and decisions negotiated. When the Reagan administration came into office in January 1981, however, the positions were summarily reversed, along with the philosophical justifications: the Auto Industry Committee was abolished as unwarranted government intervention in the industry; just as promptly, a voluntary restraint agreement was extracted from the Japanese.

In the area of regulation, the record of the two administrations features similar perverse twists. For example, in its waning weeks, the Carter administration tried to fashion a compromise on the air bag issue that not only would have put the matter to rest after years of contention but also would have benefited U.S. companies and disadvantaged the Japanese. The Reagan administration, on the other hand, simply abolished the requirement, a broad stroke that triggered a lawsuit and produced further delay and uncertainty. When the court verdict reinstated the requirement, the Reagan administration then issued a new regulation that stimulated a multimillion-dollar state-to-state lobbying battle between automakers and auto insurers—with no definitive outcome to the safety-related issue.

The inescapable conclusion is that the relationship between management and government will not be changed by agreeing first on principles and then designing new practices to enact them. In fact, the lesson of the debate over industrial policy of the last few years appears to be that discussion about the relationship between management and government that begins at that lofty level of philosophical abstraction is destined to remain at that lofty level—and destined to remain nothing but conversation.

As currently structured, the debate has three things wrong with it. First, it is about the wrong question. Second, it is being conducted at the wrong level. Third, it is being advanced from the wrong side.

The question that has been debated up to now is, "What is the proper role of government in the economy?" To address the real problem, the question should be, "What relationship between management and government will contribute to a competitive American enterprise system?" Second, rather than debating the issue at the level of macroeconomics and political philosophy, managers and government officials need to approach it at a practical level: "What overlapping activities of companies and government affect the cost and quality of American products in global competition?" Even more simply, "How can common-sense negotiations between management and government reduce the $2,000 Japanese cost advantage and also meet legitimate public policy objectives?" Finally, the discussion needs to be initiated by management, not government. In large part, the industrial policy debate has stagnated because it has smacked of big government making a further invasion of management's rights.

But the fact is that government cannot legislate, buy, or win legitimacy in its relationship with management. Management has to confer it. And it is also a fact that it is in management's own best interests to confer legitimacy on government and then to go to work with government on ways to attack the Japanese advantages.

This criticism of the debate over the management-government relationship only serves to explain why there has been so little change. It does not, however, negate the need for change. The evidence of enterprise systems around the world shows that the relationship between management and government is a critical dimension of competitiveness. And the evidence of the American relationship in the auto industry clearly demonstrates the need for change.

What is required is a fresh look at the problem, one that stands the current configuration on its head: A new management-government relationship will emerge by management focusing on an agenda of overlapping private and public policy issues that affect the cost and quality position of American companies and by negotiating trade-offs with the government over these salient issues. In effect, the task is for management to invent private sector industry policy—or to "reverse engineer" philosophy from everyday practice.

The notion of private sector industrial policy recognizes that even though governments do not compete in global industries, government policy can and does directly influence enterprise competition. This notion explicitly rejects two popular models of management-government relationships: laissez-faire capitalism and government-directed industrial policy, the latter because it does not correctly identify how the business world actually works, and the former because it does not recognize what role government can effectively play in encouraging an enterprise system to be more competitive.

The auto industry offers a number of examples of what private sector industrial policy means in practice. First and foremost, it means company management and government leaders agreeing to an agenda at a policy level more specific than macroeconomics. As the leading manufacturing industry in the world, the auto industry amply demonstrates the powerful relationship between macroeconomics and industry performance. America's recession, as the saying goes, is Detroit's depression. High interest rates, tight money, and an overvalued dollar not only shrink demand for new cars in the U.S. market but also favor imports and encourage outsourcing. Clearly, macroeconomic policies that support competitive efforts by American companies are vital to the country's future economic health.

But the auto industry also demonstrates that the relationship between management and government does not end with macroeconomic policy. The Japanese auto industry, for example, is aided by government macroeconomic policies that consistently support exports. But the fact that the Japanese automakers have products that can be exported is not a result of macroeconomics. Rather, it is at least in part attributable to company- and industry-specific trade-offs between management and government designed to reduce costs and boost quality.

In the auto industry, examples are easy to come by. Energy, for instance, is an area of particular sensitivity to the automakers: in the United States, roughly 40 percent of all oil consumed is used by cars. Moreover, as the tumultuous events of 1973 and 1979 proved, energy price and availability are at the heart of global competition in the auto industry, with direct implications for every aspect of the business, from product mix to market segmentation, competitive position between companies, and overall demand.

Nevertheless, since the passage of the Energy Policy and Conservation Act in 1975, federal energy policy and its application to the auto industry have been typically schizophrenic. The approach of the "noninterventionist" U.S. government has been to legislate strict performance standards for U.S. automakers, stipulating the corporate average fuel economy (CAFE) that must be met by each of the Big Three. It is an approach with no discernible effect on the rest of the world competitors; in essence, it continues to make government policy as if the only important market were the United States and the only relevant competitors the Big Three. It also has no relationship with the market; that is, the standard set by the government is unconnected to both the price and the availability of oil and the dictates of the auto buyer in the market. Finally, and perhaps most ironically, in noninterventionist America, it is an approach that directly and unmistakably interjects the federal government into the product-planning policy of the automakers. By establishing specific energy performance standards, the government is telling the U.S. auto industry—and only the U.S. auto industry—what kind of cars and how many of each kind to build.

In "interventionist" Japan, in contrast, the energy issue was handled far more simply, more competitively, more efficiently, more strategically, and more economically. After the first oil shock, the energy issue jumped in importance in the regular, ongoing discussions between management and government representatives. Both sides agreed, after considered negotiation, that it would be mutually advantageous if the automakers would accelerate their efforts to produce cars that were even more fuel efficient: both the national energy policy of conservation and the auto industry's business policy of exports and market leadership would be enhanced. To use the power of marketplace demand to reinforce the negotiated agreement, the government increased the gas tax, stimulating increased consumer demand for fuel-efficient cars.

This issue is important as more than a historical object lesson. Each one of the Big Three is currently engaged in a calculated gamble of tens of billions of dollars to determine whether it can manufacture competitive small cars in America. Moreover, the success or failure of the experiments will have enduring implications for each company's overall competitive posture, namely, whether the middle of the market goes to Japan and what the prospects are for hundreds of thousands of American workers. And yet as the automakers begin to lock in their investments on this high-stakes gamble, there is no negotiated strategy between management and government leadership for the single most pivotal policy issue that will shape the market into which these American-built small cars will be launched: energy.

Clearly, it would be in the interests of both American automakers, who are risking billions of dollars if not betting their companies, and American government officials, who are legitimately concerned over the country's energy use, to negotiate an approach to the issue that would serve the interests of both sides. An obvious lesson from the Japanese system would be to focus any negotiated strategy on the marketplace, rather than on the manufacturers, employing the power of consumer demand. One example of this approach would be a modest, regularly applied increase in the federal gas tax—a signal to the market to continue to place a premium on fuel efficiency and, through the market, a signal to the automakers of the kind of consumer demand to expect when launching their new small-car offerings.

A second area where the management-government relationship has a clear impact on the cost and quality of competition is regulation. As with energy policy, the history of the American relationship reveals a problem with approach: government insistence on command and control regulations that inherently distrust both the market and the manufacturer and that fail to acknowledge the differences between companies or to tap their capacity to solve a public policy problem in a way that could prove competitively advantageous to them. Again, a comparison with the Japanese is instructive. There, though adopting strict environmental regulations in part to ensure that the cars will qualify for export to the United States, the government has both used a system of company self-certification and implemented a rigorous, expensive auto inspection program—once again using consumer demand for quality as an approach to encourage each company to come up with the highest-quality product possible. Once more, both management and government would have much to gain by exploring approaches to regulations that adapt existing regulatory methods to the new competitive reality. Whether in air quality, antitrust enforcement, safety, or other regulatory areas, a negotiated strategy that seeks to emphasize both high quality and low cost would serve the interests of both sides.

These are only two examples of what is, in fact, a much longer list of public and private policy issues that directly affect the cost and quality positions of American automakers. Other areas include health care costs, which Chrysler officials have estimated add $500 to the cost of each American-made car; worker training and education, which directly affects quality and now threatens to turn GM into the largest educational institution in the country; antitrust policy, which touches both cost and quality and, in the case of the Japanese auto industry, helped promote the evolution of globally competitive companies; and trade policy, which speaks directly to the new competitive reality. In each of these areas, mutually advantageous negotiations, initiated by company leadership, could begin the critically important process of adapting the management-government relationship at the pragmatic level of day-to-day practice, rather than philosophy.

From this approach could come a number of developments essential to America's future competitiveness. One simple benefit would be new approaches to longstanding problems that could actually promote the competitive performance of American automakers in terms of cost and quality. A second benefit would be the establishment of new lines of communications between management and government, parallel to the new communications links between management and labor. Third, management could act in its own self-interest and, at the same time, help government discover new ways in which to accomplish its traditional interests, an exchange in which both sides win. These changes would not only dispel the myth of management's rights in the management-government relationship but also begin to alter the tone and import of the management-government dialogue, at last moving it away from confrontative public posturing to joint problem solving. Over the long run, however, the most important benefit from these changes may come in the evolution of the way in which both management leaders and government officials think about their ongoing relationships. By demonstrating a capacity to locate their shared interests in solving practical problems that affect both cost and quality for the companies and public policy concerns for the government, the two sides may eventually define a legitimate government role as a catalyst for competitiveness.

Without question, change is needed in the management-government relationship in the United States. From the evidence of Japan and Germany, it is hard to see how American business will be able to match the performance of foreign companies in the global competition of the 1980s and 1990s with a management-government relationship mired in the 1960s. In spite of the extensive efforts by American management and labor to reinvent their relationship, without similar progress between management and government the overall American enterprise system will continue to represent a competitive disadvantage for U.S. companies.

There are only a limited number of approaches that could apply to this situation. First, both sides could simply do nothing, continuing to play by the old rules. Second, management and government could continue to espouse the traditional philosophy of an arm's-length relationship, but at the same time government leaders could increase their pressure on foreign governments to change their systems to conform more closely to the American model. A third, and radically different, approach would be for management and government suddenly to change their prevailing view of government's role and for government leaders to begin to work on a comprehensive "competitiveness policy."

None of these three approaches, however, can legitimately hold much promise of real improvement in the competitive practices within the American enterprise system. Doing nothing seems a guarantee of competitive decline. Trying to change the competitors simply gives them the power to determine the course of the future: if they refuse to change, or fail to change, or change only superficially, or change in ways that prove unhelpful, American companies, workers, and national interests will continue to suffer. Calling for a national competitiveness policy seems also a misplaced notion, as if the government were at the center of the enterprise system and could, by virtue of a blanket policy, "make" American companies competitive.

A fourth approach seems the most pragmatic and productive: for management to identify the concrete ways in which legitimate government intervention actually affects cost and quality and then to go to work on a negotiated strategy to convert those specific interactions into American advantages. The reality of global competition is that U.S. management needs competent government participation in the enterprise system. Without the responsible participation of the government, and even with the most ideal relationship between management and labor, American companies will continue to lose out to foreign competitors who can rely on the full economic, political, and social support of their government. It would be sadly ironic if after complaining that they had lost out to the Japanese in the 1970s because of too much government, the American automakers were to lose out permanently because of too little government. Most important, the choice is for management—not government—to make.

Negotiated Strategies

The availability of new and better information, the creation of new structures that provide a location for ongoing communication among the key industrial players, and the explicit negotiation of quid pro quos related to enhanced competitiveness add up to a new context and process of strategy formulation at the enterprise level.

Formulating competitive strategy has typically been considered a function of senior executives. Indeed, with only a few exceptions in American economic history, mostly during wartime, corporate executives have themselves considered the formulation of corporate purpose and business policies to be one of their exclusive prerogatives. This notion of exclusive responsibility has been reinforced by a management ideology that asserts that top executives should participate, in the form of bonuses and other forms of incentive compensation, in the success and failure of the strategies they develop and implement.

In light of our analysis, however, we can see that established management theory and traditional practice have been outrun by events in industries such as autos. As senior managers begin to face the task of negotiating their strategies and resource requirements with labor unions and government agencies, their behavior will run counter to many orthodox beliefs about managers' exclusive "rights to manage" and authority to set policy. But the cost of sticking with these outdated orthodoxies will increase for many firms as the success of their international competitors, armed with strategies reflecting the interests and cooperation of both their work and government, continues to demonstrate that competitive advantage accrues to those firms that can line up broad support for their basic economic goals and business policies.

Negotiating the policies that make up competitive business strategy will require subtle trading: of political support for various policies and projects; enhanced career opportunities for employee support; a measure of increased job security or new payment systems for more flexible work rules; or even investment guarantees by corporations in exchange for "favorable" public policies. Although no single trade-off may improve corporate performance in a significant way by itself, a network of coordinated quid pro quos among management, labor, and government can add up over time to effective corporate strategies that have the support of relevant interest groups. In this sense, it may be appropriate to think of competitive strategy and organizational adaptation in industries like autos as resulting from multiple decisions negotiated among management, labor, and government, and to view senior managers as leaders of this process rather than as unconstrained decision makers.

LESSONS FROM THE AUTO INDUSTRY

We return, in the end, to the story of the auto industry and the lessons it has to teach the rest of the country. When we began this project, the American auto industry was in crisis. In Detroit, the largest, proudest companies in the country were facing historic losses, perhaps even bankruptcy. Across the country, hundreds of thousands of workers had lost their jobs, and the most influential, progressive union in all of organized labor was powerless to do anything about it. In Washington, successive administrations vacillated between expressions of concern and disavowals of responsibility for the plight of the industry. Around the country, the three sides took turns blaming the others and being blamed: management had been shortsighted, labor greedy, government heavy-handed. In the depths of the crisis, there were profound doubts about the nation's economic future.

By 1985, the wheel had turned. GM had transformed itself from a plodding dinosaur into a high-tech global company. Ford was close behind in diversification and, in the auto industry, substantially ahead in improving quality. Chrysler, miraculously, had not only survived but had also begun to make its own high-tech acquisitions. The UAW, smaller and still at the forefront of American unionism, was once again in the vanguard of the labor movement. And the federal government had concluded that the auto industry had made a full recovery.

But elsewhere in the economy the signs were less encouraging. Overall, the country's trade balance had plummeted to worrisome depths. For the first time in seventy years, America had become a debtor nation. For the first time there was a deficit in the balance of trade in electronics. Insiders in Silicon Valley publicly announced that the economic competition over microchips was over—and Japan had won. A round of lay-offs began in high-tech companies as investments and market share moved overseas. The part of the economy that had been presumed to be the future—the part that had been embraced during the auto crisis as the replacement for the mature, dying smokestack industries of the past—was now beginning to suffer its own competitive crisis.

Moreover, beneath the surface of the auto industry's dramatic recovery remained the unresolved dilemma of an industry struggling to make a monumental transition, an industry fighting to create a new concept of itself and to survive. The record-breaking profits and breathtaking acquisitions only masked the continued competitive disadvantage facing the U.S. automakers and the employment threat confronting the autoworkers. For the auto industry, the future was a question: new game or end game?

But beneath the surface, the facts were still stark. In simple terms, the Japanese had achieved dominance in the low end of the market and were beginning to mount successful challenges in the midsize and sporty segments. If left unimpeded by government restraints, the Japanese could realistically claim as much as 40 percent of the American market by the end of the decade. Without dramatic change, the American auto industry would face a diminishing future—a future of fewer and smaller America-based automakers, fewer jobs for autoworkers, fewer economic spinoffs into allied industries, and, ultimately, a diminished standard of living for the American people.

At the core of the competitiveness issue is a single, consistent problem: the competitive environment has changed dramatically and permanently and the American enterprise system has not. In the face of escalating global competition, involving foreign companies, unions, and governments that have developed more efficient and effective ways of negotiating strategy, the American auto industry has continued to follow the traditional relationships of a previous period. These relationships were based on conceptual principles and day-to-day practices that suited the old competitive environment. In a sheltered national environment, with competition effectively limited to just the Big Three, the disaffection of the workers and the distrust of the government made no difference.

But in global competition, the principles and practices that define the way managers, workers, and government officials think about and act toward each other have become the source of the industry's competitive disadvantage. The legacy of decades of distance and distrust is higher cost and lower quality. The result is the decline of an industry that has been central to the American economy for more than three-quarters of a century.

The broader implication of the decline of the auto industry is a powerful warning to the rest of American industry. For the principles and practices embedded in the auto industry are embedded throughout the national economy as the American way of doing business. Today, any salient industry with the potential for global competition must consider the sad fate of the auto industry.

The lesson of the auto industry is as simple as it is difficult: If America wants to compete successfully against the best in the world, the American enterprise system will have to change. It will take deep, broad, systemic change, change as fundamental as a new concept of the corporation. In the case of the auto industry, it will take reinventing not just how to build the car but more importantly how to conduct a car company—a "clean sheet" approach not just on the factory floor but in executive suites, Solidarity House, and the White House. It will require a new template for the American enterprise system.

The evidence of the recent past shows that some change is possible. But the change has been only sporadic and much too slow. It may have taken the Japanese twenty years to evolve their carefully balanced, internally consistent enterprise system. American industry does not have the luxury of this much time. For the auto industry and the increasing numbers of industries entering global competition, the mandate is clear and chilling: change or fail.

Twenty years ago, Alfred P. Sloan left General Motors and the auto industry with the same message. "No company ever stops changing," he wrote. "Change will come for better or worse. . . . Each new generation must meet changes—in the automotive market, in the general administration of the enterprise, and in the involvement of the corporation in the changing world." This generation of American managers, labor leaders, and government officials has before it the task of forging new alliances capable of meeting the challenge of global competition. How well these leaders meet that challenge will determine not only the future of the American auto industry but also much about the future standard of living and quality of life in the United States.

Competitive Product Programs and Anticipated Domestic Production and Auto-related Employment for 1990

Prepared by
John O'Donnell
for
The Harvard Business School Project on the
Auto Industry and the American Economy

SUMMARY OBSERVATIONS

• Japanese automakers have captured almost 50 percent of the U.S. small-car market, nearly 25 percent of the midsize-car market, and over 40 percent of the sports-car market. U.S. automakers have retained 100 percent of the domestic large-car market and 70 percent of the luxury-car market (Exhibit 1).

• From 1980 to 1985, Japanese and Korean automakers introduced five times as many new small cars as U.S. automakers, three times as many midsize cars, and twice as many new sports cars (Exhibits 2 and 3).

• New product announcements for the 1986–1990 period show Japanese and Korean automakers with twice as many new cars planned, as of June 1986 (Exhibits 2 and 3).

• Based on known new product plans (Exhibits 2 and 3); currently anticipated product programs and U.S. production capacity in 1990 (Exhibit 4); conservative assumptions with respect to industry sales, shifts in market segmentation, import penetration, and Canadian production in 1990 (Exhibit 5); and the anticipated distribution of imports and non-U.S. auto production in North America by major market segments (Exhibit 6),

• Existing U.S. small-car and sports-car capacity may be largely redundant in a free trade environment. The shares of the small, midsize, luxury, and sports car segments available to U.S. automakers in North America will be equivalent to only 14 percent, 43 percent, 55 percent, and 62 percent, respectively, of anticipated manufacturing capacity (Exhibit 7);

• The large-car market segment will remain the private domain of U.S. producers (Exhibit 7).

• Based on conservative assumptions with respect to U.S. auto production in major industry segments, labor hours per car by type of vehicle, number of hours worked per year by a typical U.S. autoworker, and the expected degree of vertical integration in the U.S. auto industry (Exhibit 8),

• Auto-related production employment at the four domestic auto producers will decline by 140,000 workers between 1983, a boom year for the industry, and 1990 (Exhibit 9); and

• Total auto-related production employment between 1978, a precrisis peak in domestic auto production, and 1990 will decline by 360,000 employees, or 51 percent (Exhibit 9).

EXHIBIT 1
U.S. Passenger Car Market by Size for 1985[a]
(in percent of units sold)

	% Domestic Share	% European Share	% Japanese Share
Small Cars	55	—	45
Midsize Cars	70	7	23
Large Cars	100	—	—
Luxury Cars	70	30	—
Sports Cars	54	4	42

[a]Size classification based upon *Ward's Auto World* and HBS project estimates.
SOURCE: *Ward's Automotive Yearbook,* 1985.

EXHIBIT 2
Summary of New Product Introductions and Major Redesigns
for the U.S. Market by American, Japanese, and Korean Automakers, 1980–1990
(U.S. introductions by platform type; Japanese and Korean by nameplate)[a]

	1980–1984	1985–1990[b]	Total
Small Cars			
Domestic	3 (5)[c]	2	5
Japanese/Other	15	22	37
Midsize Cars			
Domestic	4 (12)	7	11
Japanese/Other	11	8	19
Large/Luxury Cars			
Domestic	6 (17)	11	17
Japanese/Other	0	6	6
Sports Cars			
Domestic	3 (4)	1	4
Japanese/Other	8	9	17

[a]U.S. platforms and Japanese/Korean nameplates are used here as competing
product lines. Passenger car market segmentation is based upon *Ward's Auto
World,* January 1984.

[b]U.S. nameplate information for period beyond 1985 is not known at this time.

[c]Numbers in parentheses represent the number of U.S. nameplates. Note that for
U.S. automakers one platform generates as many as five nameplates, each with
several downscale and upscale models.

SOURCE: Compiled by authors from various automotive press sources and
industry interviews.

EXHIBIT 3

New Product Introductions and Major Redesigns for the U.S. Market by Domestic, Japanese, and Korean Automakers, Calendar Years 1975–1990+
(U.S. introductions by platform type; Japanese and Korean introductions by nameplate)[a]

	1975–1979[b]	1980–1984	1985	1986	1987	1988	1989	1990+
Small Cars								
Domestic	Chrysler L-body (4)[c] GM T-body (2)	Ford Erika (3) AMC/Renault Alliance AMC/Renault Encore		Chrysler P-body (2)			GM Saturn	
Japanese/ Other	VW Rabbit (U.S.)	MMC/Chrysler Colt Toyota Starlet Toyota Tercel Mazda GLC (FWD) Isuzu I-Mark Nissan Pulsar Nissan Sentra Toyota Corolla (FWD) Honda Civic Toyota Corolla SR-5 (RWD) Isuzu/GM R-body Suzuki/GM M-body Subaru DL/GL VW Golf (U.S.) Mitsubishi Mirage	Toyota/GM TVX (U.S.) Toyota Starlet Mini (FWD) Nissan March Mini MMC/Chrysler Colt Honda Civic (U.S.) Nissan Sentra (U.S.)	Mazda 323 Hyundai Excel (Korea) Toyota Starlet Mini (FWD) Nissan Micra Mini Toyota Corolla (U.S.) Subaru Justy Mini	Daewoo/GM Le Mans (Korea) Ford/Mazda 323 (Mexico) Suzuki Cultus Daihatsu Charade Kia/Ford Mini (Korea)	Chrysler/ Mitsubishi H2X (U.S.) Hyundai/ Mitsubishi Mini (Korea) Toyota Corolla (Canada) Hyundai Excel (Canada)		Suzuki/GM (Canada)

(continued)

Midsize Cars

	GM X-body AMC Eagle	Chrysler K-body (2) GM J-body (5) Ford Topaz (2) GM N-body (3)	Chrysler H-body (2)	GM L-body (2)	AMC/Renault X-58 Chrysler J-body AMC/Renault R-21 (France)	Chrysler A-body	GM-98
Domestic	GM X-body AMC Eagle	Chrysler K-body (2) GM J-body (5) Ford Topaz (2) GM N-body (3)	Chrysler H-body (2)	GM L-body (2)	AMC/Renault X-58 Chrysler J-body AMC/Renault R-21 (France)	Chrysler A-body	GM-98
Japanese/ Other		Toyota Cressida Nissan Maxima (RWD) Nissan Stanza Honda Accord Toyota Camry Mitsubishi Cordia Mitsubishi Tredia Mazda 626 (FWD) Honda Accord (U.S.) Nissan Maxima (FWD) MMC/Chrysler Vista	Honda Accord Mitsubishi Galant	Nissan Stanza Toyota Camry Isuzu Aska	Hyundai Stellar (Korea)	Mazda 626/727 (U.S.) Toyota Camry (U.S.)	

Large/Luxury Cars

Domestic	GM G-body (5) GM B-body (4) GM C-body (3) Ford Panther (3) Chrysler M-body (3)	Ford S-shell (2) Ford LS-shell (2) Ford L-shell (2) GM A-body (4) GM C-body FWD (3) Chrysler E-body (3)	GM H-body (2) Ford Taurus (2) Ford Merkur (Europe)	GM E/K-body (3) Ford Scorpio (Europe)	Chrysler C-body GM W-body Chrysler Q-Coupe (Italy)	Ford MN 12 Ford EN 25/FN9	Ford FN10

Exhibit 3 (continued)

New Product Introductions and Major Redesigns for the U.S. Market by Domestic, Japanese, and Korean Automakers Calendar Years 1975–1990+
(U.S. introductions by platform type, Japanese and Korean introductions by nameplate)[a]

	1975–1979[b]	1980–1984	1985	1986	1987	1988	1989	1990+
Japanese				Acura Legend Mitsubishi Debonair	Toyota Cressida Mazda 929	Toyota Crown Nissan Cedric		
Sporty Cars								
Domestic	Ford Fox (2)	GM Y-body (1) GM P-body (1) Chrysler G-body (2)				GM-80 (FWD)		
Japanese		Toyota Supra Mitsubishi Starion Isuzu Impulse MMC/Chrysler Conquest Nissan 300 NX Honda CRX Honda Prelude Nissan Pulsar NX	Toyota MR-2 Toyota Celica (FWD) Subaru XT	Nissan EXA Mitsubishi Starion	Mazda RX-8 Acura MRV-6	Mazda/Ford Mustang III (U.S.)		

[a]U.S. platforms and Japanese/Korean nameplates are used here as competing product lines. Passenger car market segmentation is based upon *Ward's Auto World*, January 1984.

[b]Domestic cars only are shown for the period in order to indicate approximate age of many still current platform types.

[c]Numbers in parentheses represent number of U.S. nameplates.

SOURCE: Compiled by authors from various automotive press sources and industry interviews.

Exhibit 4
Anticipated Product Actions and Manufacturing Capacity

General Motors

Body Designation	Nameplate(s)	Year of Introduction	Production Source(s)	Capacity (000)	Plan
Small Cars					
T-body	Chevette T-1000	1975	Lakewood, GA	250	Discontinued after 1987 model year.
M-body (GM-40)	Sprint	1984	Japan	17–100	Minicar sourced from Suzuki for Chevrolet. May be built in Canada in late 1980s.
R-body (GM-50)	Spectrum	1984	Japan	33–200	Subcompact sourced from Isuzu for Chevrolet.
TVX-body (GM-60)	Nova	1985	Fremont, CA	250	GM/Toyota joint venture (NUMMI) Corolla-type car for Chevrolet. Toyota may take 50,000 units for its own dealers.
—	Le Mans	1987	Korea	100	Small Kadett-type car built by Daewoo for Pontiac.
Saturn	—	1989	Spring Hill, TN	(400)	Initial production will be 250,000 by 1990.
Midsize Cars					
X-body	Citation Skylark Phoenix Omega	1979	Willow Run, MI	250	Dropped in 1985.

(continued)

Exhibit 4 (continued)

Anticipated Product Actions and Manufacturing Capacity

General Motors

Body Designation	Nameplate(s)	Year of Introduction	Production Source(s)	Capacity (000)	Plan
Midsize Cars (Cont.)					
J-body	Cavalier Sunbird Firenza Skyhawk Cimarron	1981	Janesville, WI Leeds, MO Lordstown, OH	900	Redesign in 1988. May merge with N-body plastic design in 1991 (GM-98).
N-body (GM-20)	Calais Grand Am Somerset	1984	Lansing A&B, MI	400	May merge with J-body plastic design in 1991 (GM-98).
L-body (GM-25)	Corsica Beretta	1986	Linden, NJ Wilmington, DE	500	Chevrolet's X-body replacement.
Large Cars					
G-body	Monte Carlo Bonneville Grand Prix Supreme Regal	1978	Arlington, TX St. Therese, Ont. Pontiac #2, MI	700	To be phased out during 1987–1989 and replaced by W-body (GM-10).
A-body	Celebrity 6000 Ciera Century	1982	Doraville, GA Framingham, MA Oklahoma City, OK Tarrytown, NY Oshawa A&B, Ont.	1,300	To be phased out during 1987–1990 and replaced by the W-body (GM-10).

Body	Models	Year	Capacity	Plants	Notes
Large Cars (Cont.) W-body (GM-10)	—	1987	1,500	Doraville, GA Oshawa A&B, Ont. Fairfax #2, KS	Buick, Olds, and Pontiac replacement for A- and G-bodies. To be built in 7 plants. Four lines currently scheduled for production, but others will likely be added (Oklahoma City).
B-body	Caprice Parisienne Delta 88 Le Sabre	1977	400	Fairfax #1, KS Detroit, MI Lakewood, GA	B-bodies will be built for Pontiac and Chevrolet and wagon versions only will be built for Buick and Oldsmobile in the 1990s. Lakewood will build B-body in 1987. Fairfax will close.
H-body (GM-70)	Delta 88 Le Sabre	1985	800	Flint #4 & 40, MI Willow Run, MI Wentzville, MO	FWD replacement for Buick and Olds B-bodies. Wentzville will build H- and C-bodies concurrently.
Luxury Cars C-body (FWD)	Olds 98 Electra DeVille Fleetwood	1984	500	Orion, MI Wentzville, MO	Wentzville will also build H-body in 1986 MY.
E/K-body (GM-30)	Riviera Toronado Seville Eldorado	1986	300	Hamtramck, MI	New Hamtramck plant opened during 1986 MY building redesigned E/K-body.

(continued)

Exhibit 4 (continued)
Anticipated Product Actions and Manufacturing Capacity

General Motors

Body Designation	Nameplate(s)	Year of Introduction	Production Source(s)	Capacity (000)	Plan
Luxury Cars (Cont.)					
GM-35	Cadillac Allante	1986	Hamtramck, MI	—	E/K-body luxury car for Cadillac with Italian Pininfarina body.
GM-33 D-body	Buick Reatta Fleetwood Brougham	1987 1987	Hamtramck, MI Detroit, MI	— 100	E/K-body 2-door luxury car for Buick. RWD luxury car to be continued indefinitely.
Sports Cars					
F-body	Camaro Firebird	1966	Norwood, OH Van Nuys, CA	500	Will be replaced by GM-80.
Y-body	Corvette	1983	Bowling Green, KY	100	No change.
P-body	Fiero	1983	Pontiac #1, MI	150	Midengine sports car.
GM-80	Camaro Firebird	1988	Pontiac #2, MI	250	Redesigned F-body with FWD and plastic body.

Ford

Small Cars					
Erika	Escort Lynx EXP	1980	Edison, NJ Wayne, MI Oakville, Ont.	600	Lynx to continue at least through 1987. Erika redesigned in 1985 and EXP in 1986.

Small Cars (Cont.)					
323	Lynx	1987	Mexico	130	New FWD subcompact built by Ford in Mexico based on Mazda design with Mazda components to replace Lynx.
—	Festiva	1987	Korea	100	Minicar sourced from Kia.
Midsize Cars					
Topaz	Tempo Topaz	1983	Kansas City, MO Oakville, Ont.	400	No further plans known.
Large Cars					
S-Shell	Thunderbird Cougar	1980	Lorain, OH	250	Discontinue in 1988.
MN 12	Thunderbird Cougar	1988	Lorain, OH	250	Thunderbird/Cougar RWD replacement.
L-shell	LTD Marquis	1981	Chicago, IL Atlanta, GA	250	Discontinued in 1985 and replaced by Taurus project.
Panther	Grand Marquis Crown Victoria	1977	St. Thomas, Ont.	250	Replace with FWD in 1991.
Taurus	Taurus Sable	1985	Chicago, IL Atlanta, GA	500	FWD replacement for RWD L-shell.
Luxury Cars					
LS-shell	Continental Mark VII	1981	Wixom, MI	100	Replace in 1988 and 1990.

(continued)

EXHIBIT 4 (continued)
Anticipated Product Actions and Manufacturing Capacity

Ford

Body Designation	Nameplate(s)	Year of Introduction	Production Source(s)	Capacity (000)	Plan
Luxury Cars (Cont.)					
Panther	Lincoln Town Car	1977	Wixom, MI	100	Replace in 1992 with FWD.
Sierra	Merkur XR4TI	1985	Germany	20	Low-volume luxury car from Ford Europe.
Scorpio	Lugano	1986	Germany	20	Low-volume luxury car from Ford Europe.
EN 25/FN 9	Continental Mercury "X"	1988	Atlanta, GA Wixom, MI	100	Taurus-based replacement for LS-shell.
FN 10	Mark VIII	1990	Wixom, MI	50	Taurus-based replacement.
—	—	1990	Australia	20	Luxury sedan.
Sports Cars					
Fox	Mustang Capri	1978	Dearborn, MI	270	Capri nameplate dropped in 1986 and Mustang discontinued in 1987 or 1988. May be replaced by "626" derivative.
626/727	Mustang III	1988	Flat Rock, MI	140	FWD sports sedan to be U.S. built by Mazda and sold to Ford.

SOURCE: Compiled by authors from various automotive press sources.

Chrysler

Body Designation	Nameplate(s)	Year of Introduction	Production Source(s)	Capacity (000)	Plan
Small Cars					
L-body	Omni Horizon Turismo Charger	1978	Belvedere, IL	300	Discontinue in 1987.
P-body	Sundance Shadow	1986	Sterling Heights, MI	150	Upscale small car.
—	Colt	1980	Japan	150	Subcompact sourced from Mitsubishi.
H2X	—	1988	Bloomington-Normal, IL	120	Diamond-Star Chrysler/Mitsubishi joint venture to replace L-body. Chrysler may get more than 120,000 units.
Midsize Cars					
K-body	Aires Reliant	1980	St. Louis I, MO Newark, DE Detroit, MI Toluca, Mex.	325	Discontinued in 1987 and replaced with A-body.
H-body	LeBaron GTS Lancer	1985	Sterling Heights, MI	300	Targeted at sporty compact buyers.
A-body	—	1988	Newark, DE Detroit, MI	400	Replacement for K-body. Detroit plant may close.
J-body	—	1987	St. Louis I, MO Toluca, Mex.	200	Luxury, midsize car based on H-body.

(continued)

297

EXHIBIT 4 (continued)
Anticipated Product Actions and Manufacturing Capacity

Chrysler

Body Designation	Nameplate(s)	Year of Introduction	Production Source(s)	Capacity (000)	Plan
Large Cars					
M-body	Diplomat Gran Fury Fifth Avenue	1977	St. Louis II, MO	200	No firm date for elimination. May be sourced in Mexico when St. Louis plant retooled for compact van production in 1987.
E-body	Caravelle 600 LeBaron	1982	St. Louis I, MO Newark, DE Detroit, MI	325	Discontinued in 1987 and replaced by C-body.
C-body	—	1987	Belvedere, IL	325	Replacement for E-body and possibly M-body. Targeted at four-door sedan and luxury-car market.
Luxury Cars					
—	New Yorker	1982	—	—	See E-body.
—	Fifth Avenue	1977	—	—	See M-body.
—	Q-Coupe	1987	Italy	2	Maserati-built sports car.
Sports Cars					
G-body	Laser Daytona	1983	St. Louis I, MO	100	Based on K-body. Will be split sourced with J-body in St. Louis.
—	Conquest	1983	Japan	—	Sourced from Mitsubishi.

SOURCE: Compiled by authors from various automotive press sources.

298

American Motors/Renault

Body Designation	Nameplate(s)	Year of Introduction	Production Source(s)	Capacity (000)	Plan
Small Cars					
93	Encore	1983	Kenosha, WI	150	Discontinue in 1989.
96	Alliance	1982	Kenosha, WI	150	Discontinue in 1989.
Midsize Cars					
35/38	Eagle	1979	Bramalea, Ont.	20	Should be discontinued in late 1980s (1987–1988). Split sourced with YS utility truck.
X-58	—	1987	Brampton, Ont.	180	Renault-designed intermediate car to be produced in new plant.
R-21	—	1987	France	70	New Renault designed and built in France.
R-18	Sportswagon	1980	France	10	
Sports Cars					
—	Alpine	1987	France	10	Replacement for Fuego.

Volkswagen of America

Body Designation	Nameplate(s)	Year of Introduction	Production Source(s)	Capacity (000)	Plan
Small Cars					
—	Golf	1984	Westmoreland, PA	250	Rabbit replacement. Jetta may be produced at site in the future.
—	Polo	1986	Brazil	50	

American Honda Motor Co.

Body Designation	Nameplate(s)	Year of Introduction	Production Source(s)	Capacity (000)	Plan
Small Cars					
—	Civic	1985	Marysville, OH	180	Additional capacity added to plant in 1985 and 1986.

(continued)

299

Anticipated Product Actions and Manufacturing Capacity

Body Designation	Nameplate(s)	Year of Introduction	Production Source(s)	Capacity (000)	Plan
			OTHER DOMESTIC PRODUCERS		
			American Motors/Renault		
Small Cars					
—	Civic	1988	Alliston, Ont.	40	New plant building Accords and Civics.
Midsize Cars					
—	Accord	1983	Marysville, OH	180	
—	Accord	1987	Alliston, Ont.	40	See above.
			Nissan Motor Corp., USA		
Small Cars					
—	Sentra	1985	Smyrna, TN	100	Car production added to existing truck plant. Total car-truck capacity is 240,000.
			Mazda Motors Corp., USA		
Midsize Cars					
626/727	—	1988	Flat Rock, MI	100	Sporty midsize car based on Mazda's 727 project. Split sourced with Ford.
			Toyota Motor Corp., USA		
Small Cars					
—	Corolla	1986	Fremont, CA	50	Toyota may use extra NUMMI capacity for its dealers.
—	Corolla	1988	Cambridge, Ont.	50	New plant building small cars.

(continued)

300

Midsize Cars					
—	Camry	1988	Georgetown, KY	200	New plant building Camry-derived cars.
Diamond Star Motors (Chrysler/Mitsubishi)					
Small Cars					
H2X	—	1988	Bloomington-Normal, IL	120	Chrysler and Mitsubishi split output of joint venture building Cordia/Mirage-type car.
Hyundai Motors of North America					
Small Cars					
—	Excel	1988	Bromont, Que.	100	New plant under construction with government assistance.

SOURCE: Compiled by authors from various automotive press sources.

EXHIBIT 5

Anticipated Distribution of Imports by Market Segment in 1990
(000s units)

	European	Japanese	Korean	Total
Small Cars	30	785	250[a]	1,065
Midsize Cars	250	907	—	1,157
Large/Luxury Cars	350[b]	250	—	600
Sports Cars	70	648	—	718
Total	700	2,590[c]	250	3,540

[a]Includes 100,000 GM captive imports.
[b]Includes 40,000 Ford of Europe captive imports.
[c]Includes 525,000 captive small-car imports (300,000 for GM, 100,000 for Ford, 125,000 for Chrysler). Noncaptive Japanese imports total 2,335,000 and are split 30 percent small, 35 percent midsize, 25 percent sports, and 10 percent luxury—based upon recent and expected future market trends.
SOURCE: Authors' estimates.

EXHIBIT 6

Anticipated Distribution of Foreign-based Producers' North American Production
Capacity in 1990
(000 units)

	European	Japanese	Mexican	Korean	Total
Small Cars	150	880	130	100	1,260
Midsize Cars	150	520	—	—	670
Large/Luxury Cars	—	—	—	—	—
Sports Cars	—	140	—	—	140
Total	300[a]	1,540[b]	130[c]	100[d]	2,070

[a]Comprising 150 VW Golfs and 150 Renaults.
[b]Comprising 250,000 cars from NUMMI; 440,000 cars from Honda in the United States and Canada; 120,000 from Nissan; 240,000 from Chrysler/Mitsubishi; 240,000 from Mazda/Ford; 250,000 from Toyota in the United States and Canada; and an estimated amount from Suzuki and Subaru.
[c]Comprising 130,000 small cars from Ford of Mexico.
[d]From Hyundai.
SOURCE: Authors' estimates.

EXHIBIT 7
Summary of 1990 U.S. Car Market Analysis
(000s units)

	Sales[a]	Imports[b]	Foreign Producer's N.A. Production and Sales[c]	U.S. Market Available to U.S. Automakers[d]	Canadian Sales[e]	Available N.A. Market[f]	Anticipated Big 4 N.A. Capacity[g]	Utilization of Anticipated Capacity[h]
Small Cars	2,360	1,065	1,260	35	160	195	1,400	14%
Midsize Cars	2,950	1,157	670	1,123	200	1,323	3,100	43
Large Cars	4,130	—	—	4,130	280	4,410	4,200	105
Luxury Cars	1,180	600	—	580	80	660	1,200	55
Sports Cars	1,150	718	140	292	80	372	600	62
Total	11,770	3,540	2,070	6,160	800	6,960	10,500	66%

[a]Total sales based on DRI and DOT forecasts; 1990 market segmentation based upon recent U.S. sales per *Ward's* classification: small, 20%; midsize, 25%; large, 35%; luxury, 10%; and sports, 10%.

[b]Data from Exhibit 5. Import penetration equal to 30%. European share of imports equal to 20%, or 700,000 units, and Japanese/Korean share of imports equal to 80%, or 2,840,000 units. Cars sold in the United States from Mexico counted with United States/Canadian production, not imports.

[c]Data from Exhibit 6.

[d]Column 1 less columns 2 and 3.

[e]Domestic producers' Canadian sales equal to 800,000 (per DRI and DOT) and segmented the same as the United States.

[f]Column 4 plus column 5.

[g]Summarized from Exhibit 4.

[h]Column 6 divided by column 7. Imported cars and North American production of foreign automobiles are assumed to be sold in each market segment before U.S. automakers' production because of the higher perceived quality and lower cost of foreign automakers' cars.

SOURCE: Authors' estimates.

303

EXHIBIT 8

1990 U.S. Automotive Employment Assumptions

1. Traditional U.S. auto production for 1990 is estimated to be 7 million units (from assumptions outlined in Exhibit 7, column 6);

2. Auto production in millions of units by principal market segment or size class is estimated as follows (1978 and 1983 data from *Ward's Automotive Yearbooks* and 1990 estimate from Exhibit 5):

	1978	1983	1990
Small cars	1.6	2.3	0.2
Midsize and sports cars	3.6	2.3	1.7
Large and luxury cars	5.2	3.1	5.1
	10.4	7.7	7.0

3. Based on productivity studies conducted by the U.S. Department of Transportation, each type of vehicle is assigned an hourly labor content. The following table, expressed in hours, assumes that productivity increased by 5 percent from 1978 to 1983 and will increase by *4 percent per year* from 1984 to 1990:

	1978	1983	1990
Small cars	190	181	136
Midsize and sports cars	225	215	161
Large and luxury cars	250	240	180

4. To determine the total hours of production, the total units produced in each size class are multiplied by the corresponding labor hours per car. This total is then divided by 1,950, the number of hours per year worked by a typical production employee, to determine the number of auto-production-related jobs in North America;

5. The total number of auto-production-related jobs is assumed to be split 90 percent in the United States and 10 percent in Canada, based upon historical data;

6. To determine the number of auto-production-related jobs at U.S. auto companies versus suppliers, the average degree of vertical integration is assumed to be 63 percent in 1978 and 1983 and 60 percent for 1990;

7. Based on the production and sales scenario summarized in Exhibit 7 and the six assumptions outlined above, the employment effects are presented in Exhibit 9.

EXHIBIT 9

Auto-production-related Employment at U.S. Automakers[a]
(000s employees)

1978	1983	1990(E)[b]	1983–1990	1978–1990
700	480	340	−140	−360

[a]Employment estimates represent U.S. hourly and salaried workers involved in the production and assembly of *automobiles only* at plants operated by GM, Ford, Chrysler, and AMC. These figures are not meant to represent total employment, total hourly employment, or total UAW employment in the auto industry. They are used to represent the potential magnitude of changes in employment levels associated with declines in output, changes in sourcing, and productivity improvements anticipated for the domestic auto industry.

[b]See Exhibit 8 for assumptions underlying estimate of 1990 U.S. automakers' employment.

SOURCE: Authors' estimates.

Auto Sector Policies of Major Producing Countries

Government policy, through direct and indirect means, has shaped the performance of national auto industries, influencing both the structure of production and the nature of competition and affecting the chances of profitability. Although all major governments have focused their attention on the auto sector, they have chosen to implement a diverse mix of policies. Given historic proclivities, described in chapters 3, 4, and 5, France and Japan opted for a close government role, whereas West Germany and the United States tried to keep an arm's length between the government and the auto industry. In the first instance, the French government brought its influence to bear through the ownership of the largest national producer; the Japanese government provided favorable tax treatment and, as in France, granted protection from imports and foreign investment. The West German government retained its anomalous ownership of Volkswagen, but moved away from intervening in corporate affairs while imposing tough environmental policies and effectively limiting Japanese imports. Finally, as discussed in chapter 8, the U.S. government's traditional laissez-faire approach has, from time to time, given way to periods of intense product regulation and auto-specific policies combining trade protection and emergency financial assistance.

Exhibit 1 summarizes details of the different auto sector policies of major producing countries in 1985 with respect to ownership, trade, investment, competition, financial assistance, product regulation, and fiscal matters.

EXHIBIT 1

Auto Sector Policies of Major Producing Countries, 1985

	France	Germany	Japan	United States	U.K.
Ownership	100% of Renault.	40% of VW; 5% of BMW.	None.	None.	99% of BL.
Trade	10.3% EEC tariff; unofficial OMA with Japan (3% of market); alleged NTBs.	10.3% EEC tariff.	Tariff on parts but not cars; alleged NTBs; monitors exports.	3% tariff. VER program from 1981–1985. After lifting VER, Japanese imports closely monitored.	11% EEC tariff; OMA with Japan (11% of market).
Investment	Major funding for Renault, restructuring of auto and parts industries; actively promoting investment in distressed regions; monitors foreign investment.	Economywide incentives; regional development program; open door to foreign investors.	Economywide incentives; special depreciation schedules for autos; monitors foreign investment.	States offer large subsidies for plant consideration.	Major funding for BL; actively promotes investment in distressed regions (Ford engine plant).
Competition	Encouraged collaboration in auto, components, and machine tool sectors.	Cartel office regularly challenges price hikes but allows extensive cooperation.	MITI encouraged collaboration in parts; successful in components industry.	Traditionally strong antitrust oversight; FTC investigation.	Monopoly commissioned approved BL merger, Chrysler U.K. takeover by Peugeot.
Financial Assistance	Small-scale R&D; regional and restructuring grants.	Small R&D programs under way in advanced automotive technology.	Some R&D assistance.	Major loan guarantees to Chrysler in 1979.	Small-scale R&D; regional grants.
Regulation Safety/ Design	EEC directives and local regulations; lukewarm on EEC harmonization.	EEC directives and local standards; strict inspections; favors strict, harmonized EEC standards.	Extensive MOT standards; strict inspections.	Very extensive NHTSA standards; slowdown in new standards.	EEC directives and local regulations.

(continued)

EXHIBIT 1 (continued)

Auto Sector Policies of Major Producing Countries

	France	Germany	Japan	United States	U.K.
Emissions	EEC regulations in force since late 1970s. Resisting reforms.	EEC regulations in force since late 1970s. Lead-free gas mandatory by 1986.	Standards as strict or stricter than U.S.	Very extensive standards since 1970; slowdown in implementation.	EEC regulations in force since late 1970s.
Fuel Economy	Voluntary agreement between industry and government (1979).	Voluntary agreement between industry and government (1979); methanol law.	Voluntary guidelines (12% reduction by 1985).	Mandated CAFE standards since 1975.	Voluntary agreement between industry and government (1979).
Fiscal	Progressive auto tax; high VAT; high gas tax.	VAT and progressive use tax on cars; high gas tax.	Numerous auto taxes; moderate gas tax.	Auto tax in state hands; very low gas tax.	VAT; progressive use tax; low gas tax.

OMA = Orderly marketing agreement. NTB = Nontariff barrier. VER = Voluntary export restraint. VAT = Value-added tax.

SOURCE: Mark B. Fuller, *Note on the World Auto Industry in Transition*, Case No. 9–385–332 (Boston: Harvard Business School, 1985).

Notes

PREFACE

[1] Peter F. Drucker, *The Concept of the Corporation,* rev. ed. (New York: T. Y. Crowell, 1972), p. 149.

CHAPTER 1

[1] UAW Research Department, "U.S. Auto Jobs: The Problem Is Bigger than Japanese Imports," June 1986.

[2] Some estimates now becoming public show higher totals for both the level of imports and the output of local assemblies. For example, the UAW Research Department projects 4.0 million imports and 2.6 million local assemblies out of an 11.8 million-unit market. See note 1.

[3] Chandler in John T. Dunlop, *Business and Public Policy* (Cambridge, MA: Harvard University Press, 1981), pp. 3–5.

[4] Ibid., p. 3.

CHAPTER 2

[1] These figures are for an assembly plant in the United States. In Japan, where real estate is more expensive, the comparable figures are 1.5 million square feet and 100 acres.

[2] The arithmetic is this: 300 × .01 dollars × 8 hours × 240 working days per year × 2 shifts.

[3] Based on 400,000 hourly workers in the United States.

[4] Compare the studies conducted by the U.S. Department of Transportation, Harbour and Associates, the Massachusetts Institute of Technology, and William J. Abernathy, Kim B. Clark, and Alan M. Kantrow, *Industrial Renaissance: Producing a Competitive Future for America* (New York: Basic Books, 1983).

[5] Harry C. Katz, *Shifting Gears: Changing Labor Relations in the U.S. Automobile Industry* (Cambridge, MA: MIT Press, 1985), esp. chap. 5, and references there cited.

CHAPTER 3

[1] Robert Paul Thomas, *An Analysis of the Pattern of Growth in the Automobile Industry* (New York: Ayer, 1977), p. 324; Harold Katz, *The Decline of Competition in the Automobile Industry, 1920–1940* (New York: Arno Press, 1977), pp. 28–29. See also John B. Rae, *The American Automobile Industry* (Boston: G. K. Hall, 1984), chaps. 2–3.

[2] Alfred D. Chandler, Jr., and Stuart Bruchey, eds., *Giant Enterprise: Ford, General Motors, and the Automobile Industry* (New York: Arno Press, 1980), and *Strategy and Structure: Chapters in the History of the American Industrial Enterprise* (Cambridge, MA: MIT Press, 1962).

[3] U.S. Federal Trade Commission, *Report on the Motor Vehicle Industry* (Washington, DC, 1939), pp. 29, 632.

[4] Allan Nevins and Frank Ernest Hill, *Ford: The Times, the Man, and the Company* (New York: Scribner's, 1948), pp. 342–347.

[5] Roland Henry Wolf, "General Motors: A Study of the Firm's Growth, Its External Relationships, and Internal Organization" (Ph.D. diss., Vanderbilt University, 1962); cf. Ed Cray, *Chrome Colossus: General Motors and Its Times* (New York: McGraw-Hill, 1980).

[6] Alfred P. Sloan, Jr., *My Years with General Motors* (Garden City, NY: Anchor Books, 1972), p. 74.

[7] Chandler, *Strategy and Structure,* pp. 130–162; Peter F. Drucker, *The Concept of the Corporation,* rev. ed. (New York: T. Y. Crowell, 1972), pp. 46–68.

[8] Rae, *The American Automobile Industry,* pp. 54, 65–66.

[9] Sloan, *My Years with General Motors*, p. 172. Cf. Katz, *The Decline of Competition;* Thomas, *An Analysis of the Pattern of Growth,* chap. 5; Harold G. Vatter, "The Closure of Entry in the American Automobile Industry," *Oxford Economic Papers* 4 (1952), 213–224.

[10] Thomas, *An Analysis of the Pattern of Growth,* p. 324.

[11] William J. Abernathy, Kim B. Clark, and Alan M. Kantrow, *Industrial Renaissance: Producing a Competitive Future for America* (New York: Basic Books, 1983), p. 45.

[12] Ford's and Chrysler's investments were $436.6 million and $127 million, respectively, in 1929. Ford's payroll numbered 101,069. U.S. FTC, *Report on the Motor Vehicle Industry,* pp. 498, 546, 572, 657, and 668. Chrysler was twice the size of the next largest competitor, Studebaker, and three or four times as big as any other independent manufacturer.

[13] Ibid., p. 629. Cf. David A. Hounshell, *From the American System to Mass Production, 1800–1932: The Development of Manufacturing Technology in the United States* (Baltimore: Johns Hopkins University Press, 1984), chap. 6; and Stephen Meyer III, *The Five Dollar Day: Labor Management and Social Control in the Ford Motor Company 1908–1921* (Albany: State University of New York Press, 1981), chap. 2.

[14] U.S. FTC, *Report on the Motor Vehicle Industry,* p. 631.

[15] Lawrence H. Seltzer, *A Financial History of the American Automobile Industry* (Boston: Houghton Mifflin, 1928), p. 59.

[16] Lawrence J. White, *The Automobile Industry since 1945* (Cambridge, MA: Harvard University Press, 1971), chap. 6, esp. pp. 85–86; Chandler, *Strategy and Structure,* p. 373.

[17] Sloan, *My Years with General Motors,* p. 253. James J. Flink, *America Adopts the Automobile, 1895–1910* (Cambridge, MA: MIT Press, 1970), pp. 278–288; William J. Abernathy, *The Productivity Dilemma: Roadblock to Innovation in the Automobile Industry* (Baltimore: Johns Hopkins University Press, 1978), chaps. 1–12; Abernathy, Clark, and Kantrow, *Industrial Renaissance,* chap. 2, pp. 45–46, 114–116, and Appendix D.

[18] White, *The Automobile Industry since 1945,* pp. 111–115; Cray, *Chrome Colossus,* pp. 202–203.

[19] Mira Wilkins, *The Emergence of Multinational Enterprise: American Business Abroad from the Colonial Era to 1914* (Cambridge, MA: Harvard University Press, 1970), p. 97; Wilkins, *The Maturing of Multinational Enterprise: American Business Abroad from 1914 to 1970* (Cambridge, MA: Harvard University Press, 1974), pp. 72–75.

[20] Wilkins, *The Maturing of Multinational Enterprise,* pp. 147–148.

[21] White, *The Automobile Industry since 1945,* p. 251.

[22] U.S. FTC, *Report on the Motor Vehicle Industry,* p. 29; White, *The Automobile Industry since 1945,* appendix, pp. 290–306.

[23] Allen Nevins and Frank Ernest Hill, *Ford: Decline and Rebirth, 1933–1962* (New York: Charles Scribner's Sons, 1963), chaps. 12–13; Michael Moritz and Barrett Seaman, *Going for Broke: The Chrysler Story* (Garden City, NY: Doubleday, 1981), pp. 55, 223–226.

[24] Henry Ford, *My Life and Work* (Garden City, NY: Doubleday, 1923), pp. 79–80; Meyer, *The Five Dollar Day,* pp. 12–13; Hounshell, *From the American System,* p. 220.

[25] Meyer, *The Five Dollar Day,* pp. 10, 55; Sidney Fine, *The Automobile under the Blue Eagle* (Ann Arbor: University of Michigan Press, 1963), p. 13. As Nelson Lichtenstein points out, however, the erosion of skilled workers' autonomy and the shaping of foremen's roles were not linear trends. Rather, they were slow processes that were interrupted and set back by changing responsibilities and needs during World War II. Lichtenstein, "Auto Worker Militancy and the Structure of Factory Life, 1937–1955," *Journal of American History* 67 (1980), 335–353.

[26] Quoted in Chandler, *Giant Enterprise,* p. 39.

[27] Meyer, *The Five Dollar Day*, chap. 4, esp. p. 77. See also August Meier and Elliott Rudwick, *Black Detroit and the Rise of the UAW* (New York: Oxford University Press, 1979).

[28] Clayton W. Fountain, *Union Guy* (New York: Viking Press, 1949), pp. 41–42; Fine, *The Automobile under the Blue Eagle*, pp. 15–17.

[29] Meyer, *The Five Dollar Day*, p. 80.

[30] Meyer, *The Five Dollar Day*, pp. 39–41; cf. Edmund Wilson, *The American Earthquake: A Documentary of the Twenties and Thirties* (Garden City, NY: Doubleday, 1958), pp. 219–220.

[31] Sloan, *My Years with General Motors*, pp. 457–458; Fine, *The Automobile under the Blue Eagle*, pp. 7–8.

[32] Stuart Brandes, *American Welfare Capitalism, 1880–1940* (Chicago: University of Chicago Press, 1976), chap. 14; David Brody, *Workers in Industrial America* (New York: Oxford University Press, 1980), chap. 2; Daniel Nelson, "The Company Union Movement, 1900–1937: A Reexamination," *Business History Review* (Fall 1982), 335–357.

[33] Fine, *The Automobile under the Blue Eagle*, pp. 19 and 17–21.

[34] Quoted in Alfred D. Chandler, Jr., and Richard S. Tedlow, *The Coming of Managerial Capitalism: A Casebook on the History of American Economic Institutions* (Homewood, IL: Irwin, 1985), p. 526.

[35] Fine, *The Automobile under the Blue Eagle*, pp. 155–163.

[36] Howell John Harris, *The Right to Manage: Industrial Relations Policies of American Business in the 1940s* (Madison: University of Wisconsin Press, 1982), pp. 28–29.

[37] Sloan, *My Years with General Motors*, p. 466; Harris, *The Right to Manage*, p. 142.

[38] Pat Greathouse, retired UAW vice-president, interview with the authors, December 1982; cf. Lichtenstein, "Auto Worker Militancy," p. 351.

[39] Walter P. Reuther Library, Wayne State University, WPR Speeches, Box 584, "Address by Walter P. Reuther before the Mid-Century Institute on Religion in a World of Tensions," Boston University, March 14, 1950, pp. 4–5; WPR Speeches, Box 579, "A Wage and Price Program for Reconversion," presented to the Special Executive Board of the UAW-CIO, May 24, 1945, p. 6.

[40] U.S. Department of Labor, Bureau of Labor Statistics, *Wage Chronology: Ford Motor Company, June 1941—September 1973* (Washington, DC, 1973), p. 22; Robert M. MacDonald, *Collective Bargaining in the Automobile Industry: A Study of Wage Structure and Competitive Relations* (New Haven: Yale University Press, 1963), pp. 39–40; Harry C. Katz, *Shifting Gears: Changing Labor Relations in the U.S. Automobile Industry* (Cambridge, MA: MIT Press, 1985), p. 23.

[41] MacDonald, *Collective Bargaining*, chaps. 6–7.

[42] Sumner H. Slichter, James J. Healy, and E. Robert Livernash, *The Impact of Collective Bargaining on Management* (Washington, DC: The Brookings Institution, 1960), chaps. 3–12.

[43] Victor G. Reuther, *The Brothers Reuther and the Story of the UAW* (Boston: Houghton Mifflin, 1976), chaps. 21–22; Victor Reuther, conversation with the authors, December 1981.

[44] Reuther Library, UAW GM Collection, Series VII, Box 1, Walter P. Reuther, "Labor-Management Relations—Responsibilities, Problems, and Opportunities Ahead," Speech before the Detroit Economic Club, February 4, 1963, p. 11.

[45] William Serrin, *The Company and the Union: The "Civilized Relationship" of the General Motors Corporation and the United Automobile Workers* (New York: Knopf, 1970), p. 69.

[46] Charles R. Walker and Robert H. Guest, *The Man on the Assembly Line* (Cambridge, MA: Harvard University Press, 1952), p. 51. See also, for example, Robert Blauner, *Alienation and Freedom* (Chicago: University of Chicago Press, 1964); Studs Terkel, *Working* (New York: Pantheon, 1974); Emma Rothschild, *Paradise Lost: The*

Decline of the Auto-Industrial Age (New York: Random House, 1973); B. J. Widick, ed., *Auto Work and Its Discontents* (Baltimore: Johns Hopkins University Press, 1976); John F. Runcie, " 'By days I make the cars,' " *Harvard Business Review* (May-June 1980), 106–115.

[47] Bert Spector and Michael Beer, *General Motors and the United Auto Workers*, Case No. 9–481–142 (Boston: Harvard Business School, 1981); Katz, *Shifting Gears*, chap. 4.

[48] For example, GM president Charles Wilson, Ford president Robert McNamara, and American Motors president George Romney became cabinet secretaries in the 1950s and 1960s.

[49] Flink, *America Adopts the Automobile*, pp. 114–128; John B. Rae, *The Road and the Car in American Life* (Cambridge, MA: MIT Press, 1971).

[50] Mira Wilkins, "Multinational Automobile Enterprises and Regulation: An Historical Overview," in Douglas H. Ginsberg and William J. Abernathy, eds., *Government, Technology, and the Future of the Automobile* (New York: McGraw-Hill, 1980), pp. 224–228; Alan Altshuler, Martin Anderson, Daniel Jones, Daniel Roos, and James Womack, *The Future of the Automobile: The Report of MIT's International Automobile Program* (Cambridge, MA: MIT Press, 1984), p. 17.

[51] John B. Rae, *The American Automobile: A Brief History* (Chicago: University of Chicago Press, 1965), pp. 124–127; Fine, *The Automobile under the Blue Eagle*.

[52] White, *The Automobile Industry since 1945*, pp. 121–133.

[53] Charles M. Hewitt, *The Development of Automobile Franchises* (Bloomington, IN: Bureau of Business Research, Indiana University, 1952); Stuart Macaulay, *Law and the Balance of Power: The Automobile Manufacturers and Their Dealers* (New York: Russell Sage, 1966); White, *The Automobile Industry since 1945*, pp. 156–157.

[54] U.S. FTC, *Report on the Motor Vehicle Industry*, pp. 1075–1076; Hewitt, *The Development of Automobile Franchises*, pp. 27–28.

[55] Some of these criticisms are discussed in Cray, *Chrome Colossus*, pp. 387–397. It is worth noting that the government had helped Kaiser enter the automobile industry after World War II by selling off defense production plants at a fraction of their true value.

[56] The best account of the decline of the independents is Charles E. Edwards, *Dynamics of the United States Automobile Industry* (Columbia, SC: University of South Carolina Press, 1965).

[57] The federal energy statute added no new regulatory agencies but specified fuel-economy goals for the 1985 model year and empowered the head of NHTSA to set and enforce intermediate goals before 1985.

[58] Philip B. Heymann, *Auto Safety (A)* Case No. C14–76–141.0 (Boston: Harvard University, Kennedy School of Government, 1976), p. 2.

[59] Elizabeth Brenner Drew, "The Politics of Automobile Safety," *Atlantic Monthly*, October 1966, p. 96.

[60] U.S. Congress, Senate, Committee on Government Operations, *Federal Role in Traffic Safety. Hearings before the Subcommittee on Executive Reorganization* (Washington, DC, 1965), pp. 778–779.

[61] Ibid.

[62] Quoted in Drew, "Politics of Automobile Safety," p. 99.

[63] *New York Times*, April 16, 1966, p. 27.

[64] Norman Alpert and Eugene L. Holt, "Inter-Industry Cooperative Research and the Government: Two Case Studies," in Ginsberg and Abernathy, *Government, Technology and . . . the Automobile*, pp. 334–342.

[65] Convenient summaries of the key players' positions are found in U.S. Department of Transportation, Transportation Systems Center, *Response to Federal Initiatives in*

Automobile Safety, Fuel Economy, and Emission (Cambridge, MA, September 1979), pp. 14–25.

[66] U.S. Dept. of Transportation, *Response to Federal Initiatives,* pp. 31–36; Richard H. K. Vietor, *Energy Policy in America since 1945* (New York: Cambridge University Press, 1984), pp. 251–258.

CHAPTER 4

[1] George Maxcy and Aubrey Silberston, *The Motor Industry* (London: Allen and Unwin, 1959), Appendix D, table 1, p. 223.

[2] Peter J. S. Dunnett, *The Decline of the British Motor Industry: The Effects of Government Policy, 1945–1979* (London: Croom Helm, 1980), p. 20; Roy Church and Michael Miller, "The Big Three: Competition, Management, and Marketing in the British Motor Industry, 1922–1939," in Barry Supple, ed., *Essays in British Business History* (Oxford: Clarendon Press, 1977), p. 169.

[3] Maxcy and Silberston, *The Motor Industry,* p. 13.

[4] Leslie Hannah, "Visible and Invisible Hands in Great Britain," in Alfred D. Chandler, Jr., and Herman Daems, eds., *Managerial Hierarchies: Comparative Perspectives on the Rise of the Modern Industrial Enterprise* (Cambridge, MA: Harvard University Press, 1980), p. 68.

[5] P. W. S. Andrews and Elizabeth Brunner, *The Life of Lord Nuffield: A Study in Enterprise and Benevolence* (Oxford: Clarendon Press, 1955), part IV generally, esp. chap. 2.

[6] Graham Turner, *The Leyland Papers* (London: Eyre and Spottiswode, 1971), p. 89; Church and Miller, "The Big Three," p. 176.

[7] Turner, *The Leyland Papers,* pp. 95–96.

[8] Jonathan Zeitlin, "The Emergence of Shop Steward Organization and Job Control in the British Car Industry," *History Workshop Journal* 10 (1980), 119–137.

[9] Wayne Lewchuk, "Fordism and British Motor Car Employees, 1896–1932," in Howard F. Gospel and Craig R. Littler, eds., *Managerial Strategies and Industrial Relations: An Historical and Comparative Study* (London: Heinemann, 1983), pp. 82–110; Lewchuk, "The Role of the British Government in the Spread of Scientific Management and Fordism in the Interwar Years," *Journal of Economic History* 44 (1984), 355–361.

[10] Maxcy and Silberston, *The Motor Industry,* pp. 164, 175.

[11] This section follows material in Dunnett, *The Decline of the British Motor Industry,* and an unpublished paper by Mark B. Fuller, "Government Intervention in the Auto Industry: The United Kingdom" (Boston: Harvard Business School, 1980), manuscript.

[12] Quoted in Fuller, "Government Intervention," p. 9.

[13] Dunnett, *The Decline of the British Motor Industry,* pp. 79, 107.

[14] Krish Bhaskar, *The Future of the U.K. Motor Industry* (London: Kogan Page, 1979), p. 71. Bhaskar's figures indicate the continuation of a trend begun in the mid-1960s: see H. A. Turner, Garfield Clack, and Geoffrey Roberts, *Labor Relations in the Motor Industry: A Study of Industrial Unrest and an International Comparison* (London: Allen and Unwin, 1967), pp. 104–120; and D. G. Rhys, *The Motor Industry: An Economic Survey* (London: Butterworths, 1972), pp. 444, 464.

[15] D. T. Jones and S. J. Prais, "Plant Size and Productivity in the Motor Industry: Some International Comparisons," *Oxford Bulletin of Economics and Statistics* 40 (1978), 142.

[16] Allen Flanders, Quoted in Hugh Armstrong Clegg, *The Changing System of Industrial Relations in Great Britain* (Oxford: Blackwell, 1979), p. 16.

[17] W. E. J. McCarthy, "Principles and Possibilities in British Trade Union Law," in McCarthy, ed., *Trade Unions: Selected Readings* (Harmondsworth: Penguin Books, 1972), pp. 345–365.

[18] Turner, Clack, and Roberts, *Labor Relations in the Motor Industry.*

[19] W. E. J. McCarthy, *The Role of Shop Stewards in British Industrial Relations* (London: H. M. Stationery Office, 1966).

[20] Cited in John F. B. Goodman, "Great Britain: Toward the Social Contract," in Solomon Barkin, ed., *Worker Militancy and Its Consequences, 1965–1975: New Directions in Western Industrial Relations* (New York: Praeger, 1975), p. 53.

[21] Quoted in Huw Beynon, *Working for Ford* (London: A. Lane, 1973), pp. 53–54; cf. Beynon's own observations, pp. 227–228.

[22] Quoted in Richard E. Caves, ed., *Britain's Economic Prospects* (Washington, DC: The Brookings Institution, 1968), pp. 331–332.

[23] Great Britain, Central Policy Review Staff, *The Future of the British Car Industry* (London: H. M. Stationery Office, 1975), p. x.

[24] Ibid., pp. 51–52.

[25] House of Commons, *Fourteenth Report of the Expenditure Committee 1974–75: The Motor Vehicle Industry* (London, 1975), p. 36.

[26] Quoted in Turner, *The Leyland Papers*, p. 179.

[27] Dunnett, *The Decline of the British Motor Industry*, p. 97; CPRS, *Future of the British Car Industry*, p. 70; *The Wall Street Journal*, April 11, 1975, p. 1.

[28] Bhaskar, *The Future of the U.K. Motor Industry*, pp. 46–54; CPRS, *Future of the British Car Industry*, pp. 70–72.

[29] Talbot, as the Peugeot subsidiary is known, is now a marginal producer. Most of its operations in the United Kingdom involve assembling knocked-down kits of models designed elsewhere. In 1983, Talbot suffered severe losses when business in Iran, the site of the company's largest sales, began to dry up.

[30] *British Leyland: The Next Decade* (London, 1975), p. 3, an abridged version of a report presented to the secretary of state for industry by a team of inquiry led by Sir Don Ryder. This quotation has been edited to remove italics.

[31] The account of the BL story that follows is based on interviews in July and August 1982 with Michael Carver, director of strategic planning at BL PLC; Geoff Armstrong, personnel director of BL Cars; Pat Lowry, formerly of BL but now director of the central government's Advisory, Conciliation, and Arbitration Service (ACAS); Arthur Marsh of Oxford University; and Oliver Tynan, former consultant to BL; and two books: Sir Michael Edwardes, *Back from the Brink* (London: Collins, 1983), and Paul Willman and Graham Winch, *Innovation and Management Control: Labor Relations at BL Cars* (Cambridge: Cambridge University Press, 1985).

[32] Interviews; on Ryder's involvement in company affairs, cf. Edwardes, *Back from the Brink*, p. 36.

[33] Edwardes's career at BL is described in his book, *Back from the Brink*. The account that appears draws heavily on this book.

[34] Edwardes, *Back from the Brink*, p. 218.

[35] Ibid., pp. 74, 79–80; Willman and Winch, *Innovation and Management Control*, pp. 15–16, 34–41.

[36] Edwardes, *Back from the Brink*, p. 37.

[37] Ibid., p. 88.

[38] Ibid., p. 95; cf. Willman and Winch, *Innovation and Management Control*, pp. 76–83 and chap. 7.

[39] Edwardes, *Back from the Brink*, p. 106.

[40] Ibid., pp. 113, 117.

[41] Ibid., pp. 125–127; cf. Willman and Winch, *Innovation and Management Control*, pp. 82–83.

[42] Jurgen Kocka, "The Rise of the Modern Industrial Enterprise in Germany," in Chandler and Daems, eds., *Managerial Hierarchies*, pp. 77–116.

[43] J.-P. Bardou, J.-J. Chanaron, Patrick Fridenson, and James M. Laux, *The Automo-*

bile Revolution: The Impact of an Industry (Chapel Hill: University of North Carolina Press, 1982), p. 106.

[44] Nathan Reich, *Labor Relations in Republican Germany: An Experiment in Industrial Democracy* (New York: Oxford University Press, 1938), pp. 117, 138, 152; Adolf Sturmthal, *Workers Councils: A Study of Workplace Organization on Both Sides of the Iron Curtain* (Cambridge, MA: Harvard University Press, 1964), pp. 11–16.

[45] This brief history draws on Bardou et al., *The Automobile Revolution;* Achim Diekmann, *Die Automobilindustrie in der Bundesrepublik Deutschland* (Cologne: Deutsche Instituts Verlag, 1979); and Raymond R. Sekaly, *Transnationalization of the Automotive Industry* (Ottawa: University of Ottawa Press, 1981), p. 151.

[46] Quoted in Walter Henry Nelson, *Small Wonder: The Amazing Story of the Volkswagen*, rev. ed. (Boston: Little, Brown, 1970), pp. 65–66; cf. Reich, *Labor Relations in Republican Germany*, pp. 275–276.

[47] Bardou et al., *The Automobile Revolution*, pp. 144–145; Mira L. Wilkins and Frank Ernest Hill, *American Business Abroad: Ford on Six Continents* (Detroit: Wayne State University Press, 1964), pp. 232–233.

[48] Andrew Shonfeld, *Modern Capitalism: The Changing Balance of Public and Private Power* (London: Oxford University Press, 1965), p. 240.

[49] Karl Hardach, *The Political Economy of Germany in the Twentieth Century* (Berkeley: University of California Press, 1980), p. 93.

[50] A. Muller-Armack, "The Principles of the Social Market Economy," *German Economic Review* 3 (1963); Graham Hallett, *The Social Economy of West Germany* (London: Macmillan, 1973), chap. 2, esp. pp. 17–24.

[51] Ludwig Erhard, *Germany's Comeback in the World Market* (London: Macmillan, 1954), Introduction.

[52] This account of the German industrial relations system follows several sources, including Hallett, *Social Economy*, chap. 7; Henry Christopher Wallich, *Mainsprings* (New Haven: Yale University Press, 1955), chap. 10; and Andrei S. Markovits and Christopher S. Allen, "Trade Unions and the Economic Crisis: The West German Case," in George Ross et al., *Unions and Economic Crisis: Britain, West Germany, and Sweden* (London: Allen and Unwin, 1984), part 2.

[53] Ronald F. Bunn, "Employers Associations in the Federal Republic of Germany," in John P. Windmuller and Alan Gladstone, eds., *Employers Associations and Industrial Relations* (Oxford: Oxford University Press, 1984), p. 172; Clark Kerr, "Collective Bargaining in Postwar Germany," in Adolf Sturmthal, ed., *Contemporary Collective Bargaining in Seven Countries* (Ithaca: Cornell University Press, 1957), p. 171.

[54] Collective Bargaining Agreement Act (1949); modified in 1952.

[55] Markovits and Allen, "Trade Unions and the Economic Crisis," p. 95.

[56] Wallich, *Mainsprings*, p. 310.

[57] Hallett, *Social Economy*, p. 86.

[58] Hardach, *Political Economy*, p. 161; Eric Owen Smith, *The West German Economy* (New York: St. Martin's Press, 1983), chap. 3; Hallett, *Social Economy*, pp. 71–72; Michael Kreile, "West Germany: The Dynamics of Expansion," in Peter J. Katzenstein, ed., *Between Power and Plenty* (Madison: University of Wisconsin Press, 1978), p. 192.

[59] Nelson, *Small Wonder*, p. 136. The narrative follows Nelson and Reinhard Doleschal and Rainer Dombois, eds., *Wohin läuft VW? Die Automobilproduktion in der Wirtschaftskrise* (Reinbek bei Hamburg, 1982), esp. chaps. 1 and 3.

[60] Quoted in Nelson, *Small Wonder*, p. 152.

[61] Ibid., p. 144.

[62] Ibid., pp. 139–140; Wolfgang Streeck, *Industrial Relations in West Germany: A Case Study of the Car Industry* (New York: St. Martin's Press, 1984), chap. 4, esp. pp. 46–48.

[63] Despite Germany's enviable postwar record, few American management experts

have studied German manufacturing techniques. Two who have are Robert H. Hayes and Steven C. Wheelwright, *Restoring Our Competitive Edge: Competing through Manufacturing* (New York: Wiley and Sons, 1984), chap. 11.

[64] Mark B. Fuller, "Government Intervention in the Auto Industry: Germany" (Boston: Harvard Business School, 1980), manuscript, pp. G-14 and G-15.

[65] Smith, *The West German Economy*, pp. 73–74; Hallett, *Social Economy*, pp. 66–68.

[66] Smith, *The West German Economy*, chap. 4, esp. pp. 33, 49.

[67] Wolfgang Streeck and Andreas Hoff, "Industrial Relations in the German Automobile Industry: Developments in the 1970s," in Streeck and Hoff, eds., "Industrial Relations in the World Automobile Industry—the Experiences of the 1970s" (Science Center Berlin, International Institute of Management/Labor Market Policy, 1982), pp. 334–336 and 342–346.

[68] The following paragraphs are based on Streeck, *Industrial Relations in West Germany*, chaps. 5–6; Fuller, "Government Intervention," pp. G-25 to G-32; and Joachim Beickler and David Benello, "Volkswagen's Decision to Invest in the United States," (Boston: Harvard Business School, May 1982), manuscript.

[69] Fuller, "Government Intervention," p. G-11.

[70] Streeck, *Industrial Relations in West Germany*, pp. 67–74.

[71] See M. S. Salter and W. A. Edisis, *The Volkswagen Group*, Case No. 9-385-333 (Boston: Harvard Business School, 1985).

CHAPTER 5

[1] U.S. Department of Transportation, *The U.S. Automobile Industry* (Washington, DC, 1980); William J. Abernathy, Kim B. Clark, and Alan M. Kantrow, *Industrial Renaissance: Producing a Competitive Future for America* (New York: Basic Books, 1983); studies of James Harbour; interviews with strategic planning staff at Ford Motor Company.

[2] J. D. Powers surveys, 1984.

[3] Japan Institute for Social and Economic Affairs, *Japan 1985: An International Comparison*, pp. 21, 22, and 42.

[4] Taishiro Shirai, "A Theory of Enterprise Unionism," in Shirai, ed., *Contemporary Industrial Relations in Japan* (Madison: University of Wisconsin Press, 1983), p. 130.

[5] Miriam S. Farley, *Aspects of Japan's Labor Problems* (New York: J. Day, 1950), p. 7.

[6] Interview with the authors, Tokyo, Japan, January 1982.

[7] Ronald Dore, *British Factory, Japanese Factory* (Berkeley: University of California Press, 1973), p. 338.

[8] Interview with the authors, Toyota City, Japan, January 1982.

[9] Farley, *Aspects of Japan's Labor Problems*, p. 218.

[10] Taizo Yakushiji, "Dynamics of Policy Interventions: The Case of the Government and the Automobile Industry in Japan, 1900–1960" (Ph.D. diss., MIT, 1977), p. 185.

[11] Haruo Shimada, "Japan's Economic Viability and Labor-Management Relations," *Journal of Japanese Trade and Industry* 3, 2 (March-April 1984), 14.

[12] Farley, *Aspects of Japan's Labor Problems*, p. 82.

[13] Shirai, "A Theory of Enterprise Unionism," p. 130.

[14] Farley, *Aspects of Japan's Labor Problems*, p. 88. Cf. Andrew Gordon, *The Evolution of Labor Relations in Japan: Heavy Industry 1853–1955* (Cambridge, MA: Harvard University Press, 1985).

[15] William Duncan, *U.S.-Japan Automobile Diplomacy* (Cambridge, MA: Ballinger, 1973), p. 74.

[16] Yakushiji, "Dynamics of Policy Interventions," p. 199.

[17] Duncan, *U.S.-Japan Automobile Diplomacy*, p. 72.

[18] Interview with the authors, Tokyo, Japan, January 1982.

[19] Toyota Motor Sales, interview with the authors, Tokyo, Japan, January 1982.

[20] Ibid.

[21] Interview with the authors, Toyota City, January 1982.

[22] Ibid.

[23] Michael A. Cusumano, *The Japanese Automobile Industry: Technology and Management at Nissan and Toyota* (Cambridge, MA: Harvard University Press, 1985), chap. 3, esp. pp. 149–160.

[24] Interview with the authors, Tokyo, Japan, January 1982.

[25] Ibid.

[26] All Toyota Federation of Automobile Workers Union, *Handbook* (Toyota City, 1982), p. 4.

[27] Interview with the authors, Toyota City, January 1982.

[28] Yakushiji, "Dynamics of Policy Interventions," pp. 217–224.

[29] Rodney Clark, *The Japanese Company* (New Haven: Yale University Press, 1979), p. 54.

[30] Shirai, "A Theory of Enterprise Unionism," p. 216.

[31] Interview with the authors, Toyota City, January 1982.

[32] Ibid.

[33] Professor Konosuke Odaka of Hitotsubashi University, interview with the authors, Tokyo, January 1982.

[34] Duncan, *U.S.-Japan Automobile Diplomacy*, p. 2.

[35] Ibid., p. 7.

[36] Ibid., p. 36.

[37] Ibid., p. 44.

[38] Satoshi Kamata, *Japan in the Passing Lane* (New York: Pantheon, 1982), p. 198.

[39] Ibid., p. 86.

[40] Ibid., pp. 27–30.

[41] Interview with the authors, Toyota City, January 1982.

[42] Ibid.

[43] Ibid.

[44] Julian Gresser, *Environmental Law in Japan* (Cambridge, MA: MIT Press, 1981), p. 271.

[45] Interview with the authors, Toyota City, January 1982.

[46] Gresser, *Environmental Law in Japan*, p. 272.

[47] See William Tucker, "The Wreck of the Auto Industry," *Harper's*, November 1980.

[48] Quoted in Kim B. Clark, *Toyo Kogyo Co., Ltd. (A)*, Case No. 9–682–092 (Boston: Harvard Business School, 1982), p. 4.

[49] Interview with Naohiro Amaya in *Journal of Japanese Trade and Industry* 1 (1982), 23.

[50] Interview with the authors, Tokyo, January 1982.

[51] Ibid.

[52] Ibid.

[53] Ibid.

CHAPTER 6

[1] Interview with authors, July 8, 1982.

[2] There are many market segmentation schemes for passenger cars. In this chapter, we use the classification of *Ward's Auto World*. Small cars are defined as having interior space less than 85 cubic feet and overall length less than 197 inches. The comparable numbers for midsize cars are between 80 and 95 cubic feet and overall length between 170 and 185 inches. An example would be Chrysler's Reliant and Aries models. A large car is 95 to 115 cubic feet and 185 to 220 inches. An example would be GM's Buick Century. Sports and prestige cars are classified not only by size but also by

price, image, performance, and consumer demographic profiles. See *Ward's Auto World,* January and February 1984.

[3] U.S. Department of Transportation, "Restructuring of the Auto Industry and Its Impact on Employment," February 1982.

[4] Interview with John Smith, formerly GM's director of worldwide product planning, August 24, 1982.

[5] U.S. Department of Transportation, "Restructuring of the Auto Industry."

[6] Ibid.

[7] Estimated on the basis of data presented in National Academy of Engineering, "The Competitive Status of the U.S. Auto Industry" Washington, DC, 1982). See also estimates of Harbour and Associates, reported in *Automotive News,* February 24, 1986.

[8] Interview with the authors, November 1, 1984.

[9] *Ward's Auto World,* January 1984, p. 26, and February 1984, p. 26.

[10] *Automotive News,* February 13, 1984.

[11] Interview with authors, November 26, 1984.

[12] Press conference, December 19, 1983.

[13] Interview with Alex C. Mair, GM's vice-president and group executive for technical services staffs, February 15, 1984.

[14] *Detroit Free Press,* January 30, 1983.

[15] Interview with authors, January 15, 1984.

[16] Philip K. Fricke, Goldman Sachs and Co., Report on General Motors Corporation, March 19, 1984, pp. 12–13.

[17] "Resolution—1984 Collective Bargaining Program," UAW, March 6–8, 1984.

[18] John Holusha, "General Motors: A Giant in Transition," *New York Times,* November 1, 1982, p. 78.

[19] *New York Times,* September 5, 1982.

[20] *Ward's Auto World,* May 1983, p. 34.

[21] Interview with authors, February 19, 1984.

[22] Interview with authors, March 24 and June 30, 1982.

[23] Ibid.

[24] Ibid.

[25] Interview with authors, March 24, 1982.

[26] *New York Times,* November 2, 1983.

[27] *Ward's Auto World,* February 1984, pp. 46–47, and *The Wall Street Journal,* November 30, 1984.

[28] *Automotive News,* April 23, 1984, p. D-1.

[29] *Fortune,* December 23, 1985, p. 22.

[30] *Automotive News,* August 20, 1984.

[31] 1985 annual reports of General Motors, Ford, and Chrysler.

[32] Interview with authors, June 30, 1982.

[33] Ibid.

[34] Ibid.

[35] Interview with Robert Decker, July 8, 1982.

[36] Interview with authors, November 26, 1982.

[37] Interview with authors, August 24, 1982.

[38] Interview with authors, July 8, 1982.

[39] Ibid.

CHAPTER 7

[1] See Appendix A, exhibit 11. Cf. Alan Altshuler, Martin Anderson, Daniel Jones, Daniel Roos, and James Womack, *The Future of the Automobile: The Report of MIT's International Automobile Program* (Cambridge, MA: MIT Press, 1984), p. 204.

[2] William Serrin, "The Union Movement Looks in the Mirror," *New York Times,* February 24, 1985, p. E5.

[3] Information supplied by the UAW Research Department.

[4] As of May 1983, Ephlin headed the GM Department and Yokich administered several more: Ford, Organizing, and the Skilled Trades. Vice-President Marc Stepp, head of the Chrysler and the Technical, Office and Professional Workers (TOP) departments, had been an officer since 1977. Other vice-presidents were Odessa Komer (Women's Department; Independent Parts and Suppliers; first elected 1974); and Bill Castevens (Agricultural Implements; elected 1983).

[5] UAW Public Relations Department, *Brief Background on the UAW* (May 1983).

[6] "The UAW's Finances: A Summary of the Union's Financial Report for 1984," *Solidarity,* November 1985, pp. 16–19; cf. UAW Board of International Trustees and International Secretary-Treasurer Raymond Majerus, *Report, January 1, 1982 to December 31, 1982,* pp. 4–5; *Report of Secretary-Treasurer Raymond Majerus to the Twenty-seventh Constitutional Convention* (May 1983), pp. 3–8.

[7] Interview with the authors, June 16, 1982.

[8] Interview with the authors, February 25, 1982.

[9] "Q&A: Bieber Talks on Industrial Policy, Concessions, Organizing, and the Rank and File," *Solidarity,* June 1983, p. 5; UAW Public Relations Department, "Fraser Reacts to Reagan Speech," *News from the UAW,* September 25, 1981, pp. 1–2.

[10] Interview with the authors, June 16, 1982; "Fraser Assails Failure of U.S. to Adopt Industrial Policy to Deal with Continuing Employment Crisis," *News from the UAW,* July 22, 1981, p. 1.

[11] Interview with the authors, August 23, 1982.

[12] Interview on "The Phil Donahue Show," Donahue transcript no. 03112, p. 9; cf. p. 23 for similar comments by autoworkers in the audience.

[13] Owen Bieber, "Why a Higher Auto Wage Isn't Too Much to Ask," *The Wall Street Journal,* August 27, 1984, p. 12; Remarks by Owen Bieber, Vice-President and Director, UAW General Motors Department, to the IMF-UAW-GM Workers World Auto Conference, June 25–26, 1981, pp. 46–47. Cf. Douglas A. Fraser, "The Myth of the Overprivileged Auto Worker," *The Wall Street Journal,* April 27, 1981.

[14] Donald F. Ephlin, Letter to the Editor, *Harvard Business Review* (November–December 1981), p. 76.

[15] Interviews with the authors, July 1982 and May 1983. In 1983 the UAW commissioned an independent consultant to analyze the cost differential using data supplied by the UAW and sources in the labor movement worldwide. The report was completed prior to the 1984 bargaining round but has never been made public.

[16] "Statement of Douglas A. Fraser," President, International Union, United Automobile, Aerospace and Agricultural Implement Workers of America (UAW) before the Subcommittee on Commerce, Transportation, and Tourism, House Committee on Energy and Commerce on H.R. 1234, The Fair Practices in Automotive Products Act," *Federal Register* (Washington, DC: GPO), April 12, 1983, p. 15. Fraser made the same charge in his testimony on H.R. 5133 in the previous Congress. See also "Mission to Japan: Owen Bieber Goes to Tokyo," *Solidarity,* May 1984, pp. 4–6.

[17] "Statement of Douglas A. Fraser," p. 14, and Appendix A.

[18] The General Motors contract, settled in April 1982, was patterned after the Ford contract except for some terminology and specific details.

[19] Ford Motor Company, "Highlights, 1982 Ford-UAW National Agreements," p. 7.

[20] Interview with the authors, June 1, 1984.

[21] See the articles by Thomas J. Pascoe and Richard J. Collins; Marshall Goldberg; Ernest J. Savoie; and Gary B. Hansen, in Barbara D. Dennis, ed., *Industrial Relations Research Association: Proceedings of the 1985 Spring Meeting* (Madison: University of Wisconsin Press, 1985) pp. 519–553.

[22] Interview with the authors, May 20, 1983.

[23] Interview with General Motors Industrial Relations Staff, December 5, 1985.

[24] Interview with the authors, July 1, 1982.

[25] Interview with the authors, December 12, 1982.

[26] Chrysler and AMC never evinced much interest in QWL and have limited themselves to establishing quality circles instead.

[27] See above, chapter 3, for a brief account of the origins of QWL and EI programs. See also Harry C. Katz, *Shifting Gears: Changing Labor Relations in the U.S. Automobile Industry* (Cambridge, MA: MIT Press, 1985), esp. chap. 4.

[28] Other well-publicized QWL programs operate at the Buick complex in Flint, Michigan, and at an assembly plant in Tarrytown, New York.

[29] Neil De Koker and Joe Malotke, "GM-UAW Saturn Study Center Update," presented to the President's Commission on Industrial Competitiveness, April 30, 1984; Memorandum of Agreement between Saturn Corporation and UAW, July 1985, p. 6.

[30] William Serrin, "Saturn Labor Pace Assailed by a UAW Founder," *New York Times*, October 28, 1985, p. A13.

[31] Interview with the authors, December 10, 1982.

[32] Remarks by Owen Bieber to the 27th UAW Constitutional Convention, May 19, 1983, pp. 17–18.

[33] Raymond E. Majerus, "Workers Have a Right to a Share of Profits," *Harvard Business Review* (September–October 1984), pp. 42–50.

[34] The UAW's general political views are spelled out in the triennial president's report and resolutions of the constitutional convention.

[35] UAW, Community Action Program, *U.S. Auto Content Law, Background Information* (1982); Fraser, "Statement . . . before the Subcommittee on Commerce, Transportation, and Tourism, House Committee on Energy and Commerce," April 12, 1983.

[36] "On the Road to Job Security," *Solidarity*, May 1982, pp. 11–13.

[37] U.S. Congressional Budget Office, *Domestic Content Legislation and the U.S. Automobile Industry. Analyses of H.R. 5133, The Fair Practices in Automotive Products Act* (Washington, DC, August 16, 1982), pp. 49–50. The Congressional Research Service and the Department of Commerce released similar critical reviews of local content in 1982. See also Martin Anderson, "Local Content Legislation in the U.S. Auto Industry: Risks and Realities," unpublished paper, Future of the Auto Program, Massachusetts Institute of Technology, 1982.

[38] "UAW Proposes Industrial Policy Program Aimed at Full Employment and Renewed Growth," *News from the UAW*, May 19, 1983, p. 1.

[39] UAW, *The UAW Blueprint for a Working America: A Proposal for an Industrial Policy*, May 1983, pp. 9–10. The *Blueprint* explains social accounting more fully: the purpose is "to measure more widely the return to society of an investment made or not made. . . . When decisions are being debated on whether to close an 'unprofitable' plant, for example, we must factor in such things as the cost to society of jobless benefits, other Treasury losses, the destruction of the community's social structure, and the potential viability of alternative products that could be produced there." The concept of social accounting draws heavily on the work of economist Barry Bluestone (son of Irving), a consultant to the UAW.

[40] Ibid., pp. 11–13.

[41] Ibid., pp. 16–17. The UAW has since reaffirmed the *Blueprint*: see UAW, *Building America's Future: Alternatives to Economic Decline*, pp. 18–20. This document was prepared for the 1986 UAW convention.

[42] UAW Public Relations Department, *Brief Background on the UAW* (May 1983); UAW Research Department.

[43] Walter P. Reuther Library, Wayne State University, WPR Papers, Box 137/8, "Confidential: Organizing Problems Facing the UAW," n.d. The year may be 1959.

[44] A survey of certification and decertification elections conducted between 1960 and 1980 bears this out.

[45] Carl Dean Snyder, *White Collar Workers and the UAW* (Ithaca: Cornell University Press, 1962). According to Jack Stieber, *Governing the UAW* (New York, Science Editions 1967), p. 105, the UAW had about 50,000 white-collar members in the early 1960s. Compare the 1982 figure cited above. Doug Fraser, interviewed in May 1984, challenged Stieber's estimate as much too high.

[46] Interview with the authors, September 23, 1982.

[47] *Report of Secretary-Treasurer Raymond Majerus to the Twenty-seventh Constitutional Convention* (May 1983), p. 5.

[48] Interview with the authors, September 23, 1982.

[49] Stieber, *Governing the UAW*, pp. 149–153.

[50] Muriel Beach, "The Problem of Skilled Workers in an Industrial Union: A Case Study," *ILR Research*, Fall-Winter 1961, p. 9.

[51] Interview with the authors, December 10, 1982.

[52] LOC spokesmen claim that the Ford ratification, carried by a margin of 73 percent to 27 percent, gives no real indication of worker support for concessions. LOC argues that many Ford workers commented on the contract by not voting at all. Only 60,000 of 160,000 eligible workers voted on the Ford contract.

[53] Interview with the authors, July 6, 1982.

[54] Dale D. Buss, "Unions Say Auto Firms Use Interplant Rivalry to Raise Work Quotas," *The Wall Street Journal*, November 11, 1983, pp. 1, 31.

[55] William Serrin, "A 'Superstar' for Canadian Labor," *New York Times*, April 7, 1985.

[56] Interview with the authors, June 16, 1982.

CHAPTER 8

[1] Douglas H. Ginsberg and William J. Abernathy, eds., *Government, Technology, and the Future of the Automobile* (New York: McGraw-Hill, 1980), p. 393.

[2] Interview with authors, Washington, DC, October 10, 1985.

[3] Ibid., October 9, 1985.

[4] Ibid.

[5] Ibid., October 11, 1985.

[6] Ibid., January 18–31, 1983.

[7] Ibid., October 11, 1985.

[8] Ibid., January 18–31, 1983.

[9] Ibid.

[10] Ibid., October 8, 1985.

[11] Testimony of Robert G. Dederick, assistant secretary for economic affairs, before the Subcommittee on Trade of the Senate Finance Committee, December 1, 1981, p. 6.

[12] Interview with authors, Washington, DC, October 9, 1985.

[13] For a comprehensive treatment of the implicit and explicit auto-specific policies of the world, see Wayne A. Edisis, *Note on the World Auto Industry in Transition,* Case No. 9-385-332 (Boston: Harvard Business School, 1985), pp. 19–29.

[14] Interview with the authors, Washington, DC, January 18–31, 1983.

[15] John Holusha, "What Deregulation Means for G.M.," *New York Times*, November 1, 1981.

[16] Interview with authors, Washington, DC, October 10, 1985.

[17] Ibid.

[18] Ibid.

[19] See Federal Trade Commission consent agreement dated December 22, 1983, File Number 821–0159.

[20] Interview with Michael Finkelstein, National Highway Traffic Safety Administration, Washington, DC, October 11, 1985.

[21] Interview with the authors, Washington, DC, October 10, 1985.

[22] Alexander Hamilton, James Madison, and John Jay, *The Federalist: A Commentary on the Constitution of the United States* (1788; New York: Tudor, 1937), p. 65.

[23] Interview with the authors, Washington, DC, October 10, 1985.

[24] Ibid., January 18–31, 1983.

[25] Ibid., October 10, 1985.

[26] Ibid., October 9, 1985.

[27] Ibid.

[28] Ibid.

[29] Ibid., October 10, 1985.

[30] Ibid., January 18–31, 1983.

[31] Ibid., October 9, 1985.

[32] Ibid., October 11, 1985.

[33] Ibid., October 10, 1985.

[34] Ibid., October 11, 1985.

[35] Ibid., January 18–31, 1983.

[36] Ibid., October 10, 1985.

[37] Ibid., January 18–31, 1983.

CHAPTER 9

[1] GM-UAW Saturn Project Joint Study Center report (mimeo, 1984).

[2] Ibid.

[3] Ibid.

[4] Ibid.

[5] Ibid.

[6] Interview with authors, NUMMI plant, Fremont, California, January 10, 1985.

[7] From NUMMI press release, speech by Tatsuro Toyoda, January 1985.

[8] Interview with authors, NUMMI plant, Fremont, California, January 10, 1985.

[9] Ibid.

[10] Ibid.

[11] Ibid.

[12] Ibid.

CHAPTER 10

[1] Peter F. Drucker, *The Concept of the Corporation*, rev. ed. (New York: T. Y. Crowell, 1972), pp. 247–249.

[2] Interview with authors, Washington, January 1985.

[3] Interview with authors, Washington, January 1982.

[4] Interview with authors, Washington, February 1985.

CHAPTER 11

[1] Interview with authors, Tokyo, Japan, January 1982.

[2] Interview with authors, St. Louis, Missouri, May 1985.

[3] Interview with authors, Washington, DC, October 10, 1985.

[4] Interview with authors, St. Louis, Missouri, May 1985.

[5] Interview with author, Lansing, Michigan, February 1985.

[6] Quoted from state of Michigan proposal to General Motors for Saturn Project siting decision, 1985.

Index